BEYOND COMPLIANCE

A New

Industry

View of the

Environment

WORLD
RESOURCES
INSTITUTE

Edited by Bruce Smart

April 1992

Kathleen Courrier
Publications Director

Brooks Clapp
Marketing Manager

Hyacinth Billings
Production Manager

Pamela Reznick
Cover Design

Each World Resources Institute Report represents a timely, analytical treatment of a subject of public concern. WRI takes responsibility for choosing the study topics and guaranteeing its authors and researchers freedom of inquiry. It also solicits and responds to the guidance of advisory panels and expert reviewers. Unless otherwise stated, however, all the interpretation and findings set forth in WRI publications are those of the authors.

CONTENTS

FOREWORD

Around the world, societies are pursuing two potentially conflicting goals: a cleaner environment and sustained economic growth. Reconciling these goals will require a sweeping technological transformation—essentially an eco-industrial revolution—that brings human impacts back into balance with nature's regenerative powers.

More than any other factor, the sheer magnitude of human economic activity has brought us to this challenge. Since World War II, world population has doubled and the size of the world economy has quadrupled. For the first time, human numbers and impacts have grown so large that they are threatening on a global scale the systems that support life. Looking ahead, this phenomenal growth in the scale of the human enterprise is projected to continue. World populations will likely double again by mid-century, and the world economy could multiply fivefold. What if the production of climate warming gases, industrial wastes, and other pollutants and the consumption of energy, water, and other natural resources keeps pace with those growth curves? Pollution and resource consumption would skyrocket, making today's difficult problems into tomorrow's insurmountable ones.

A workable future is possible only if we rapidly replace current technologies with new and "greener" ones—in every sector, from energy generation and transportation to manufacturing, housing, and agriculture. Environmental damage can't be cut down to size until the pollution generated and the raw materials used per unit of output—both strongly influenced by technological factors—decline much faster than economic output grows. For starters, the need to replace old stocks in the economy with new, ecologically modern capital equipment and consumer durables is there for all to see.

Given this situation, the business community can confidently expect a future in which public demand for environmental protection—already high—will rise steadily in intensity. As this happens, environmental performance will increasingly determine economic viability. Dirty or dangerous activities and products will be regulated or priced out of the market. Environment-friendly processes and consumer goods will have a competitive advantage, enjoy customer approval, and gain early market share. A premium will be placed on new environmentally advantaged technologies like emissionless vehicles, photovoltaic electricity, bioengineered pest resistances, and pollution prevention in manufacturing. Environmental demands will thus create major economic opportunities.

Companies that see these opportunities and seize them at the appropriate time stand to prosper. Moreover, because the rising demand for environmental protection will be virtually universal (if not uniform) around the world, environmental requirements and international competitiveness need not conflict. Indeed, environmental improvements and greener technologies should provide a competitive edge to companies and to nations. Strict environmental laws—at least those that encourage innovation and efficient, cost-effective approaches—should actually strengthen national competitiveness.

The companies whose reports are presented in *Beyond Compliance* see themselves at the beginning of this ''eco-industrial revolution.'' They are responding to the rising demand for environmental quality and to their own growing understanding of the interdependence of economic and ecological systems. Important as pressure from environmentalists and governmental direction are to stimulating change, in the end only the corporate community can efficiently provide the necessary organization, technology, and financial resources needed to design and implement change on the scale required. Companies that are trying to be leaders on a new path to a sustainable future merit our encouragement and support, just as the inevitable backsliders deserve a vigorous shove onto the trail.

Beyond Compliance traces the recent experiences of a selection of companies that have publicly stated a determination to move toward environmental excellence. It shows how new products, processes, and programs—in the front office, the plant, and the community at large—grew out of a combination of community, government, stockholder, employee, and market forces. It reviews how companies set environmental goals, how they allocate responsibility for meeting them, and how they measure their success. Contributors share stories of how they took their message to the public, which carrots and sticks worked and which didn't, and how they are building on both successes and failures to plan for the future. A few also tell of efforts at industry-wide reform.

Recounted in the words of the companies that are changing, these corporate reports are not intended to be audits of company environmental performance. It would, in fact, be a surprising reversal of human nature if the descriptions gave as much attention to shortcomings and failures as to success. We do believe, however, that the changes described are for the great part commendable, that the difficulties in making them are real, and that enthusiastic and constructive corporate participation in the search for sustainable development is essential to reaching that shared goal. With that in mind, WRI hopes this volume, skillfully edited by Bruce Smart, himself a former CEO of a Fortune 100 company, will inform business leaders and others interested in corporate environmentalism and help spur the extensive change needed now. If it stimulates debate on the degree of change that has actually occurred or the best means of promoting progress in the future, so much the better.

Financial support for this book was provided by Louisa C. Duemling and the Curtis and Edith Munson Foundation, Inc. We deeply appreciate the generosity of both.

James Gustave Speth
President
World Resources Institute

ACKNOWLEDGMENTS

Books such as this are inevitably the work of many hands and minds, some of them unknown to an editor whose privilege it is to try to blend their work together into a coherent whole. Those company representatives who made the valuable contributions of material on which *Beyond Compliance* is based are listed in Appendix I. Without them there would be no book, and we thank them both for their submissions and the patience and cooperation with which many of them endured the editorial process. As for their anonymous associates who also helped, we ask forgiveness for our inability to recognize them specifically, but thank them heartily as well.

A dozen outside reviewers gave wise counsel and editorial input that has usefully influenced the final product. They include John Adams and his associate Catherine Lassila, Richard Ayres, Edwin "Toby" Clark, Thomas Gladwin, David Hales, Steven Jellinek, Nathan Karch, Jeffrey Leonard, Edward Strohben, and Vickie Tschinkel. Since most of them now work or previously worked for environmental organizations, their observations on the corporate material stimulated editorial comment that might otherwise have been omitted. We thank them all, including one or two who at their request remain unnamed, for their perseverance and the care with which they examined and critiqued the text and the conclusions drawn from it.

No WRI-sponsored publication escapes unscathed from internal peer review. We received helpful lessons from Alan Brewster, Kathleen Courrier, Jessica Mathews, Walt Reid, Robert Repetto and particularly from Donna Wise, who also served as pathfinder through the complexities of the review process. The book is better, and the editor more enlightened because of them.

Editorial, production, and marketing help came from Kathleen Courrier, Robbie Nichols, Hyacinth Billings, and Brooks Clapp. It is also their book, literally "from cover to cover."

No editor can survive without an alter ego to catch errors and fill in voids, which Nina Kogan did with skill and grace. Her many contacts with contributors were especially helpful in keeping the project reasonably on schedule. It also helps to have a cheerful and skilled support staff, a role that fell to Elaine Young, assisted on occasion by Georgia Moyka. Together they have typed, proofread, duplicated, collated, and bound nine drafts of *Beyond Compliance*.

Finally, and most important, it is necessary to thank Gus Speth. His enthusiasm for the project from concept to publication has been unwavering. His recognition of the central role that corporations must play in worldwide environmental improvement is the foundation for WRI's support of this effort, and his counsel on how to treat subjects on which there are bound to be differing views has been wise and well founded. We are in his debt.

Bruce Smart
April 1992

I.
WHYS AND WHEREFORES

During the last two decades, understanding of industry's impact on the world's environment has increased enormously. This expanding body of scientific knowledge is the principal basis for environmentalists' alarm over the risks of "business as usual" and for the resulting public pressure for change. Although a few atypical corporations are seen by observers to have had their environmental antennae up for years, public conventional wisdom currently has it that American business managers automatically oppose all such calls for environmental improvement, and respond to them only after bitterly contested laws and regulations force their reluctant compliance.

Yet, recent actions by a significant number of leading American companies and industry groups appear to be signaling a sea-change in the scope of corporate environmental understanding and response, calling that bit of conventional wisdom into question. At the forefront of this change in approach are a number of well-known firms whose products and processes have been found to be hazardous or highly polluting. Perhaps because these enterprises are the most visibly threatened, or have learned from the controversies in which they have been embroiled, they also may be ahead of industry in general in spotting environmental imperatives and opportunities.

The purpose of this book is to encourage this trend toward greater corporate environmentalism, a trend that has tremendous promise for all who seek an "eco-revolution" in industrial environmental attitudes and behavior.

The Audiences

These chapters are written primarily by, for, and about business. Their intent is to encourage more companies to recognize the

1

benefits to them of a positive approach to environmental challenges and to learn from the experiences of the organizations whose stories make up most of the text. For companies already committed to a new philosophy, this book can broaden their knowledge of what others are experiencing and help them coax recalcitrants within their ranks to accept management's new environmental thinking. Those still sitting on the environmental sidelines may find inspiration and discover that it is in their own self-interest to consider and then act on what their neighbors, consumers, and the environmental and scientific communities are telling them. Through the experiences of those included here, fence-sitters may also find guidance in how to go about changing to the corporate policies, organization, culture and operational programs that the future demands.

Since education is a precursor to change, it is also hoped that the company stories and the editorial comments that surround them will prove of value to business schools and other educators seeking to expand the environmental understanding of students of any age and calling.

Environmentalists should find this book both interesting and provocative; some are sure to bristle. Naturally enough, participating companies have generally put their cleanest foot forward and kept the other foot back out of sight. And they don't give the environmental community much credit for setting business on a new path. But since it is progressive company efforts that are most likely to set the pace of change and convince other firms to move forward, no attempt has been made to accompany these positive reports with a critic's litany of negatives, though several companies forthrightly admit that much is yet to be done.

Current State of Play

The extent to which a nascent eco-industrial revolution is unfolding is not yet entirely clear. Certainly, the changing environmental practices of its leaders are neither fully refined or extensively emulated. Some in industry still appear to take environmental criticism lightly, or react to it by offering scientific defenses of past actions, rather than by trying to understand and respond to the problems and perceptions that critics raise. Similarly, valid corporate claims of recent environmental improvements are discounted by some observers as "full of sound and fury, signifying nothing." But others note and welcome significant shifts in attitude and practice in important sectors of the industrial landscape.

This book presents what two dozen companies report they are doing, why they are doing it, and what victories and setbacks they are experiencing as they seek to alter their approach to the environment. The stories disclose why these companies believe the steps they are taking are both important and beneficial to them:

- Pollution is waste, and preventing it at the source can save money in materials and in end-of-the-pipe remediation.
- Acting voluntarily now can minimize future risks and liabilities, make costly retrofits unnecessary, and aid in the design of more efficient regulations.
- A company moving "ahead of the curve" on environmental issues will find competitive advantage over those struggling to keep up.
- New "green" products and processes can increase consumer appeal and open up new business opportunities.
- A reputation for being environmentally progressive improves recruitment, employee morale, investor support, host community acceptance and management's self-respect.

Besides suggesting what to do, the case histories identify a number of conditions that companies consider obstacles to cost-effective environmental progress. Policy research, analysis, and debate may define these present, emerging or deepening problems and suggest paths around them.

Industry's Place in the Sustainable Development Equation

Because modern industry controls so much of the world's store of technology, financial resources, and organizational strength, sustainable development—defined as "meeting the needs of today's people without compromising future generations' ability to meet theirs"—is unlikely to be achieved without industry's full and willing participation.

Especially critical to this process are the large multi-national corporations best positioned to develop, implement, and diffuse replacement technologies that are more environmentally benign

3

than the ones now in common use. Without sustainable development—including both quantitative and qualitative progress in global
standards of living—the world's social and political stability, and
the natural resources and ecosystems on which the global economy
depends, will be damaged or destroyed, taking modern industry
down along with them.

The potentially damaging effect of human economic activity
on the workings of the natural environment has been recognized
and reported for generations, from the conservation movement
prominent in the 19th century, to Rachel Carson's *Silent Spring* in
1962, to the 1987 Brundtland Commission, which challenged the
world to find a path to global sustainable development. Indeed,
calling public attention to these conditions had been a major *raison
d'être* for and contribution by the environmental movement.

As world population has grown and as industrial activity has
increased even more rapidly, the impact of people on their surroundings has accelerated, in more and more cases breaching the limits of
natural systems' restorative powers. Paralleling this growth in polluting activities has been an increase in scientists' ability to recognize
and measure damage and to establish cause-and-effect relationships.

Some in business and industry continue to be guided by an
outmoded philosophy. For a long time, industry took for
granted two basic assumptions: one was that resources for industrial development and production would always be available somewhere on the globe and enable industrial growth to
proceed without constraints; the other was that the earth could
absorb the byproducts of industrial societies indefinitely without undergoing fundamental environmental changes. These assumptions no longer hold—if in fact they ever did.

■ *Edgar S. Woolard, Jr., Chairman and
CEO, Du Pont*

*From Chapter IX "Beyond Compliance: A New Industry View of the Environment"—
1992*

As these realities have become more widely identified by environmentalists and recognized by the public, it is not surprising

that demands for change have mounted and that business enterprises—particularly large and visible ones—have come under pressure. Even with the current gaps in scientific knowledge, this demand for industrial change is rational, timely, and legitimate, and its satisfaction essential to humankind's future.

To understand how central industry's position is to environmental improvement, consider the factors that contribute to large-scale environmental deterioration. The industrial environmental burden on the world's resources can be expressed by the following equation:

**Global Industrial Environmental Burden =
(Population) × (Industrial GNP per Capita) ×
(Environmental Impact per unit of Industrial GNP)**

Demographers predict that the present world population of 5+ billion will roughly double by the middle of the next century. Absent a cataclysmic disaster, the momentum of current birth and death rates strongly supports this projection. Almost all of the forecast growth will take place in the less industrialized countries, where environmental damage caused in part by the related factors of population and poverty is already rampant, and where industrial development is necessary to check its further increase.

Similarly, it is apparent that increasing industrialization and consumer aspirations will keep pushing industrial GNP per capita upward worldwide, following the experience of the last several decades. In fact, without such an increase, especially in less developed countries, social and political stability will be seriously threatened around the globe. According to one estimate, by the year 2050, total world GNP per capita will be two and one half times today's, which, together with population growth, would quintuple the current level of world economic activity.

If these figures prove even close to correct, it is obvious that to hold the global environmental burden constant or, better yet, to reduce it, will require a *dramatic reduction* in industrial environmental impact per unit of GNP—probably a cut in excess of 80 percent, to less than 20 percent of today's level.

Corporations are inherently responsive entities that react out of self interest to the economic, legal, and social forces around them. Their first step toward change must thus be greater recognition of

5

emerging environmental realities and the social pressures they are generating. In response to this new awareness, the sensitive corporation will come to see that its self-interest is best served by a new approach. That managers may also perceive it as "the right thing to do" will give them a personal, as well as a corporate, incentive to proceed along a path in which newly crafted policies are followed by changes in organization, behavior, and attitude, eventually resulting in implanting an environmental ethic throughout the workforce. Such results, diffused through industry, can make the corporate world a powerful instrument for sustainable development—and thus an institutional resource of major environmental significance.

Constraints on Business

Despite the necessity of a new approach, it will not come quickly, cheaply, or easily. Large companies and entire industries readjust slowly, even when led aggressively in a new direction. Imbedded but outdated technologies, existing facilities, old ways of doing things, limits on financial and human resources, prescriptive regulations, consumer preferences, and competitive markets all represent inertia to be overcome. Managing large companies differently and well will prove more difficult than identifying their shortcomings.

Years of adversarial encounters have left some veteran business people with a reservoir of mistrust of the motives and tactics of business critics, which may be compounded by differences of age, education, and perspective. For these people, listening is hard, frustrating work. For example, engineers—the educational discipline of many CEOs—tend to look at science and risk/reward calculations as the soundest bases for policy. The social activists and lawyers, who staff many environmental organizations, may place intangible human values and public wishes higher. It is difficult for any person to concede that an adversary has a point, much less acknowledge one's own past error. Yet, such concessions by both sides may be necessary beginnings for the cooperative effort needed to best solve environmental problems.

Given these constraints, some observers will find the progress reported to be remarkable, while others may see it as still inadequate and unproven. Perhaps it is "all of the above."

How the Book was Prepared

The corporate actions taken and lessons learned are reported in this book in the words of the companies that are experiencing them. Much of the text was submitted as complete company "case histories" written specifically for use here. Other pieces were drawn from corporate publications or from articles and speeches by senior corporate officials or other knowledgeable observers. The companies' words, statements, goals, and claims are their own. All the company material used has been written or approved by a high corporate official, often the chief executive officer, and thus represents the company's official view on the subjects discussed. A list of authors and approving authorities is included as Appendix 1, and, where appropriate, their names are noted in the text.

Extracts from these submissions have been assembled into chapters describing where corporate environmentalism stands in two dozen companies, which events and actions led up to it, how it is perceived by the public, and where the companies expect it to go in the future. Authors of the corporate submissions have approved all the editing for context and accuracy. To introduce each section, to provide connective tissue, and to draw conclusions from corporate experiences, the editor has woven commentary into each chapter; this material is presented in italics, as are pertinent quotes from a number of outside observers. The editor is also entirely responsible for the first and last chapters: "Whys and Wherefores" and "Afterthoughts."

The result is a composite case history of the current state of corporate environmentalism reported by twenty four companies that see themselves in the forefront of corporate environmental initiative, rather than just responding after the fact to regulations imposed on them. As with autobiographies, and especially those vulnerable to critical or even litigious assault, the company stories tend to accentuate the positive. Observers will correctly point out that much is still not right in the contributing companies, let alone in industry at large. Environmentally aware companies will need to focus on their remaining shortcomings just as vigorously as they report on their improvements. Even the best have a lot left to do. Industry's critics should remain watchful lest progress stall, and they must participate in the debate on how to broaden and accelerate corporate environmental efforts. The hope is that they will do so with a positive attitude.

How the Participating Companies Were Selected

All the industries represented in this book make products or employ processes that are having a major current environmental impact, including particularly chemicals, petroleum, power generation, packaged goods, and electronics. Each individual company chosen has publicly stated a determination to change and reports some success in doing so. And most have been recognized by some outside body or bodies as leaders in this effort. A description of each of the participants and, where applicable, the environmental recognition accorded each appears in Appendix 2.

Most of the companies represented in these pages have also been identified as significant contributors to pollution. As such, they hold dominion over industry's greatest opportunities to make major environmental improvements, and their experiences can provide the most significant lessons in how—and sometimes how not—to do so.

Because North America is the largest per capita user of environmental resources, almost all of our examples come from companies with headquarters here. Because the most intractable problems are global, most participants are large multinationals and therefore well known. But since medium-sized and smaller companies, perhaps facing different environmental problems, have equally interesting issues to manage, a few are included to highlight both the similarities and the differences in approach that size dictates and to stimulate medium-sized and smaller companies, along with large ones, to raise their sights "beyond compliance." The companies selected are not the only members of industry that are seeking a new way; others have stories just as interesting to tell, but space necessarily limits the number included here. Nor does inclusion imply that their processes and products are any "greener"—or less "green"—than those of their competitors.

Since this book is addressing the shifts in policy of well-established companies facing their own environmental problems, it does not include those who sell remediation services or equipment, or otherwise aid in pollution abatement. Their actions, of course, are also important ingredients of the changes needed to reach sustainable development and are of great interest to "green" investors, but their management problems are the conventional ones typical of any growth industry, rather than ones that call for changes in policies and culture.

This book barely touches on agriculture, which faces equally difficult though different challenges, and it does not address the need to make transportation systems, building design, and land-use policies more sustainable. While companies in these fields can take important environmental initiatives, and some are doing so, they cannot bring their full powers of innovation to bear until government starts calling for and supporting changes to these energy, water, and land-intensive systems, as it already has done in the fields of air, water, toxic chemicals and emissions, chlorofluorocarbons, power generation, and solid waste management.

Sponsorship

Funding for the preparation and publication of this book has come entirely from non-corporate foundation grants, individual donors, and World Resources Institute (WRI) endowment income. WRI does receive a limited amount of financial support from a number of corporations, in total amounting to about 3 percent of WRI's 1991 budget. While some participating companies are current WRI supporters, most are not. A company's status in this regard (see Appendix 2) has had no bearing on its selection, and no corporation has provided any financial support for this project.

Editorial Observations

No attempt has been made to judge or evaluate the candor or balance of the corporate submissions included in this book, nor to edit their tone. Certainly, there are alternative views on the situations the companies describe, and in some instances they have been included to highlight the realities of the terrain the participants are traversing.

A number of company case histories submitted dwell at some length on past events, including their early efforts at environmental protection. While these are interesting, today's concerns lie

9

principally with today's and tomorrow's problems. For brevity's sake, most of this historical material has been excised unless needed to dramatize change. Similarly, so many readers are familiar with concepts such as "sustainable development" and "global warming" that detailed descriptions of these issues are not included here. These omissions—made to allow the reader to get directly to the point of the current corporate experience—should not offend the thoughtful and cooperative contributors on whose efforts this book depends. The goal has been to ensure room for their descriptions of what their companies are doing, what is working well, what less so, and what the future holds—the heart of their messages.

As is the custom with WRI publications, the chapters and comments written by the editor reflect only his own opinions and experience. As an organization, WRI has been strongly supportive of the concept underlying this project, but the views expressed in this book are those of the authors and the editor.

Bruce Smart
Editor

II.

COMPANY PROGRAMS AND RESULTS

The key questions any environmental observer will ask a company are "What is your problem?", "What are you doing about it?", and "How are you coming along?" Not surprisingly, almost every participating company submitted interesting material in an effort to answer those questions. For this initial chapter, the programs of thirteen companies have been selected and arranged into four categories to provide a wide view of the current state of play of corporate environmental efforts:

- *Reduction of wastes and emissions,*
- *Source reduction, recycling, and solid waste management,*
- *Conservation and renewable sources of energy, and*
- *Forest management and the preservation of biodiversity.*

In subsequent chapters, these and other companies tell why they are taking a new look at the environment, what changes in policies, organization, and corporate culture are called for, how their actions have been received beyond the corporate community, and what they see in their environmental future.*

Reduction of Wastes and Emissions

The public generally identifies environmental degradation with highly visible or frightening situations: toxic chemicals, oil spills, smog, and overflowing garbage dumps. But a company does not have to be located at a point of critical attack to realize that pollution is waste and that its prevention may have economic as well as environmental benefits.

---

*As noted in Chapter I, italicized text in Chapters II–XII has been written by the editor.

11

3M *(from the company case history)*

Pollution prevention became a way of life at 3M in 1975 when the company initiated its Pollution Prevention Pays (3P) program, the first time a major company made pollution prevention an integral and permanent element of operations and implemented it company-wide in an organized way. 3M's 3P program is directed at all media—air, water, and land. It is a conservation-based approach to environmental management, seeing pollution as a waste, an inefficient use of resources.

In 1975, with the advent of 3P, pollution prevention became first choice in the hierarchy of 3M waste management, listed here in order of priority:

- Prevent pollution at the source.
- Recover and recycle manufacturing by-products and other assets for internal reuse or external sale.
- Treat wastes that can't be prevented or recycled, using control equipment and other methods to reduce toxicity and volume.
- Dispose of treatment residue through appropriate methods.

3P is a voluntary program to motivate employees worldwide to look for innovative ways to eliminate pollution at the source. It is aimed primarily at 3M's thousands of technical employees in laboratories, manufacturing, and engineering.

3M's chief executive officer and the Board of Directors assigned responsibility for implementing 3P to the vice president of the Environmental Engineering and Pollution Control (EE&PC) staff group. EE&PC environmental engineers are assigned to business unit facilities to assist in 3P implementation.

3P focuses on preventing the generation of waste and on recycling.

Preventing Generation of Waste:
- Raw material substitution—eliminating a hazardous constituent used either in the product or during manufacture.
- End-product substitution—producing a different product that accomplishes the same functions with less pollution than a previous product.

- Process modification—changing the process design to reduce waste generation.
- Equipment redesign—changing the physical design of the equipment to reduce waste generation.
- Direct recycling—reusing materials directly in the manufacturing process.
- Good housekeeping—instituting new procedures, such as preventive maintenance to reduce waste generation.
- Inventory control—minimizing quantities of raw materials in stock to eliminate surplus that could become waste when the product is changed or discontinued.

Recovery and Recycling:
- Segregation—separating waste streams to reduce the volume of hazardous waste handled or to allow for reuse and recycling.
- Recovery/reuse/recycling—recovering generated waste for reuse or recycling by 3M or outside companies.

Any employee or group of employees may identify a need and develop a project. Most projects must be approved and funded by the operating unit most affected by the project. Once projects are approved for funding, they may be submitted for official 3P recognition.

A pollution prevention project must meet established criteria to be recognized as an approved 3P project:

- It must, through process change, product reformulation, or other preventive means, eliminate or reduce a pollutant that currently is a problem or has the potential to become a problem in the future.
- It should exhibit, in addition to reduced pollution, environmental benefit through reduction in energy consumption, more efficient use of raw materials, or improvement in the use of other natural resources.
- It should involve a technical accomplishment, innovative approach, or unique design.
- It must have some monetary benefit for 3M. This may be through reduced or deferred pollution control or manufacturing costs, increased sales of an existing or new product, or other reduction in capital requirements or expenses.

13

Since 3P started in 1975, more than 3,000 approved projects worldwide have resulted in the prevention of more than 575,000 tons of pollution. 3P success stories include:

- A 3M manufacturing facility in Missouri used an acid solution to clean copper sheeting for making circuit boards, a process that created 40,000 gallons a year of hazardous waste that required expensive disposal techniques. Technical employees found that a slurry of water and pumice could clean the copper just as well and produce no hazardous waste. It did, however, create non-hazardous residue that had to be disposed of. A subsequent change to a mild citric-acid cleaning solution answered that problem.
- Production line scrap that once was landfilled was turned into new products at a South Dakota plant. The products are oil and liquid sorbent minibooms and industrial pillows, a miniature version of the type 3M makes to contain and absorb oil spills at sea. Minibooms, which are used in machine shops and other industrial settings, are made from residue materials generated in the manufacture of face masks. The new product is profitable, and 3M realized big savings in disposal costs.
- 3M's pharmaceutical plant in California developed a water-based medicine tablet coating, replacing a solvent base. The change cost $60,000, but eliminated the need for $180,000 in pollution control equipment. It also saved materials and reduced air pollution.

Savings from all of the 3P projects since 1975 total more than $530 million. Savings come from pollution control facilities that did not have to be purchased and installed, from reduced pollution control operating costs, from reduced manufacturing costs, and from retained sales of products that might have been taken off the market as environmentally unacceptable.

[Ed. Note: 3M also lists other benefits flowing from the 3P program, including materials conservation, reduced regulatory compliance paperwork, fewer potential liabilities, improved competitive position, improved company reputation, and lowered waste-disposal costs. It has also provided a base of experience from which to help others improve their environmental

performance. Recently 3M decided to take the 3P program a step further. The 3M story continues:]

While the 3P program had been very successful, 3M decided in 1989 to expand its voluntary commitment to improve environmental quality. In 1989, the 3P+ program was established, setting specific challenging waste reduction goals for the 1990s and for the year 2000.

Under the 3P+ initiative, 3M intends to reduce all hazardous and non-hazardous releases to air, water, and land by 90 percent and to reduce the generation of all waste by 50 percent by the year 2000. This is in addition to a 50-percent reduction already achieved through 3P projects. Beyond the year 2000, 3M's goal is to come as close to zero emissions as is technically possible.

Primary emphases are on development of new processes, products, and packaging that have a minimum impact on the environment. This effort will take 3M from a position of compliance with environmental regulations to being substantially under limitations established by environmental quality standards.

A major step toward achieving year 2000 goals is an air emissions-reduction program designed to cut these emissions from 3M facilities worldwide by 70 percent by 1993. This program involves using the best pollution control technology and techniques available on all major emitting sources, both existing and future facilities. The cost of the air emissions reduction program is $175 million.

Reducing air emissions with pollution controls is seen as an interim solution. For the longer term, 3M looks for permanent innovative pollution-prevention solutions to achieve and improve upon year 2000 targets. The principal focus of these efforts is removal of solvents used in coating processes.

Waste minimization teams are being formally established in every operating division to identify source reduction and recycling opportunities and develop plans to address them. These interdisciplinary teams consist of representatives of manufacturing, laboratories, engineering, marketing, packaging engineering, and other units needed to ensure the broadest perspective possible.

A pollution prevention staff has been established in the Environmental Engineering and Pollution Control Department (EE&PC) and assigned a variety of responsibilities. This group is essentially

15

the program facilitators. Its job is to help make 3P+ happen. Among the responsibilities of the pollution prevention staff is monitoring and reporting to management on the progress of 3P+. 3M management expects to be kept fully apprised of problems, technical breakthroughs, and overall progress of the program. Staff's quarterly reports plot progress against a 1990 baseline year.

The pollution prevention staff encourages the sharing of good ideas and technical breakthroughs among the company's divisions. It also monitors legislative and regulatory activity that might affect the program and goals of 3P+. And, of course, one of the staff's most important responsibilities continues to be the encouragement of the pollution prevention concept through recognition programs.

3M does not profit from air emission credits earned through its efforts. Under company policy, the credits are usually turned back to local or state environmental agencies for improvement in air quality. A variation on that theme occurred at a 3M facility in California. 3M sold emission credits to a neighboring company, enabling the purchaser to proceed with a job-creating expansion. 3M then donated the $1.5 million proceeds to a public environmental fund to be used for air quality improvement.

Another assist toward year 2000 goals will occur through Challenge '95, a new five-year corporate productivity program. Challenge '95 sets a 1995 goal of a 35-percent reduction in waste generated, a significant step toward the 50-percent year 2000 goal. A second target of Challenge '95 is a 20-percent reduction per unit of production in energy use by 1995. This is in addition to a 50-percent energy reduction per unit of production already achieved since 1975. Many of 3M's operating groups have established their own environmental goals that complement Challenge '95. Challenge '95 marks the first time a 3M productivity program has incorporated environment-related goals.

Because 3M's 3P program has been going for 16 years, 3M describes what can be achieved over time. But it is also worth noting that the company has upgraded and expanded its program over that span from 3P to 3P+ and Challenge '95, in each case increasing the level of protection sought while bringing the environment closer to the center of strategic and operational planning. Thus, the 3M experience presents not a snapshot of the present but a moving picture of corporate environmental effort as it has evolved in one company over the last decade and a half.

Their philanthropic approach to air emissions credits is testimony to 3M's understanding of public attitudes.

3M's 3P concept has been emulated in a number of more recent waste-reduction programs elsewhere in industry. In the mid-1980s, Dow initiated its "Waste Reduction Always Pays" program and Chevron began its effort to "Save Money and Reduce Toxics." Both companies report significant reductions in operating costs and waste discharges, using techniques very similar to 3M's.

■ ■ ■

AT&T carries the 3M process a step further. The company has initiated a program to design future waste out of the production system before it ever has a chance to appear.

AT&T *(from the company case history)*

The fifth guiding principle of quality management is prevention through planning. This principle is illustrated by what's happening as AT&T prepares for the future. At AT&T Bell Laboratories Engineering Research Center, Hopewell, New Jersey there is a group with fascinating challenges. The group's charter is to prevent future environmental problems by planning. By taking a broad look at the complete environmental picture. By looking two years—five years—even twenty years down the road.

The group chose waste as its first project. Not only waste in the traditional sense at AT&T—wood pallets, packing material, cable scrap, etc.—but also air emissions, rinse water, and solvents. The group worked in the Richmond plant as a "living laboratory" because it has several chemical-intensive internal business units. They had to develop a "systems," or "cradle-to-grave," view of waste— to the products that go out the door—even to recovery of those products at the end of their life.

The project is driven by a vision: AT&T factories producing high-quality products competitively through closed-loop operations. Materials leave only as finished products or as benign waste. No hazardous waste leaves.

17

The 13-member team is very close to developing a documented waste-minimization process for all AT&T plants. Next, they'll see if they can design waste out of the process altogether.

AT&T scientists and engineers are also experimenting with sophisticated tools to monitor plant operations—in real time—from factory floor to loading dock. The aim is to substantially reduce the potential for spills or accidental emissions.

The company is exploring the potential of information technology—the combined use of communications and computers—to help solve environmental problems. Such tools can provide timely information that enables people to use resources more efficiently while generating less waste. AT&T believes it's up to those in the industry to create widespread awareness of such information and make it available to others.

In addition to designing techniques to improve its products and processes, AT&T sees an opportunity to sell its goods and services to help others do likewise.

■ ■ ■

In many cases, new and better technologies are currently available to replace older more environmentally harmful products or processes, but society lacks sufficient incentives to hasten their introduction into widespread use. Thus, the lag time between knowing how to do something, and actually getting it done, allows environmental damage to persist and even to grow. Unocal came up with a novel idea to attack this problem in the smog-ridden Los Angeles Basin.

Unocal *(from its 1991 brochure on its South Coast Recycled Auto Program—SCRAP)*

On most days, the people of Los Angeles breathe the dirtiest air of any community in America. As the city's battle with smog enters its fifth decade, increasing attention has focused on mobile sources of pollution—automobiles, trucks, and buses—as key contributors to the region's air quality problem.

Mobile sources account for about 60 percent of all ozone-precursor emissions (hydrocarbons and nitrogen oxides) in the Los Angeles Basin. Petroleum refineries and electric power plants account for about 5 percent. Other sources (some of which have yet to be regulated), such as dry cleaners, bakeries, and even private homes, make up the difference.

While technology has sharply reduced emissions from the tailpipes of late-model automobiles and trucks, nearly 400,000 pre-1971 vehicles—all of which have little or no pollution-control equipment—continue to operate on Southern California's streets and freeways. Mile for mile, these old cars are the worst polluters on the road. Although pre-1971 vehicles are a serious source of air pollution—accounting for about 15 percent of all emissions from mobile sources in the L.A. Basin—little has been done about them.

Fleet Profile: L.A. Area			
	Pre '71	**All Cars**	**Pre '71 as % of Total**
Number Cars, 1000s	380	6,000	6
Number Miles, Millions	2,280	73,278	3
HC, Tons Per Day	57	266	22
CO, Tons Per Day	345	2,275	15
NO_x, Tons Per Day	30	234	13

[Ed. Note: Pre '71 figures shown in the fleet profile chart are those available to Unocal before the testing of actual vehicles described below. Based on what these tests showed about emissions and mileage, the pre '71 cars, 6 percent of the total fleet, account not for 15 percent but about 24 percent of the emissions listed.]

Retrofitting these old cars with up-to-date pollution-control systems would cost more than many of them are worth.

In mid-1990, Unocal proposed a new approach to the problem. The company announced a demonstration program to eliminate several thousand of these vehicles through a voluntary purchase plan in which Unocal would pay $700 for each car, then turn it over to a scrap yard to be crushed and recycled.

Unocal's South Coast Recycled Auto Project—SCRAP, for short—started with a budget of $5 million, enough to purchase and scrap 7,000 cars. The company estimated that taking this many pre-1971 vehicles out of circulation would cut L.A.'s air pollution by about 6 million pounds in the first year alone. Other people soon joined the effort—more than 100 individuals, plus major firms like Ford Motor Company and Cypress Semiconductor, and regulatory agencies like the South Coast Air Quality Management District (SCAQMD). All contributed additional money. Another 1,400 cars could be retired, cutting air pollution that much more.

But the biggest surprise was the final tally on exhaust emissions actually eliminated. Unocal tested the tail pipe emissions of every old car purchased for SCRAP. Early results suggested that these vehicles were far dirtier than air quality models had predicted. As a result, Unocal arranged to have rigorous emissions tests performed on 74 cars selected at random from the SCRAP vehicles. The results were eye-opening: On a per-mile basis, the average hydrocarbon (HC) emissions of the sample group were triple our expectations, and carbon monoxide (CO) was double. Only in emissions of nitrogen oxides (NO_x) did cars in the sample group prove "cleaner" than expected, although they were still 11 times dirtier than a 1990 vehicle.

Unocal's SCRAP program actually removed nearly 13 million pounds of pollutants from Southern California's air, or twice as much as projected when the program was launched. From an emissions standpoint, this was the equivalent of removing about 150,000 brand-new cars from the roads.

We also learned that SCRAP vehicles were driven on average 5,500 miles per year or about 90 percent as far as average old cars. Thus, SCRAP vehicles were driven somewhat less than average but emitted far more [total] pollution than expected.

These pre-1971 cars were among the least energy-efficient vehicles on the road, averaging 12 miles per gallon in city driving, about half the fuel economy of 1990 cars. In fact, had the SCRAP vehicles been sold as 1990 model-year cars, they would have been subject to an average "Gas Guzzler Tax" of $2,500 each!

SCRAP planners had to deal with several pressing issues before the program could begin.

First of all, what would the owners of such cars do for transportation once their vehicles were scrapped? Would $700 be enough to buy a replacement car? Unocal surveyed the used car market in Southern California and learned that, indeed, many post-1975 cars were priced below $700. These autos were equipped with smog controls, so that replacement transportation would be not only affordable, but cleaner as well. Second, Unocal wanted to be sure the cars purchased for SCRAP were in running condition and registered in the Los Angeles Basin for at least six months.

Finally, Unocal had to find a way to speed up the administrative process of scrapping the vehicles. Ordinarily, it takes five to ten days to complete the paperwork before a car can be legally crushed and shredded in Southern California. The Department of Motor Vehicles assigned special personnel to the project. These individuals handled the paperwork right where the cars were crushed, cutting processing time down from several days to a few minutes.

The success of SCRAP highlighted the opportunity for regulators to create conditions that would make programs like SCRAP economically feasible for many companies in the Los Angeles Basin. The device that could make this work is called an "offset," and regulators began viewing it with renewed interest.

Offsets are credits that companies could receive for cleaning up air pollution from mobile sources—air pollution caused by some other organization or individual. These credits could temporarily offset the same amount of the company's own pollution "debt" (i.e., emissions from its own stationary sources). Offsets would not necessarily cancel a company's pollution debt; they might simply defer it, providing time to explore more cost-effective technologies and systems for cleaning up the air.

Through a program of innovative offsets supplementing the existing regulatory framework, companies and public agencies could be encouraged to focus their efforts on the most cost-effective and immediate environmental programs. Properly used, offsets could accelerate the cleanup process, get the easiest (and often worst) causes of smog cleaned up first, and save money for the consumer, who ultimately pays the cost of pollution abatement and control.

Unocal's SCRAP program suggests some possible elements to be considered in designing an environmental improvement strategy:

- *Go after the most cost-effective improvements first. As in economic investments, easy targets offer the greatest return for the dollar spent.*

- *Go after the pollution that can be quickly eliminated. Environmental expenditures will earn an immediate return instead of lying fallow during a long implementation period.*
- *When it is impractical to get polluters to clean up their own mess promptly, consider giving other organizations an incentive to do it for them.*

The goal is to solve the problem as quickly, cheaply, and completely as possible, perhaps by increasing the rapidity with which the capital stock of polluting equipment is turned over. In the case of the Los Angeles Basin, if all cars were replaced by 1990 models in proper operating order, the smog-causing gasses would be reduced by 82 percent.

■ ■ ■

Small companies also have opportunities to reduce wastes and in so doing improve both their environmental performance and their bottom line. But, because of their more limited resources, they often must find outside financial and technical help in order to design and implement innovative solutions. The experience described below tells how one such small company went about the process of environmental improvement.

Briggs Nursery, Inc. *(as submitted by Dr. James Robbins of Briggs)*

Briggs Nursery, Inc., is the largest wholesale nursery in western Washington, selling ornamental nursery stock to 38 states and 17 foreign countries. Nursery stock is produced on a 150-acre site in Olympia and a new 400-acre farm near Elma. The workforce averages 150 employees. Orson Briggs established the nursery in 1912 on 15 acres of land for the production of field grown fruit crops. Three generations later, Briggs Nursery remains a family-owned business recognized as an industry leader for the production of ornamental trees and shrubs from tissue culture.

Production of container-grown plants by traditional methods requires significant inputs such as irrigation water, fertilizers, and agricultural chemicals. Concern exists over the potential impact of some of these materials on the environment and whether quality plants can be grown in systems requiring fewer resource inputs.

Based on a request from the nursery industry, Dr. James Green of the Horticulture Department at Oregon State University proposed the original concept for the Closed, Insulated Pallet System (CIPS). CIPS is designed to address six environmental and production needs facing the nursery and greenhouse industry:

- elimination of production-related waste discharge,
- conservation of resources,
- better pest management alternatives,
- improved working conditions,
- reduction in root zone temperature extremes, and
- increased materials handling efficiency of container-grown crops.

Design aspects of CIPS are actually quite simple. *(See Figure 1.)* Basic principles involved in the system's design include:

- a moisture-impermeable surface;
- an opaque, reflective, box-like structure for growing and moving a number of pre-spaced plants; and
- a capillary subirrigation system utilizing a large water reservoir.

Figure 1. A Cross-Sectional View of a Closed, Insulated Pallet

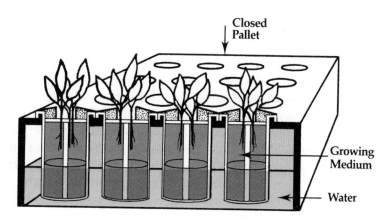

Closed
Pallet

Growing
Medium

Water

Source: Dr. James Greene, Oregon State University, 1991

The "closed" nature of the system eliminates runoff from production areas and the sealed, insulated growing system reduces extremes in media temperatures and the amount of water required. Combined, the various simple components of CIPS result in what is called a "plant driven system." Because the plants determine the timing and amount of water and fertilizer use, CIPS results in a reduction in resource inputs and a potential savings in manpower.

Briggs Nursery's longstanding commitment to new technology and to the environment led to its involvement in this innovative and challenging research. A project of this size by a small business such as Briggs Nursery requires significant financial and personnel resources, often in excess of in-house capabilities. For financial support, the nursery pursued a number of grant programs designed specifically to support research projects involving small businesses. The company successfully applied for Small Business Innovation Research (SBIR) grants from both the U.S. Department of Agriculture (USDA) and EPA and has received additional funding from the EPA's Pollution Prevention By and For Small Business program.

A unique aspect of the research program at Briggs Nursery is its participation in a multidisciplinary team involving individuals from industry and academia. Although a significant number of Briggs Nursery employees possess expertise critical to this project (engineering, plant pathology, horticulture, accounting), outside participation was essential for the nursery to increase its human and technical resource base in a cost-effective manner.

The Briggs Nursery philosophy that you should actively work on solutions to such challenges is not universally shared. The CIPS approach has raised eyebrows in the industry because it deviates significantly from current approaches and involves a large number of changes within a short period of time. This lack of support and encouragement by a significant segment of the industry has certainly not been reassuring to Briggs and its cooperators.

A project of this magnitude calls upon resources far in excess of normal business operations. The size, complexity, and detail of this basic research project has provided some unique challenges for the employees of Briggs Nursery. Scaling up for a "soft funded" research project of this size, while trying to balance on-going R&D needs for the company, has proven to be an interesting juggling act. The uncertainty of requested grants and rigid guidelines for funded projects makes long-term planning difficult.

As with many things in life, hindsight is always 20:20. Many shortcuts and lessons have been learned during this process. As a small company that is outside the research loop and not backed by extensive technical resources, Briggs has found the process sluggish at times. The lack in breadth of resources makes associations with academic institutions even more critical.

The research effort has shown that a Closed, Insulated Pallet System is a technically feasible concept. Preliminary results indicate that when plants are grown in CIPS, water use can be reduced by 90 percent and runoff totally eliminated compared to traditional spaced, overhead irrigated, container-production methods. The sealed media surface eliminates the need for herbicides and reduces the need for certain insecticides. The insulated, well-watered root environment appears to improve the effectiveness of certain biocontrol/biostimulant organisms, which could reduce the amount of chemicals and fertilizers used to grow plants in the future.

Spared dealing with citizens' protests over hazardous wastes, and without the high public profile of large companies, smaller businesses may be quite satisfied to leave current methods well enough alone. The use of government grants to small risk-taking enterprises like Briggs thus becomes another useful technique for finding better ways to reduce the environmental impact of highly fragmented industries.

■ ■ ■

The hypothesis that chlorofluorocarbons (CFCs) damage the ozone layer, first advanced in the 1970s, has been scientifically confirmed. As a result of the global threat CFCs pose, in 1987 a number of nations negotiated the Montreal Protocol, an international agreement that, as recently strengthened, calls for the elimination of CFC production in developed countries by 2000, and in less developed ones by 2010. More than 50 countries are now signatories. A global fund, administered by the World Bank and overseen by contributing signatory nations, has been created to help developing countries adopt alternatives to CFCs for refrigeration, aerosol propellants, (where still permitted), plastic foam blowing, cleaning of electrical components, and other established uses. Very recent and alarming data have now led to a decision by the President to phase out U.S. production of CFCs by the end of 1995.

CFCs represent a somewhat atypical category of emissions, differing from most others because:

- Their harmful impact is global, not restricted to production or end-use locations.
- There is a gestation period of several years between CFC release and subsequent damage to the ozone layer. Even when their manufacture and use are totally discontinued, it will take many decades for the ozone layer to heal.
- Their manufacture and use are now regulated by the Montreal Protocol.
- The U.S. government has imposed a tax on them, at a rate that escalates annually to discourage their use prior to Montreal Protocol deadlines.

For these reasons, there is an urgent need for affected industries to find substitutes for CFCs, to redesign processes and systems to accommodate those substitutes, and to aid in the rapid global diffusion of the new technologies as they are developed. Thus, efforts to eliminate CFCs can demonstrate both the complexities and the techniques involved in removing other hazardous materials from the global industrial scene.

Most environmental attention has been focused on large, multinational companies in pollution-intensive industries. As the Briggs Nursery case indicates, however, smaller companies are not immune to environmental difficulties, and some have addressed them vigorously and creatively. Small companies face less daunting internal communications problems, and they are less subject to the glare of public scrutiny. Of course, their resources to deal with environmental matters are substantially smaller as well.

Zytec Corporation, an electronics firm employing about 750 people, is another company that believes that leadership pays. In fact, the company has recently been awarded one of the three Malcolm Baldridge Quality Awards for 1991. While good descriptions of programs to eliminate CFCs were provided by AT&T, Dow, Northern Telecom and Xerox, the Zytec story is presented here because it illustrates the sophisticated approaches that even a smaller company can take.

Zytec Corporation *(from the company case history)*

CFCs, formerly presumed stable and chemically benign, have now become leading culprits in a potential global tragedy.

In the electronics industry, CFCs have been utilized in removing the corrosive materials from electronic circuit boards produced during the soldering process. A circuit board functions only if its thousands of copper-to-copper connections are properly formed. In a mass production environment the circuit board and component leads are coated with a "solder flux" that strips the surfaces of oxides and other contaminants prior to exposure to the bath of tin/lead solder.

Removal of post-solder bath flux residues by means of CFCs or water wash cleaning equipment is well developed and highly effective. Many national and international agencies (including the U.S. military) have formulated standards of circuit board cleanliness that strongly relate to the use of CFCs as the cleaning agent.

The Montreal Protocol created a truly chaotic situation. A well established process needed significant modification or elimination, but no mature CFC-free processes with industry-wide acceptance were available.

For Zytec, the reaction to the Montreal Protocol and subsequent Environmental Protection Agency (EPA) comments was somewhat less traumatic because an alternative process that left fewer flux residues had already received preliminary evaluation. Thus, it was possible for Zytec management to quickly formulate goals for reducing the use of CFCs. The Montreal Protocol originally called for a 50-percent reduction in the use of CFCs by 1998. In April 1989, Zytec released a position paper to all of its customers and suppliers asking for their cooperation in attaining complete elimination of CFCs by 1991. Specifically, the goal was to reduce usage from over 65,000 pounds in 1988 to less than 32,500 pounds in 1989 (a 50-percent reduction), and to zero in 1990.

The development of Low Solids Fluxes (LSF) for soldering electronic assemblies required several procedural and organizational modifications. Because of the reduced chemical activity of the solder flux, it became necessary to pay more attention to improved soldering practices. These included greater cleanliness of incoming circuit boards, improved solderability of electronic components, expanded utilization of first-in-first-out (FIFO) inventory control, enhanced storage facility temperature/humidity control, and elimination of potentially harmful packaging materials.

The manufacturing organization was modified by using the talents of Zytec's Value Analysis (VA) group for technical support of all soldering operations. Soldering was still the responsibility of individual product assembly lines, but the VA group assisted with training, process development, applications of Statistical-Process-Control (SPC), and defect analysis.

The visibility of the VA group increased as they became more involved with performing soldering process-optimization experiments, interacting with suppliers and customers, and providing documentation for publication. The VA group utilized sophisticated Design of Experiment (DOE) statistical approaches for optimization testing in the standard production environment, and Surface Insulation Resistance (SIR) laboratory testing and environmental stress testing at offsite locations.

Value Analysis allowed central information gathering for dealing with suppliers, customers, and other interested parties. It soon proved necessary also to accumulate supplier data for a host of available solder fluxes, review the information, and propose additional experiments or production trials.

Each customer presented unique requirements for quality, reliability, appearance, and other final product performance parameters. VA correlated customer specifications with available performance data. Finally, the VA group assisted in publicizing Zytec's efforts by:

- publishing technical papers,
- making presentations at appropriate conferences,
- assisting with media announcements and articles,
- making presentations to customer groups, and
- conducting tours.

Early in the LSF conversion program, Zytec's management decided that all aspects of the process not related to a customer's proprietary data would be freely available. Therefore, the VA group prepared an LSF information booklet that was issued on request to all interested companies or individuals.

By early 1991, all Zytec customers had approved processes that allow for complete freedom from cleaning with CFCs, and the goal of "zero use" was met with added benefits in process simplification, cost reduction, and quality improvement. By mid-August, 1991, Zytec soldered its millionth circuit board with the LSF process. The successful application of LSFs has also allowed for improved utilization of current factory floor space, decreased use of scarce water resources, and yielded significant reductions in the need for electrical power and compressed air.

Is the program now complete? Absolutely not! Compliance with the Montreal Protocol mandate is only a first step. Further quality and environmental improvements are all continuous goals. Success is not achieved with a one-time effort, but by a long-term strategy requiring evaluation of new materials and technology, process modification and optimization, training, and quality and reliability enhancements.

Along with creativity, organizational skills, and technical sophistication, the Zytec story illustrates that no company stands alone in the industrial economy. A change anywhere affects outside relationships—in Zytec's case, both suppliers and customers—and must be engineered into the total system with cooperation and support of many affected parties. And, as a process is re-engineered for one purpose, many other benefits may accrue along the way, an example of how environmental improvement can heighten overall competitiveness. With the recent decision to mandate a faster phaseout of CFC's, Zytec's forehandedness serves it well.

■ ■ ■

Source Reduction, Recycling, and Solid Waste Management

A growing mountain of household trash is the environmental problem most visible to millions of citizens. With the exception of some relatively low-volume hazardous products—such as used batteries, paint, waste motor oil, and certain household chemicals—the great bulk of today's trash is ecologically harmless. But disposing of it is both an environmental and an economic matter—because of the costs of collection, transportation, and landfilling at increasingly expensive or remote sites and because of the economic value and environmental savings inherent in recovering the materials and energy input contained in the trash when it is segregated and recycled.

If the present burden of society's trashpile can be reduced by techniques such as:

* *Source reduction*
* *Better product quality to provide longer service life*
* *Design for disassembly and reuse of components*
* *Recycling*

29

then both the amount of eventual waste and the all-in costs of dealing with it can be reduced. While citizens' willingness to do their part is increasing, and some local governments are demanding programs such as mandatory segregation and recycling, neither group alone or together can establish all the conditions necessary to close the solid waste loop effectively. Solutions to these complexities require both involvement and changes by industry if they are to succeed.

Ideally, market forces should play a major part in the development of solid waste management schemes. In some cases deposit systems stimulate returns for recycling. In others unit charges for household waste disposal have already reduced the amount of trash generated. However, it is difficult for host local governments to charge householders full cost for collection and landfilling, both because of political opposition and because high disposal costs imposed directly on consumers could encourage the improper disposal of wastes. Nor is the environmental cost differential between virgin and recycled feedstocks easily calculated or factored into manufacturers' economics. As a result, many products made from recycled materials are less serviceable or more expensive than those made from their virgin counterparts, or both. In addition to the qualitative goal of "less waste," quantitative economic measures need to be developed to incorporate all the presently unmeasured costs into the solid waste calculus.

Close coordination with users of recycled materials, and with users of products made from them becomes part of any post-consumer recycling program or cradle-to-grave systems redesign. High percentages of aluminum cans and scrap steel are already recycled through established systems, based on market forces. Waste paper is perhaps the most ubiquitous candidate for increased post-consumer recycling. Here is how several major San Francisco area companies are planning to develop both a larger supply of waste fiber and a greater market for products made from it, as reported by one of the initiators of the project.

Bank of America (et al.) *(supplied by Richard Morrison, senior vice president)*

Three large San Francisco Bay Area companies have created a coalition to try to improve the market for recycled paper. Bank of America, Pacific Gas and Electric Company, and Chevron plan to sign a charter which commits them to increase their purchases of recycled paper products. Other Bay Area companies are currently considering membership. Each corporation is a major purchaser of paper products.

The group met regularly since the summer of 1991 to develop the provisions of the charter under which they will voluntarily increase both their purchases of recycled paper products and the post-consumer waste content of the paper products purchased. The group also advocates expanding recycling programs and devoting new efforts to using paper products more efficiently. They have met regularly with printers, paper converters and manufacturers, and equipment manufacturers. Some of these companies also plan to sign the coalition charter.

The coalition hopes its actions will demonstrate sufficient long-term demand for recycled paper products to encourage investment in new recycled paper plants, de-inking plants and improved printing equipment. The coalition invites other organizations to become members to further enhance the effectiveness of its efforts.

The following is a draft of the coalition charter, which is expected to be finalized in March of 1992.

RECYCLED PAPER COALITION CHARTER

Preamble

We, the Members of the Coalition agree on the need for paper users to conserve natural resources and reduce waste through purchasing environmentally preferred paper products and by maximizing efficiency in the overall consumption of paper products. This effort initiated by the private sector is intended to encourage paper recycling and stimulate demand for recycled paper products made from materials that would otherwise be discarded.

Definition of Environmentally Preferred Paper Products

- Environmentally preferred paper products are those which minimize the impact on the environment throughout the process of manufacture, distribution, use, recycling and disposal.
- Most importantly, while all recovered paper should be considered in determining recycled content, environmentally preferred paper products should be made from recycled

31

materials using the highest percentage of post-consumer waste technically and legally feasible.

Membership

Members embrace the goals and commitments of the Coalition. To reflect this commitment membership is based on the following:
  a. Adoption of policies and/or programs that reflect the goals and commitments of the charter.
  b. Reporting as specified in the reporting section of the charter.

Goals of the Coalition

1. To reduce waste by using paper products efficiently.
2. To increase demand for environmentally preferred paper products by:
   a. committing as individual organizations to increase the use of environmentally preferred paper products.
   b. adding other companies and organizations to the coalition.
3. To maximize the content of post-consumer waste in paper products purchased. This may be achieved by the following:
   a. increasing the amount of environmentally preferred paper products as a percentage of total paper products purchased.
   b. increasing the percentage of post-consumer waste content in significant categories of paper products.
4. To overcome barriers and problems concerning availability, quality, and cost of environmentally preferred paper products.
5. To enhance the supply and quality of recycled pulp by committing to comprehensive paper recycling collection programs.

Commitment—Members of the Coalition will

1. Reduce waste by using paper products efficiently.
2. To the extent technically and legally feasible, embark on a purchasing program to satisfy paper requirements with

environmentally preferred products containing, as the initial goal, at least 10 percent post-consumer waste.

3. Give preference to competitively priced paper products with higher percentages of post-consumer waste and higher percentages of total recovered paper content.
4. Work with paper and equipment manufacturers to increase post-consumer waste content as quickly as technology will permit.
5. Ultimately, purchase 100 percent environmentally preferred paper products where technically and legally feasible.
6. Implement a comprehensive recycling program as widely as possible.

Reporting

Annually, by the end of the first quarter, each member will submit to the Coalition administration its plan of implementation for that calendar year. The plan shall reflect the member's action steps to accomplish the goals of the charter. Each new member will submit its plan within three months of joining the Coalition.

By the end of the first quarter each year, each member will report against its plan of the previous year the accomplishments and barriers encountered, if any. The report shall include as much specificity as possible. Two examples are attached. The use of the matrix format is encouraged but not required. The member's reports will be consolidated for the Coalition to use for possible reporting.

All individual members reporting to the Coalition will be confidential. Each member shall determine what information, if any, it will make available to the public.

Legal Attachment to be Published with the Charter

Membership in this Coalition is voluntary. No Member of the Coalition shall have any legal obligation arising out of this coalition: (a) to any other Member, (b) to any paper or equipment manufacturer or seller, (c) to any government agency, (d) to anyone else for any reason whatsoever, nor shall the coalition create any legal obligation among buyers as a group with sellers as a group.

The Members of the Coalition do not intend that this charter be used by either proponents or opponents of mandatory recovered paper content limits to support their positions. While individual members are free to express their own views, the Coalition as a group is neutral on this subject.

The format for reporting covers current results and future projections for paper purchases and waste paper generated, broken down by various categories. It has been omitted here in order to save space. The legal caveats in the final section recognize the complexities that even a simple voluntary association can raise for participants in the litigious world in which business operates.

If a system existed by which the environmental costs of making, using, collecting, and reusing paper fibers were incorporated into presently recognized economics of manufacture distribution and disposal, market forces would have already created an efficient closed-loop system, eliminating the need for the Coalition to develop one based on intuition and social pressure. Absent the ability to internalize these costs quantitatively, the Coalition's effort provides a commendable alternative.

■ ■ ■

Faced with the need to reuse, recycle or otherwise reduce the volume of waste materials quite specific to the company's products and systems, Xerox introduces the concept of remanufacture (incorporating discarded parts into new machines) and is designing copiers to accept paper made from recycled fibers, and copiers with features that reduce the amount of paper needed to perform the intended service.

Xerox *(from the company case history)*

In the resource conservation area, Xerox has been reclaiming and recycling materials used in manufacturing processes, including metal-alloy photoreceptors used in products (1.6 million pounds of nickel, aluminum, and selenium, annually). In addition, in the U.S. alone, over 35 million pounds of metal and other material are being recovered and recycled annually from scrapped products and parts.

Recognizing customer concerns about disposable products, Xerox has developed procedures for retrieving and recycling customer-replaceable copy cartridges. The company has now established design standards for its future products, including copy cartridges and toner containers, that provide an integrated approach to extended life, reduced cost, recycling, and remanufacturing compatibility. Customers participate in partnership with Xerox, returning copy cartridges.

Xerox is investigating new uses for waste toner from the company's manufacturing operations. Several promising solutions, including masterbatch pigmentation for plastics, asphalt additives, gaskets, and plastic lumber are in various stages of implementation. Tons of waste toner will be diverted from landfills to constructive uses, resulting in expected savings of over a million dollars a year.

The quality improvement process was applied by packaging engineers to reduce the environmental impact of our supplier and product packaging. Several teams working on packaging problems achieved the following:

- Instituted reuse of packaging and pallets based on a standardized design. This will avoid about 10,000 tons of waste and save up to $15 million annually.
- Developed Recyclable Corrupad cushioning from post-consumer recycled material, as a substitute for expanded polystyrene.
- Specified that when white corrugated shipping containers are desired they have an outer surface layer made exclusively from repulped, office waste paper that has not been de-inked. For other containers mixed wastepaper brown (MWP Brown) material is to be used, having a 50-percent post-consumer waste content.

Many product ideas conserve energy and reduce waste, including on-demand printing made possible by high-speed, masterless duplicators and the recently introduced DocuTech Publishing Series. DocuTech is a new reprographic machine for automated printing of books on demand, as well as 2-up and 4-up printing on paper sizes up to 11 by 17 inches. Since it prints on demand, it avoids overproduction and its ability to shrink page and type size allows more information to be printed on fewer pages.

Xerox, Rank Xerox, and Fuji Xerox all offer xerographic paper with post-consumer recycled content. In 1990, Xerox introduced a recycled copy paper in the United States and Canada comprised of 50-percent recycled fiber, including 10-percent post-consumer waste. In addition, Rank Xerox markets an "environmental paper" in Europe that is manufactured without using chlorine bleach and optical brighteners. Another Rank Xerox recycled paper uses 100-percent recycled wastepaper and is made without using chlorine bleach or optical brightening agents. This paper has been awarded Germany's coveted "Blue Angel"—the country's emblem of environmental acceptability—which requires that at least 50 percent of the content come from "low-grade" wastes, such as newspapers, phone books and magazines.

■ ■ ■

Procter & Gamble is one of the world's largest producers of consumer packaged goods, and it is a major manufacturer of wood pulp and pulp-based products, including disposable diapers. Its products and packaging are visible components of the solid waste stream.

In his report to shareholders at the October 1990 Annual Meeting, Chairman Edward L. Artzt spoke as follows on the company's efforts to deal with the solid waste problem in both Europe and America.

Procter & Gamble *(from a speech by Chairman and CEO Edward L. Artzt)*

Let me start with our environmental policy. We at Procter & Gamble feel a real responsibility to help preserve our world's environment through research, education, and action. Our policy is to be proactive—to be out front—and not merely responsive to pressure on environmental issues.

Today, I want to focus on solid waste. Our policy there starts with an objective—a vision of the future. We envision a world in which a bare minimum of products and packaging is tossed away. We envision that what does get thrown away will be reused, recycled, composted, or incinerated—with landfills used only as a last resort.

How are we doing? Well, just last week, the Company was presented the Keep America Beautiful "Vision for America" award in recognition of our leadership and many initiatives to help clean up the environment. We are proud and grateful for this recognition, but we're not kidding ourselves. We have a great deal yet to do.

One of our managers recently gave a talk on P&G's environmental policy. The audience was a mixture of students, representatives from environmental and consumer groups, and managers from other companies like ours. His written report of the meeting contained a statement that stuck in my mind. It said, "words won't cut it anymore. Important, meaningful, effective action is required."

Our consumers are also telling us that we still have a lot of work to do. We hear from environmentally aware consumers every day on our toll-free phone lines and through the mail—telling us to keep reducing the amount of packaging we use and to use recycled or recyclable materials whenever we can. We find ourselves very much in tune with our consumers on these issues. Let me give you some specific examples of what the Company has been doing to help relieve the solid waste crisis.

We have already reduced the cubic volume of our disposable diapers—Pampers and Luvs—by 50 percent when we introduced thin superabsorbent gel cores. We have also switched from bulky cardboard cartons to polybags, and that move cut our diaper packaging volume by 80 percent.

[Ed note: P&G's move from cartons to polybags saves volume and hence reduces pressure on landfills. Plastics, however, because of their varied chemical makeup and general lack of biodegradability, present a special recycling problem. Of course, a superior material may later become available. Meanwhile, P&G's choice of polybags responds to their evaluation of present environmental needs.]

Worldwide, Procter & Gamble has been in the forefront of compact detergent technology, which requires less packaging material. We've also introduced liquid refill packages, which reduce packaging up to 85 percent, and concentrated liquid products designed to be mixed with tap water in the home.

On recycling, we are working closely with local governments in such diverse cities as Baltimore, Maryland and Coburg, Germany to develop the collection systems, processors, and end-use demand to make recycling a commercial reality. We have committed ourselves to using recycled materials whenever we can. Our new Spic & Span bottle is 100 percent recycled plastic, and all of our U.S. laundry detergent cartons are made from recycled paper. We've also been using recycled plastic to produce our Liquid Tide, Cheer, Downy and Bold detergent bottles. These brands use high density polyethylene from recycled milk bottles that would have otherwise gone to landfills.

But the biggest opportunity for reducing solid waste in landfills has yet to be tapped. It's municipal solid waste composting. Up to 60 percent of the waste going into landfills today is organic compostable material and about half of that amount is wood pulp-based—that is, newspapers, magazines, telephone books, and paper and cardboard packaging.

Disposable diapers are a small part of this paper and pulp-based group. While they make up only 2 percent of the total, we feel that there is an urgent responsibility for finding new ways to significantly reduce the volume of diapers going into landfills. People always ask us—"Why don't you just make a biodegradable diaper? Wouldn't that solve the problem?" The answer, unfortunately, is no.

So-called biodegradable diapers simply would not degrade in landfills. A landfill is designed to be as water-tight and as air-tight as possible to prevent seepage and contamination, particularly of underground water supplies. Therefore, virtually nothing degrades in landfills, not even newspapers, food scraps, and yard wastes. We need to deal with our organic solid waste in a different way. We need to grind it up and compost it and return it to the environment as nutrient-rich totally sanitary humus. That may sound like a wild idea, but I assure you it is not. Municipal composting is exciting technology, and it really works. The heat sanitized humus produced by composting is a perfect soil conditioner and mulch for parks, farms, nurseries, greenhouses, and golf courses. It's also a natural for commercial landscapers.

When tilled into the earth, compost improves the soil's texture, water retention, and drainage. Nutrients can cling better to soil particles so farmers and gardeners need less chemical fertilizer. Compost can also help replace the billions of tons of top soil lost each year to erosion.

There already are 10 municipal solid waste composters operating in various parts of the United States. More than 150 are being developed. Only two years ago, there were no commercial solid waste composting facilities in Canada. Today, nine are planned there. Europe is already well ahead of the United States, with more than 200 municipal composting facilities up and running.

Procter & Gamble is committed to accelerating this worldwide development of municipal composting. I'm pleased to announce that we are taking two major steps to encourage further development of composting as a practical solution to solid waste management.

First, we are committing $20 million to fund projects that will advance municipal composting. This will include:

- Projects to demonstrate how composting should be integrated into the community's total solid waste system. We're talking about large waste systems that handle as much as 800 tons of garbage a day.
- Projects to show how composted solid waste humus can improve the quality of topsoil. For example, we've already initiated a five-year project with the U.S. Bureau of Mines to use solid waste compost to reclaim open-pit ore mines. And, we're funding research at the University of Minnesota to test compost for growing crops such as corn, alfalfa, and barley.
- Projects to advance composting technology for high population areas to meet the huge waste stream of cities like New York, Boston, and San Francisco.

My second major announcement today covers the Company's commitment to develop and introduce compostable disposable diapers. We have already demonstrated that our current Luvs and Pampers diapers are compatible with municipal composting systems, both in the U.S. and overseas. Currently, about 80 percent of the material in our diapers is already compostable. The rest is screened out during the composting process. Our goal is to make our diapers as fully compostable as possible, by replacing non-compostable materials with compostable ones as soon as materials can be developed and checked out in test markets.

Our next big step will be to replace the plastic backsheets on our diapers with fully compostable materials. We hope to have these new products in test markets during 1991, and assuming a favorable reception from consumers, we aim to expand the new diapers broadly over the next few years as municipal composting facilities become more and more widely available.

[Ed. Note: In February 1992, P&G reported that it has developed and is testing compostable diaper backsheets with encouraging results. A year after Mr. Artzt's speech, Procter & Gamble's case history provided this status report on the composting project:]

Currently, there are nineteen solid waste compost facilities either operating or in the start-up phase in eleven states in the United States and an additional 150 under development in thirty states. Five new state-of-the art model plants in the United States will begin operations during 1991. Plans are also under way to build solid-waste composting facilities in three major U.S. cities: Baltimore, Houston and San Diego. Worldwide, there are over 500 composting facilities and if one considers composting facilities for only leaf and yard waste, the number soars past 2,000.

P&G has provided funding to twelve communities in seven states to support their compost development efforts. In addition, the Company has sponsored several scientific and technical seminars in the United States, Switzerland, Belgium, and Germany for literally thousands of waste management professionals. P&G also has sponsored the development of educational materials for waste management and composting plant operators in Switzerland.

Further, the Company has joined with the Ohio State University, the U.S. Department of Agriculture and the U.S. Environmental Protection Agency, among others, in planning an International Composting Research Symposium to be held in Columbus [Ohio] in May 1992. Other activities include local market studies in six states to examine end uses for compost, currently being conducted by the Battelle Institute, and twelve research projects, now under way at eight universities on compost quality and technology.

The concept of source reduction, recycling, and reuse of recovered materials—call it "closing the loop" or "cradle to grave" systems design—consists of a number of steps:

- *Design the product to contain a minimum amount of material that must eventually be discarded.*
- *Design the product to facilitate recovery and reuse of its materials or components.*
- *Establish a post-consumer segregation, recovery, and return system.*
- *Change manufacturing processes to accommodate recycled materials in lieu of virgin input.*
- *Increase market demand for recycled materials and products made from them.*
- *Assist intermediate and end users in accommodating to any product performance changes caused by use of recycled materials.*
- *Eventually dispose of worn-out products and materials in a cost-effective and environmentally benign fashion.*

No one has more incentive to promote these changes than companies like Procter & Gamble and Xerox whose products are threatened by public dissatisfaction with the solid waste problem. And no one has a greater ability to work with consumers, waste collectors, recycled materials users and governments to close the loop than these companies. However, not all critics support the types of recycling proposed by Procter and Gamble and Xerox. For example, Ross Brockley, writing in the July/August 1991 issue of Multinational Monitor *states:*

> *''The problem with plastics recycling, however, is that it is not really recycling. As [Barry] Commoner explains, the 'system is not closed.' Plastics can only be recycled into lower grade plastics. Used styrofoam cups, for example, might be used to make a picnic table, but they cannot be recycled as styrofoam. New styrofoam will have to be manufactured to create new cups. Essentially all recycling plastics does, Commoner says, is create one more market for the industry.''*

Most people seem, however, to agree that some recycling progress now is preferable to delay in the hopes of eventual perfection.

Conservation and Renewable Sources of Energy

All modern economic systems rely to one extent or another on electric energy, derived in great part from the combustion of fossil fuels or biomass. Thus, power generation contributes heavily to lowered air quality, including

41

atmospheric build-up of carbon dioxide (CO_2) with its potential for global warming and resulting climate change.

In this section, three electric power companies describe their role in minimizing this threat. Assuming that economic activity will continue to require electric energy, power companies have three principal areas to consider in devising a strategy for emissions improvement. They can:

- *Reduce fuel consumption through greater efficiency in the production, transmission, and use of energy (often called conservation).*
- *Switch from coal or oil to less polluting fuels or to renewable energy sources.*
- *Capture harmful stack gasses before they escape into the atmosphere.*

The third option, the "end-of-the-pipe" solution, is pretty well incorporated into most modern power plants, though Japanese research is seeking ways to solidify CO_2 from stack gases, a distant though potentially revolutionary addition to remediation technology. The greatest opportunities for near-term improvement thus lie mostly in the first two areas. Here are some of the programs being implemented:

New England Electric System (NEES) *(from the company's brochure, "NEESPLAN 3")*

We have chosen air emissions for priority attention because air quality is substantially affected by the burning of fossil fuels to generate electricity and because our regulators have emphasized further improvements in this area. Growing concerns about the possible warming of the global atmosphere due to the emission of carbon dioxide and other "greenhouse gases" underscore the importance of these efforts.

The aggregate goal of a 45-percent reduction *[weighted for environmental impact]* is based on initial targets that NEES has set to reduce primary air emissions, as follows:

1) a 53-percent reduction in the tonnage of SO_2, representing a reduction of 74,000 tons per year between 1990 and 2000;
2) a 50-percent reduction in the tonnage of NO_x, representing a reduction of 30,000 tons per year between 1990 and 2000; and
3) a 20-percent reduction in the emissions of CO_2, and other greenhouse gases, including CO, CH_4, N_2O and CFCs, when

netted against our actions to offset these emissions. This net reduction represents the equivalent of approximately 3 million tons of CO_2.

NEES has developed a single index to measure the impact of air emissions so that we can readily monitor progress. This index reflects emissions from all power sources on which NEES relies to meet our customers' needs, including both our own generation and purchased power, as well as actions we take to offset these emissions. The index includes eight air emissions:

- Sulfur Dioxide (SO_2)—a contributor to acid rain;
- Nitrogen Oxides (NO_x)—contributors to ozone formation and acid rain;
- Carbon Dioxide (CO_2)—a greenhouse gas;
- Particulates—dust and ash, which can affect breathing;
- Volatile Organic Compounds (VOCs)—contributors to ozone formation;
- Carbon Monoxide (CO)—a respiratory irritant and a greenhouse gas;
- Methane (CH_4)—a greenhouse gas; and
- Nitrous Oxide (N_2O)—a greenhouse gas.

[Ed. Note: To arrive at its "weighted" index of emissions, NEES collaborated with independent expert consultants and the Massachusetts Department of Public Utilities to establish monetary values that express the environmental benefit of avoiding the emissions normally associated with burning each ton of a fuel. Using these values, they constructed a weighted total of all NEES emissions from which to measure reductions. Obviously, assigning different relative values to the various gasses would alter the percentage by which any specific program would reduce the weighted total. Despite its empirical nature, the NEES technique is an important effort to monetize environmental impact as a first step in designing and prioritizing emission-reduction programs.]

The year 1990 is the starting point for measuring our goal. Our 1990 emissions data reflect the substantial efforts NEES had already undertaken before 1990 to reduce emissions, making our goal of further reductions more challenging.

NEES's goal is to achieve a 45-percent reduction in the net air emissions from our operations between 1990 and 2000 even though our energy requirements in 2000 are projected to be 14 percent higher than in 1990. On a per-kilowatt hour basis, this goal would reduce net air emissions by more than 50 percent over the decade.

NEES intends to accomplish its overall air emissions reduction goal through a variety of programs:

- 11 percent improvement will come from actions to comply with federal and state clean air legislation, ahead of schedule where possible. These actions include modifying our 440 MW *[Megawatt]* Brayton Point Unit 4 to enable it to burn natural gas; using lower sulfur oil and coal to reduce SO_2 emissions; installing NO_x reduction technology on major generating units; and refurbishing pollution-control equipment.
- 10 percent will come from using non-utility generation predominantly fired by natural gas.
- 9 percent will come from repowering NEES's Manchester Street Station as a gas fired combined-cycle plant, which will greatly improve its efficiency and reduce emissions. This project, which has been included in rates by the Federal Energy Regulatory Commission, is expected to enter service in 1995.
- 6 percent will come from other new power sources entering service between 1990 and 2000, including the purchase of hydroelectric energy from Hydro-Quebec. We are also seeking relicensing of our own hydroelectric facilities and are repowering our Vernon hydro station to increase its efficiency, while adding 20 MW of capacity.
- 4 percent will come from continued C&LM *[conservation and load management]* efforts, expected to eliminate the need for about 850 MW of resources, thus preventing growth in environmental emissions.
- 5 percent will come from actions beyond our current commitments.

Renewables

Renewable resource technologies are methods of generating electricity without consuming fossil fuel. They include relatively well-developed technologies, such as hydroelectric generation, and newer technologies, such as the generation of electricity from wind, solar, biomass, waste, and methane released by landfills.

NEP [New England Power Company] plans to solicit [proposals for] advanced renewable energy projects from non-utility suppliers. Although there is not a need for additional power at present, the current lack of urgency will allow us to explore new technologies in a way that would not be possible at a time of energy shortage.

New renewable resources procured in this initiative can be valuable in three ways. First, some renewable plants may be a source of energy at a price comparable to existing and new fossil fuel generation. Second, renewable resources may provide emission reductions to complement other air emission reduction strategies or offset opportunities. Finally, some renewable projects can provide valuable information about the feasibility, value, and potential for expansion of technologies that are not yet proven in New England.

While NEES has experience with many renewable technologies, we have no experience with advanced biomass plants that use a fast-growing wood supply as a fuel source. This technology allows the CO_2 released during combustion of the wood to be substantially offset on a continuing basis by CO_2 intake through photosynthesis during tree growth. Development of a small project would give us greater knowledge of the future feasibility and value of larger advanced biomass projects.

We have similar lessons to learn about the development and adaptation of wind technology to this region. Our initiative will allow us to put such technologies to the commercial test and to gain experience with procurement, siting, and licensing.

NEES is planning to explore methods of offsetting emissions of greenhouse gases, which have been associated with the warming of the global environment. While scientific controversy exists over the net effect of increases of such gases on global temperature and climate, NEES plans to follow the recommendation of the National Academy of Sciences that utilities and others implement low-cost measures to mitigate the further buildup of greenhouse gases.

Greenhouse gases can be reduced or prevented at their source before being released into the atmosphere. They can also be reduced by taking actions at other locations to counterbalance or "offset" the emissions. The most commonly cited example of an offset is planting trees to absorb CO_2 from the atmosphere.

NEP plans to solicit proposals for programs to offset greenhouse gases. The proposed solicitation will allow us to test several different offset strategies during the next few years. These may include offsets available in our service area, such as the recycling of CFCs from refrigerators and air conditioners, and offsets available globally, such as tree planting to remove CO_2 from the environment. Other strategies that may be available at low cost include reusing solid waste such as coal ash; recovering methane released in the mining of coal; and enhancing marine algae growth to absorb carbon dioxide.

Our C&LM efforts can serve as a model for our new environmental initiatives. NEES's C&LM programs have been researched, developed, and implemented in concert with the Conservation Law Foundation (CLF). The programs are reviewed by a Demand-Side Management Advisory Board that includes representatives of environmental groups (including the CLF), our customers, and the academic community. Most important, our C&LM efforts have received the full support of our regulators in the three states we serve. Regulators in Rhode Island, Massachusetts, and New Hampshire broke new ground in allowing NEES to earn an incentive on the savings produced by our C&LM programs.

To help develop, implement, and oversee its environmental initiatives, NEES is creating a new environmental collaborative. This collaborative will include representatives of the environmental, consumer, business, and academic communities. The collaborative will focus on our environmental targets, including the identification of the most cost-effective means of achieving them. The group will help to develop the details of NEES's renewables initiative, greenhouse gas offset initiative, and other efforts, such as further exploration of offsets for NO_x and SO_2 emissions.

In addition to programs to reduce greenhouse gases, New England Electric reports environmental initiatives aimed at using fly ash as concrete aggregate, recycling paper, reducing the number of chemicals used, increasing car pooling, and conducting environmental training programs.

In its emission reductions effort, the company makes particular note of its close working relationship with regulators. This is especially important because investments in environmental protection, including energy conservation, are being allowed by regulators as inclusions in a power generation company's capital or operating costs in an increasing number of states. Recovery of or a return on these environmental investments may then be included in prices to be paid by electric power customers. At the margin, the higher prices also tend to reduce power usage. In this situation, a regulated utility can pass on its conservation expenses to consumers more easily than can a manufacturer whose products compete in international markets with less environmentally burdened rivals, assuming that in doing so the power company does not lose out to the competing forms of energy that may bear different social or environmental costs.

Also of interest are the close working relationship New England Electric has developed with environmentalists and the company's aggressive plan for studying the potential of renewables by means of outside contracts for pilot projects. Like many other corporate environmental improvement programs, however, New England Electric's is in its early stages, and results projected are not yet in hand.

■ ■ ■

Like New England Electric, Southern California Edison sees energy conservation as a key step to environmental improvement. Its commitment to reduce CO_2 emissions by 20 percent is described in Chapter XII. Another one of its strategies is to develop and demonstrate energy saving technologies that can benefit its customers.

Southern California Edison *(from the company case history)*

In January 1991, Edison created the Customer Technology Application Center (CTAC) located in Irwindale, California. CTAC is the largest and most comprehensive facility of its kind, communicating energy solutions that promote energy efficiency and help improve the environment to thousands of Southern California companies. CTAC hosts seminars and demonstrations for customers, as well as engineers, architects, government leaders and employees.

CTAC contains an extensive selection of commercially available electric technologies. The 23,000-square-foot facility includes industrial, commercial, residential, commercial food preparation, lighting design, and learning centers. Each features tested electric technologies plus related informational materials.

The Industrial Technology Center exhibits industrial lighting fixtures and three individual lighting systems. Demonstrations

47

educate customers in low emissions and energy-saving innovations, such as ultraviolet and infrared curing and microwave and radio frequency drying. Showcased in the Commercial Technology Center are high efficiency heat pumps, a power quality demonstration, thermal energy storage systems, and alternatives to internal combustion engines. The Residential Technology Center features a 1,000-square-foot "House-of-the-Future." Heat pumps, electronic meters, home automation systems, water conservation techniques, and an electric fan are demonstrated here. The Commercial Cooking Center contains the latest in commercial cooking technology, including a conveyor convection oven, a braising pan and a steamer convection oven. The Lighting Design Center features 150 lamp fixtures designed to increase productivity and energy efficiency. Color booths demonstrate how different fixtures and lights alter the perception of color.

The 100-seat Learning Center, which accommodates conferences and seminars, provides a glimpse into the future in conference presentations with podium control of lighting and all audio-visual capabilities. Since opening, CTAC has had more than 15,000 customers visit.

Several additional outreach programs are housed at CTAC. Clean Air Coatings *[for example]* was developed to help customers throughout Edison's service area meet increasingly strict air-quality regulations. Edison demonstrates the most advanced techniques for meeting air-quality compliance standards in many industries, including the wood finishing, auto body, metal, and plastics industries. Methods such as ultraviolet- and infrared-curing techniques, as well as high volume, low pressure, and waterborne technologies, are demonstrated side-by-side in CTAC—a one-stop shop for technologies. Customers are encouraged to bring samples of their products to CTAC. Edison coatings experts also visit customers to demonstrate new methods and to discuss technology upgrading.

■ ■ ■

Pacific Gas and Electric Company is the nation's largest investor-owned gas and electric utility serving most of northern and central California. PG&E has adopted a comprehensive environmental program that is integrated into all aspects of its business. Key elements of the program include improving the efficiency with which customers use electric power, the development of environmentally preferred power production technologies such as renewables, and the promotion of clean air vehicles. Because it is in the business of distributing natural gas, it is also trying to increase use of that fuel as a replacement for more polluting alternatives. Here is how these programs were presented to PG&E's Board of Directors:

Pacific Gas and Electric Company *(from the company's 1991 Annual Report ''Commitment to Environmental Quality'')*

In 1990, Pacific Gas and Electric Company adopted a corporate goal to improve the quality of the environment, reflecting the increasing awareness and concern about environmental quality on the part of its shareholders, customers, and society in general. And it announced PG&E's commitment to lead in environmental work among energy utilities in the United States.

Also in 1990, PG&E adopted a policy statement—to describe how the company plans to achieve the new environmental goal. In the policy statement, PG&E set out specific objectives in seven areas: Customer Energy Efficiency, Electric Resources Planning, Clean Fuels, Clean Air Vehicles, Natural Resources Stewardship, Employee Involvement, and Environmental Management.

[Ed. Note: The first, third, and fourth program are discussed immediately below. The fifth, Natural Resources Stewardship, is covered in Section E of this chapter.]

Programs to increase efficiency in the use of energy constitute PG&E's largest energy resource and its most environmentally benign energy strategy for the 1990s. Customer Energy Efficiency (CEE) is the centerpiece of the company's Electric Resource Plan. For every megawatt (mw) of new electric capacity that will be added in PG&E's system in the 90s, PG&E expects to save three mw—or ''negawatts,'' as they are becoming known—through CEE. These savings will be achieved primarily through new and improved technologies, rather than through traditional conservation techniques, which many customers associate with some sacrifice of comfort and convenience.

PG&E's confidence in its CEE plans is based on its history of success in encouraging customer conservation and energy efficiency.

49

Over the last 15 years, PG&E has invested $1.5 billion in energy-efficiency measures, avoiding 1,800 mw of new power plant construction and saving customers more than $3.5 billion.

In mid-1990, PG&E began a major expansion of its CEE programs, with plans to spend about $2 billion on energy efficiency in the '90s, more than double what it spent in the '80s. During 1991, about $185 million was spent on more than 40 programs. That was an increase of about $47 million over 1990.

PG&E's strategy is to use financial incentives and education to motivate customers to install and use more energy-efficient lighting, appliances, building systems, heating and air conditioning, landscaping techniques, and other available technology. For example:

- 18-watt compact fluorescent bulbs produce as much light as 75-watt incandescent bulbs, but use less energy and last 12 times longer. Energy savings over the 10,000-hour life of the fluorescent will total $60. To encourage customers to install the fluorescents, PG&E will rebate $7 of the $12 cost of each bulb.
- Today's high-efficiency refrigerators use 50 percent less energy than models sold in the 70s. PG&E provides rebates to help customers buy the high-efficiency appliances. PG&E also advocates increasingly higher appliance efficiency standards.

In both examples, while the initial purchase price to the customer is higher than for traditional equipment, the total life-cycle costs to the customer are reduced. 1991 CEE activities throughout PG&E resulted in savings of about 607 million kilowatt hours (kwh) of electricity, equal to the annual use of about 100,000 PG&E area households; 37 million therms of natural gas, equal to the annual use of 50,000 PG&E area households, and offset the need for 119 mw of electric generating capacity, enough to serve an area of about 120,000 people. These savings come from all groups of customers and a variety of measures taken in 1991 including lighting efficiency improvements that will save more than 200 million kwh per year; agricultural programs, including, pump repairs and adjustments, modern irrigation pipe and greenhouse heating curtains that will save more than 100 million kwh per year; heating, ventilation and airconditioning that will save more than 70 million kwh per year; high-efficiency refrigerators for home use that will save more than 4.5 million kwh per year, and industrial process improvements such as more efficient motors and better boilers that will save more than 40 million kwh per year.

PG&E exceeded its 1991 CEE electric energy goal by 92 percent, its natural gas goal by 151 percent, and its electric capacity goal by 15 percent.

First-year emission reductions from measures taken in 1991 will total some 445 tons of nitrogen oxides, 120 tons of sulfur oxides and 340,000 tons of carbon dioxide from entering the atmosphere. The pollution savings, since the CEE programs began in 1990, are the equivalent of taking about 70,000 cars off California's roads.

PG&E's CEE-related earnings in 1991, under new regulations that allow the company to earn a profit linked to its success in saving energy, were $45.1 million before taxes.

Education and research are also vital elements of the CEE program. For example:

- In 1991, PG&E opened its Pacific Energy Center in San Francisco, a $7.5 million technology center to demonstrate energy-efficient technologies and design techniques to residential and commercial architects, engineers, builders, and developers.
- In 1990, PG&E contracted for a $10-million study with the Rocky Mountain Institute, the Lawrence Berkeley Laboratory and the Natural Resources Defense Council to demonstrate new energy-efficient technologies in homes and businesses. The project is testing the hypothesis that modern high-efficiency technologies can produce energy savings of up to 75 percent, at or below the cost of new energy supply. In 1991, retrofit design of the first commercial building site was 95 percent completed, with indications that electric use can be reduced 75 percent and gas use can be reduced by 90 percent.

With CEE, everybody wins. The environment benefits because power plants produce less energy and therefore fewer emissions than they otherwise would, and the need for new power plants, power lines and substations is reduced. Participating customers save on their energy bills. If the participating customer is a business, this enhances its competitiveness. All customers benefit because it costs less to save energy than to build the facilities to produce it. And PG&E shareholders win because of the profit incentives available to California utilities.

Clean Fuels

To ensure an adequate future supply of natural gas to the California market, PG&E and Pacific Gas Transmission Company (PGT), a wholly-owned subsidiary of PG&E, in 1991 began preliminary construction on a 900-mile, $1.7 billion pipeline expansion project to bring an additional 755 million cubic feet of gas daily to California starting in 1993. Natural gas delivered through the new pipeline will avoid the use of at least 10 million barrels of oil a year in California. This means that about 4,000 tons of nitrogen oxide and 1½ million tons of carbon dioxide will not enter the atmosphere each year.

In September 1991, PG&E announced an agreement in principle to sell its wholly-owned subsidiary, Pacific Gas Transmission Company, which owns and operates the portion of the pipeline between California and Canada, to TransCanada Pipelines, Ltd. Terms of the planned sale include a commitment by TransCanada to complete the expansion.

PG&E also supports the development of clean fuel technologies. The company is participating in a joint venture to build the world's first molten carbonate fuel cell power plants. The first such plant, a 100-kilowatt test facility at PG&E's Research and Development Center in San Ramon, California, went into operation in 1991.

This type of fuel cell could eventually be used at existing generating sites to replace conventional steam-thermal units. Clean-burning and quiet, it would also be a candidate for use in a "distributed utility generation" setting, producing power in the same neighborhood in which it would be consumed.

[Ed. Note: Fuel cells emit no NO_x and, since their anticipated fuel efficiencies are greater, they emit proportionately less CO_2 per unit of power delivered than a central power plant fueled by natural gas (the most environmentally benign fossil fuel). Like the conventional gas-fired power plant, fuel cells emit essentially no SO_2. Both gas-based systems emit less CO_2 per btu of fuel used than coal or oil-fired power plants. In short, fuel cells are very promising environmentally, but fall somewhat short of being

a no-emissions "silver bullet" solution because of their remaining CO_2 discharges. Whether they can deliver electricity at a competitive cost is yet to be determined.]

Clean Air Vehicles

Improvement in California's air quality will depend to a large extent on reducing emissions from motor vehicles. In March 1990, at its service center in Concord, PG&E opened the state's first publicly accessible fueling station for vehicles equipped to operate on natural gas. By the end of 1991, full or limited public access was available at 14 stations in PG&E's service area, with 13 more to be completed in 1992. PG&E's goal is to serve 125,000 fleet vehicles by the year 2000, or 25 percent of the 500,000 fleet vehicles in the service area suitable for conversion to natural gas. PG&E's Natural gas vehicle (NGV) gasload in the year 2000 is expected to be 17.6 billion cubic feet, or about 3% of gas sales. PG&E is also participating in the research and development of electric vehicles, which hold the greatest long-range promise for the reduction of air-polluting vehicle emissions.

The fleets of delivery trucks, vans, and buses that operate in and around major population centers are ideal candidates to run on natural gas. These vehicles typically log many miles of stop-and-go city driving, fuel at the same locations, and have space for natural gas tanks. And there are lots of them—800,000 in PG&E's service area, of which 500,000 are suitable for conversion to natural gas. PG&E's goal is to serve 25 percent of this market, or 125,000 vehicles, by the year 2000. In PG&E's service area, 250 fleet vehicles, including 135 belonging to the company, were operating on natural gas at the end of 1990.

On a per-mile basis, vehicles that run on natural gas rather than gasoline produce about 80 percent less reactive organic gases (ROG), which contribute to ozone; 60 percent less benzene and formaldehydes, both carcinogenic gases; 50 percent less carbon monoxide, a toxic gas; and 25 percent less carbon dioxide, the principal greenhouse gas. NGVs already exceed most of California's 1994 standards for light duty vehicles, the strictest standards in the nation.

To increase the convenience of NGV fueling, PG&E had seven natural gas stations operating in its service area at the end of 1990.

53

Figure 2. Vehicular Air Emission Reductions
(Percentage reduction using natural gas versus gasoline)

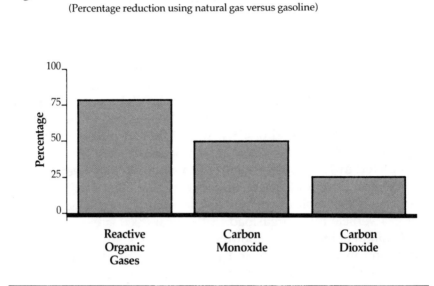

Source: Commitment to Environmental Quality—1990 Annual Report to the Board of Directors of Pacific Gas and Electric Company, p. 4

In early 1991, PG&E opened five more. Of the total, five are fully accessible to the public and six have limited access. By the end of 1992, the number of fueling stations at PG&E and customer sites is expected to total 33. Other NGV milestones in 1991 included:

- PG&E's agreement with Shell Oil Company for installation of the first natural gas dispenser at a retail service station. The dispenser, at a Shell service station in Sacramento, was opened to the public on April 16, 1991.
- An agreement by General Motors and 10 utilities, including PG&E, under which GMC Truck will build at least 1,000 dedicated natural gas three-quarter ton trucks in late 1991 and 1992.

[Ed. Note: Interestingly, the practicality of gas-powered fleets is already well established elsewhere. Essentially all of the taxicabs in Tokyo and Seoul are already running on propane, with initial and operating cost of new vehicles at least competitive with gasoline-powered alternatives, according to the U.S. Embassy in Tokyo.]

In its electric vehicles effort, PG&E is participating in the national evaluation of the G-Van, a full-sized prototype van powered by lead-acid batteries. The vehicle is being tested for market acceptability. These vans recharge in eight to ten hours from a 240-volt outlet. When recharging is done at night, commercial fuel costs are about three cents per mile.

■ ■ ■

The environmental programs described by the three power companies differ markedly in one major respect from the manufacturing examples that preceded them. In two cases, the central thrust of the program is conservation—centered around a reduction in the demand for their product resulting from company-supported consumer efficiencies. This reversal of the stereotypical situation, in which companies are accused of stimulating excessive use of products to build sales and profits, has a simple cause. There is an economic benefit to saving because the rate-setting agencies allow the companies to recover and earn a return on energy-saving investments in the system. So, these companies are not just changing to save their right to operate, they are changing to help their bottom lines.

In one form or another, power company investments in energy conservation are now incorporated into the rate-setting process in about 30 states. The extent of the programs of our three reporting companies, and the environmental benefits that accompany them, underscore the wisdom and power of putting market forces to work to help the environment.

Forest Management and the Preservation of Biodiversity

It is an ecological truism that "everything affects everything else." Recently, it has become apparent that a similar inter-relationship exists between the "everythings" of nature and the "everythings" of economic activity.

This link is clearly evident in the impact of both power generation and forestry on the workings of nature's carbon cycle, the process by which the carbon discharged as CO_2 gas to the atmosphere through combustion or natural causes is sequestered by means of photosynthesis and refixed as solid matter in the form of trees and other vegetation, reducing the increased concentration of atmospheric CO_2 that would otherwise exist. And, as economic activities disturb forests, they also change the nature of the forest as habitat for a multitude of plant and animal species.

55

Here are two examples of how one company, working with World Resources Institute, conceived of a way to operate that would prevent its activities from having any net impact on the global CO_2 balance and, at the same time, would help to alleviate poverty and preserve biodiversity in tropical countries.

The AES Corporation (AES) *(from its booklet "Carbon Offset Programs—Summer Update—1991")*

Because AES power facilities burn fossil fuels and emit carbon dioxide (CO_2), the largest contributor to global warming, the company decided several years ago to explore possible ways to offset the carbon it releases in case scientific concerns about global warming prove accurate.

AES's strategy involves balancing carbon released from its new power plants with carbon sequestration, the process of increasing the carbon that is stored in forests and other living matter. This strategy is possible because carbon is absorbed from the air through photosynthesis and makes up roughly half the mass of a tree.

Because CO_2 has a global circulation pattern, AES can target any part of the world for a carbon offset. When evaluating projects, AES looks for additional benefits that can include improving economic conditions for communities in areas hard-hit by deforestation and preserving endangered plant and animal species in those areas.

Guatemala Agroforestry Project

Guatemala once had one of the richest and most diverse forests in Central America. Due to population pressures experienced over the past 35 years, however, fully half of the Guatemalan forests have been cleared for fuelwood, lumber, and agriculture.

[Ed. Note: Concentrated land ownership and need for export earnings have also generated pressures to clear forests.]

This continued deforestation has led to extensive soil erosion, which damages valuable farmland and decreases the life of the country's hydropower resources by siltation of reservoirs.

The Guatemala Agroforestry Project was created to regain lost biomass and to control the soil erosion problem through reforestation programs and soil-conservation measures. The project is based on "multiple use sustainable forestry." Local farmers are being trained in farm and forestry practices by United States Peace Corps volunteers, Guatemalan forestry extension agents, and CARE (Cooperative for American Relief Everywhere) personnel. The project aims to involve 40,000 Guatemalan farm families in self-sustaining agroforestry and forest and soil-conservation programs. The programs include the planting of 52 million mixed species trees by the year 2000.

[Ed. Note: Several organizations are contributing to the Guatemala project, including the U.S. Peace Corps, US-AID, and CARE, which is managing the effort.]

Figure 3. Relative Contribution Toward Carbon Sequestration

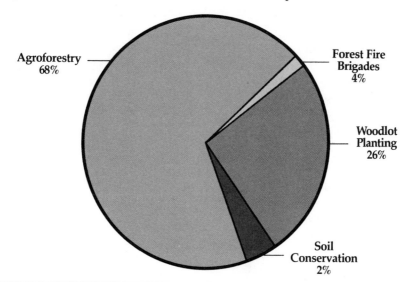

Agroforestry
68%

Forest Fire
Brigades
4%

Woodlot
Planting
26%

Soil
Conservation
2%

Source: World Resources Institute Report, *Forestry as a Response to Global Warming*

AES Thames plant's contribution of $2 million to CARE will establish an endowment that will help to fund project activities for the 10-year project period and beyond.

The AES Thames plant anticipates emitting approximately 15.5 million tons of carbon into the atmosphere over its 40-year-life. The Guatemalan programs in agroforestry, forest fire brigade training, soil conservation, and woodlot planting are expected to generate enough biomass to sequester 18 million tons of carbon over the same 40-year period.

[Ed. Note: Progress towards the project's goals are illustrated in Figure 4.]

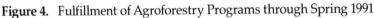

Figure 4. Fulfillment of Agroforestry Programs through Spring 1991

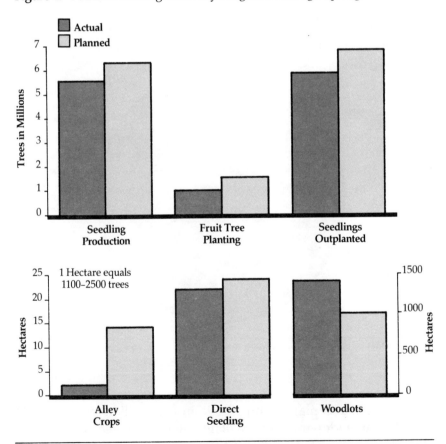

Source: "AES Carbon Offset Programs Summer Update 1991," p. 3

Alley cropping is a method of agriculture in which nitrogen-fixing trees are planted in conjunction with crops, increasing productivity. CARE still anticipates achieving the goal of planting 310 hectares of alley crops by the end of the project period. Wood-lots are trees planted for lumber, building, and other harvestable purposes. The project plans call for planting 12,500 hectares of woodlots by the year 2000.

Mbaracayu Conservation Project

AES Barbers Point is a 180-MW cogeneration plant currently under construction in Hawaii. This plant will emit about 14.8 million tons of CO_2 over its 35-year life. This volume requires a carbon-mitigation program roughly similar in scale to the AES Guatemala project. To achieve this goal, AES Barbers Point is currently working with the Nature Conservancy and the Moisés Bertoni Foundation to fund a major forest-conservation project in Paraguay.

It was recently estimated that 250,000 acres of tropical forest are cleared each year in Paraguay, and at present rates the whole country could be deforested in 15 years. At risk from such deforestation is the Mbaracayu, a 142,800-acre tract that contains some of the last dense humid sub-tropical forest in Latin America. The Conservancy and its Paraguayan partner, the Moisés Bertoni Foundation, recently purchased the tract from the International Finance Corporation. The Mbaracayu is home to 19 distinct plant communities and many unique and endangered species. It is also the historic home to the Ache, an indigenous tribe of hunter-gatherers who rely on the forest's threatened wildlife and plants for their traditional livelihood.

Conservation groups and the National Parks Directorate in Paraguay determined that purchasing the Mbaracayu was the only possible way of fully protecting it. Competing bidders to the International Finance Corporation for the land included lumber companies who would selectively remove timber prior to burning the forest to clear the land for farming. By helping to prevent the destruction of the forest, AES will halt the release of much of the forest's millions of tons of sequestered carbon.

AES Barbers Point will provide up to $2 million of the $3.75 million needed for start-up funds for the first three years of the project. The application of such funds is indicated in Figure 5.

Figure 5. Application of Funds

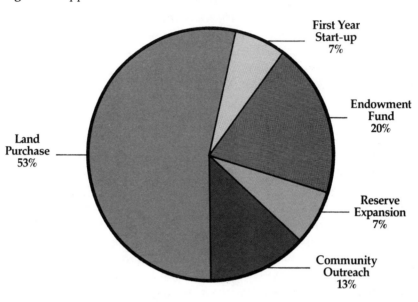

Source: "AES Carbon Offset Programs Summer Update 1991," p. 3

Additional land for buffer zones around the park will be purchased using other funds. Economic development programs for
local communities based on sustainable use of natural resources
will be established. Science expeditions and nature tourism are also
planned to be an integral part of the project. The Nature Conservancy and the other parties involved have just closed with the International Finance Corporation to purchase the Mbaracayu. Over
the long term, the value of these projects in sequestering carbon
will be measured by the average mass of vegetation present on the
land compared to the amount that would have been there without
the AES-supported programs. In this way, the effect of trees dy-
ing and decaying, and their harvest for fuelwood can be factored
into the calculation of net carbon removed from the atmosphere.

■ ■ ■

*It is not necessary to go to exotic tropical countries to help preserve bio-
diversity. Plenty of opportunities to protect habitat lie within the United*

60

States. When a company's operations are as widespread as utilities' are, individual employees have a special responsibility to minimize their impact on the natural world in which they work. Here is the approach of one company operating in the ecologically sensitive area of Southern California.

Southern California Edison *(from the company case history)*

The company's environmental experience ranges from air quality improvement, to creating an artificial reef at its San Onofre Nuclear Generating Station near San Clemente, California, to the discovery and protection of a Pleistocene Age horse *[skeleton]* at a desert construction site. However, it is Edison's Endangered Species Alert Program that has emerged as one of the utility's environmental flagships and that is another example of a program primarily directed to employees.

California is home for some of the most rare, most threatened, and most endangered species of any state in the nation. More than 750 species of animals and about 5,200 plant species exist naturally in the state, many of which are found nowhere else in the world. Of these, approximately 80 wildlife and 180 plant species are officially designated by either the federal or state government as endangered or threatened with extinction. More than 100 threatened or endangered species can be found within the company's diverse 50,000-square-mile service area.

During the past 100 years, burgeoning agricultural and urban growth have dramatically depleted the state's once pristine natural habitat. And, as the population continues to grow, the continual loss of habitat will undoubtedly and unfortunately increase the number of endangered species.

As part of Edison's effort to help reverse this decline, the company designed an Endangered Species Alert Program to avoid impacts on these species and their respective habitats. The program consists of a detailed employee information program that educates construction workers about the presence and characteristics of the many species they could potentially encounter.

At the heart of this program is a heavily detailed and abundantly illustrated manual that has been distributed to the utility's field personnel. The manual serves as a valuable tool to spot potential

61

threats to species before they develop. Further, the manual serves as a guide to alert employees about possible violations of the federal Endangered Species Act of 1973, as well as the California Endangered Species Act.

Other specific Edison environmental programs support protection of birds of prey and enhancement of marine life. For example, big hawks, eagles, and ospreys can be electrocuted if their expansive wings touch two energized lines at once on transmission towers and power poles. Edison engineers have installed elevated perches and inverted "V-shaped" fixtures on top of its power poles to encourage perching on safer roosts. Edison also identifies areas with the highest concentration of birds of prey so that it can avoid them when building lines and structures. Also, Edison is helping the Department of Fish and Game in the California Condor Release Program by modifying or "undergrounding" some of its facilities in the targeted release area.

Along the Southern California coastline, Edison has made use of abalone in power plant operations to verify the absence of toxins in our effluent discharges to the ocean. However, over the years, the abalone population has been depleted in Southern California due to excessive harvesting and ocean contaminants. Edison researchers began breeding the mollusks in the lab and developed new techniques for safer abalone placement and survival in the wild. Since that program's inception, Edison divers have returned more than 250,000 abalone to Pacific waters. This research also has enhanced the prospect for commercial abalone farming in the future.

■ ■ ■

Together with clearing land for agriculture, harvesting trees for lumber, fuelwood, and fiber represents a major drain on the world's natural forests and the species that depend on the complex ecosystems that natural forests provide. Yet, the products of the forests are essential for the economies of both developed and developing countries. The question becomes how to provide for those needs with minimum impact. It is not an easy one to answer. Here is what Weyerhaeuser, long known as "the tree growing company" has to say:

Weyerhaeuser *(as submitted by the company)*

Increasing world population will place extraordinary demands on both tropical and temperate forests to supply the wood and paper products that modern society requires, while at the same time providing wildlife habitat, watershed protection, and other elements of sustainable forest ecosystems. As we approach the next century, it is imperative that both public and private forestlands be managed to meet the broad range of economic, ecological, and social needs of future generations.

Weyerhaeuser Company recognized as early as the 1930s that successfully regenerated and more intensively managed forests would be needed to meet the demand for forest products on a long-term, sustainable basis. This idea was viewed as a radical departure from the forest practices typical of the industry at that time.

> "This is not for us, nor for our children—but for our grand-children."
>
> ■ *Frederick Weyerhaeuser, 1900*

Nevertheless, the philosophy of managing forestlands for the long term became established as a Weyerhaeuser "core value." We began with the basics: aggressive protection of forestland from the ravages of wildfire, research in tree planting and other forest regeneration practices, and basic soils research provided the scientific foundation for today's management prescriptions.

By the mid-1960s, long-term world population projections and Weyerhaeuser's previous quarter century of forestry research combined to support the next incremental change in forestland management practices—from *extensive* to *intensive*.

Known as High Yield Forestry, our intensive forest management strategy was launched in 1966. An increase in management intensity would:

- dramatically increase per acre productivity of useable wood fiber,
- provide an attractive investment opportunity,
- help meet the increasing demand for forest products, and
- relieve some of the pressure on public lands that were being increasingly managed to emphasize non-timber resource values.

The results of these intensive forest-management practices are very impressive. In 1992, the growth rate of conifers on our U.S.

63

ownership is among the highest in the world. On our highest site [i.e., *most productive*] lands, we are producing more than twice the annual growth on each acre compared to unmanaged forests. With intensive management on productive sites, the world's needs for wood and paper products can be satisfied with significantly less acreage than would be otherwise required.

This success has been supported by producing forest tree seedlings in our own nurseries, understanding and utilizing the genetic variation of our forest tree species, and improving the survival and growth rates of planted seedlings. We grow 300 million seedlings annually in our nurseries—one third of which are destined for Weyerhaeuser forests and the remainder sold to other landowners.

Impressive as this tree-growing record is, it isn't enough. Today the public expects more. In 1992, it's not enough to be best at growing and renewing trees. It isn't even enough to be very efficient at using the trees we grow and at reusing some of the wood fiber through recycling. Thus, the third incremental change in Weyerhaeuser's forestland management: managing to enhance public resource goals.

Regeneration is essential. Most of our lands support healthy second- or third-generation forests that are managed on a sustainable basis. We plant 300 to 600 new trees on each acre we harvest, for a total of 2.1 billion trees planted to date. These healthy second- or third-generation forests play another very significant environmental role: they perform the important function of sequestering carbon and releasing oxygen.

Managing our forests for biological diversity is also important. It's not a question of whether to, but rather, how best to achieve biological diversity objectives. We believe the answer lies in sound environmental research, and in understanding the trade-offs between forest productivity and wildlife habitat. We believe that, by managing the public and private forests as a landscape of forest types we can both meet the wood needs of the nation and provide for a wide spectrum of diverse habitat types.

In both the Northwest and the Southeast, we maintain riparian zones in a natural condition, whether or not required by law. The wildlife resource is of particular interest to our company and the public. Research on how wildlife is influenced by our forestry practices began in the early 1950s. In addition to game species, threatened and endangered species, non-game wildlife, and the interaction of forest management and wildlife are receiving increased attention. For example, the effect of forest roads and timber harvest on water quality, seasonal flow patterns, and fish habitat conditions has received significant research attention.

Much of our ongoing research involves cooperative studies with federal and state agencies, native American tribes, universities, and environmental organizations. Such cooperation not only ensures that the broader, public interests are being considered, but also enhances communication, application, and acceptance of the research findings.

In some cases, biologically, culturally, and aesthetically unique sites have been sold, exchanged, or donated to public agencies. Examples include the over 10,000 acres of wetlands in North Carolina donated to the Nature Conservancy to help form the Great Dismal Swamp National Wildlife Refuge and our sale and donation of land to the Arkansas Nature Conservancy and the State of Arkansas to help establish the Cossatot River State Park-Natural Area.

[Ed. Note: Since such donations qualify as charitable contributions for income tax purposes, the environmentally minded donor company is partially compensated for turning over a valuable asset to the cause of conservation, and thus encouraged to do so.]

Through intensive management of forests that are capable of producing high volumes of wood, we can reduce the need to harvest timber on less productive publicly owned forestlands. While biological diversity may be modified in forests where timber production is the primary objective, the opportunity to maintain greater species diversity on other forestlands will be increased. The more effectively the United States manages its forestlands, the less demand will be put on other, more sensitive, global forest systems by the world's growing population.

Frederick Weyerhaeuser did not begin a practice of sustainable forestry because he saw it as a method of protecting biodiversity. Rather, he recognized that if he could make his land continuously productive, the sustainable yields it provided would be an economic legacy for his children and grandchildren. But he had the beginnings of a very good idea.

As the Weyerhaeuser story points out, intensive management will produce more useable wood fiber—and store more carbon—per acre than natural forests of equal age. As it does so, a sustainable world can meet its forest products needs from less forest area, leaving more land to remain in a natural state as habitat, and as a place of recreation and beauty. Along with efficient use and reuse of forest materials, sustainable forestry thus becomes an important element of sustainable growth.

But the Weyerhaeuser example also calls a deeper problem to mind. Frederick Weyerhaeuser looked ahead to his grandchildren. He could do so because he owned and controlled the use of the land. But much forest land today has many claimants to ownership: private citizens who hold legal title; governments who either own land or regulate land use; citizens who see it as a birthright; workers who depend on it for a livelihood; its resident flora and fauna; and generations of people yet to come. Not all these claimants see a personal stake in sustainable development or act in the interests of the environmental future.

For example, any government that sells natural forest stumpage at below cost may temporarily subsidize employment and thus help its political position, but the private landowner's investment in sustainable forestry is undercut and discouraged by the government's below-cost pricing. And when any government considers the gross proceeds of natural forest harvests to be current income rather than in part a liquidation of a capital asset, it may delude itself into thinking that its policies make economic sense.

At the heart of an environmental ethic must lie responsibility and stewardship. Until there is collective political will to take the long view on biodiversity, global warming, agricultural practices, and soil conservation—as well as forestry—in short, to replace current exploitation with conservation for someone else's future—the world will find it difficult to reach the goal of sustainable development.

■ ■ ■

The programs described in this chapter have a number of interesting characteristics in common.

First, most of them are new (3M and Weyerhaeuser being the exceptions). Thus, while promising, success is usually still conditional or yet to be realized. If industry is to be enlisted widely in the search for sustainable development, projects such as these must generate real benefits for their sponsors and serve as opening wedges to stimulate other companies to do likewise for fear of being left in the dust of competition.

That thought leads to a second set of characteristics—the principal forces that gave birth to the programs. While all have important environmental underpinnings, five also promise significant direct economic benefits sufficient to justify them on a stand-alone basis. Six are motivated, directly or indirectly, by pressures generated by growing public environmental awareness. Two (Briggs and Unocal) seem to spring from intellectual curiosity—a search for greater environmental understanding and to demonstrate a better way of doing things. Only one (Zytec) is in direct response to regulations.

While this back-of-the-envelope analysis is by no means statistically defendable, it does suggest that companies respond vigorously to environmental challenges when they see it in their own interest to do so, whether because of the "carrot" of economic gain or the "stick" of public disapproval. The fact that they write about their efforts with obvious pride also suggests that, whatever the other incentives, seeing themselves and being seen as environmentally progressive is important to them.

III.

COOPERATION AMONG COMPANIES

Companies have traditionally formed industry-wide organizations to deal with common problems where cooperative effort is not constrained by anti-trust concerns. Such organizations range in scope from the International Chamber of Commerce, the National Association of Manufacturers, and the Business Roundtable to industry trade associations and local business associations or clubs. It is not surprising that rising concern for the environment has broadened the role of some organizations and spawned a number of new ones, including, among many others, Keep America Beautiful, the Global Environmental Management Institute (GEMI), two gatherings of the World Industrial Conference on Environmental Management (WICEM I and II), and The Business Council for Sustainable Development—an international group of chief executives developing business positions on environmental policy for the United Nations Conference on Environment and Development (UNCED), scheduled to meet in Rio de Janeiro in June of 1992.

Three of these that were mentioned by several participating companies deserve special notice for their significant contributions to advancing corporate environmentalism.

Responsible Care*

For decades the Chemical Industry has seen itself as a benefactor of society by its application of science to create a wide array of new products of value to modern living. But it has also—in many cases unwittingly—been producing wastes—toxic and otherwise—that are damaging its surroundings.

---

*"Responsible Care" is a registered mark of the Chemical Manufacturers Association.

From Silent Spring *and* Earth Day 1970 *on, the industry has been in-dicted by the public for these by-products of its operations, and as a conse-quence has suffered from public mistrust and extensive government regu-lation. As this book documents later on, placing full reliance on internal scientific skills and conclusions on risk, accompanied by closed-door poli-cies toward the public, has not solved all environmental problems and has failed to overcome unfriendly public perceptions.*

In the late 1980s, a growing number of chemical companies' senior executives began seeking a better way of conducting both their businesses and their communications with stakeholders. Their answer has been Responsible Care, patterned after a similar program already in place in Canada. By endorsing Responsible Care, they committed themselves and their companies to a new business culture, along the lines of total quality improvement, through which they would continuously upgrade their com-panies' environmental performance.

While the process of fashioning Responsible Care's "Guiding Princi-ples" and "Codes of Management Practices" was coordinated by the indus-try trade group, the Chemical Manufacturers Association (CMA), the specific policies are the product of committees of industry executives, aided by panels of non-technical neighbors, environmentalists and academics, and ultimately approved by the company CEOs that make up the CMA Board of Directors.

Responsible Care has received virtually total endorsement by the U.S. chemical industry, and adherence to its principles is a prerequisite for mem-bership in CMA. Since the program is new and since, as one executive put it, "We're trying to design this program to keep companies in, not get them out,"* no sanctions have yet been imposed on any member, though a "due process" procedure has been adopted to deal with future backsliders.

Here is how one sponsoring company sees its involvement in Respon-sible Care:

The Dow Chemical Company *(from the company's case history)*

In 1988, CMA conducted a survey to assess public opinion of the chemical industry. The results of this survey came as no sur-prise to some of us. The chemical industry's low standing with the

---

*Quote from the Harvard Business School case on Responsible Care, 1991.

public is matched only by the tobacco and nuclear industries. And that low perception is of major concern to us. That perception influences young people's decisions about working for our industry; that perception influences how our customers feel about buying our products and doing business with us; and, that perception influences the kinds of regulation and legislation that the public demands.

The only way to improve perception is through consistent, long-term action designed to improve performance. Hence the Responsible Care initiative, developed to respond to public concerns regarding the chemical industry through an industry-wide commitment to continuous improvement in the performance of our operations. Our counterparts in the Canadian chemical industry already had a similar program in place to inspire and guide the CMA effort. Many Dow employees were active in drafting the program's original Guiding Principles and continue to serve on committees developing the Codes of Management Practices that pertain to specific areas of our operations. Four of these codes are already in effect: Community Awareness and Emergency Response (CAER), Pollution Prevention, Distribution, and Process Safety. Two more codes will be initiated during 1992: Employee Health and Safety and Product Stewardship.

Besides committing participants to comply with the Guiding Principles and operate according to the Codes of Management Practices, Responsible Care encourages the formation of community citizen advisory panels and has formed a national Public Advisory Panel [PAP] to review issues of the chemical industry and help develop programs that are responsive to public concerns.

At the local level, Dow, like other CMA members, has begun establishing community advisory panels at its manufacturing sites. These panels give the public the opportunity to ask questions and express concerns, and they have proven extremely effective in increasing our communications with the public.

Another element of the Responsible Care initiative is a provision for member company "self-evaluation"...a report card, if you will. Public skeptics of Responsible Care may doubt the credibility of a self-policing industrial program relying on annual self-reporting. We think that seeing our continuing reductions of emissions and incidents will lead to believing. However, we also believe that we

71

need to develop some means of independent validation of our progress if Responsible Care is to have ultimate credibility with the public.

[Ed. Note: This subject is currently under discussion within the CMA. Dow's statement establishes its position on the matter; if performance is not independently validated a skeptical public is likely to remain so.]

Under the Responsible Care initiative, Executive Leadership Groups, consisting of representatives from CMA membership, meet periodically to discuss member-company concerns and offer mutual assistance. The success of Responsible Care is dependent on the performance of the entire chemical industry. The groups support and facilitate each member's continual improvement efforts.

Responsible Care is now going global. Through the efforts of our U.S.A.-based multinational companies and CMA staff, a Responsible Care initiative is currently active in nine countries and under development in approximately a dozen more. Each individual country initiative is unique in certain respects, yet includes the fundamental features of the CMA Responsible Care program.

What lessons have we learned from Responsible Care? First, Responsible Care is not a public relations or advertising program, though public communications is an important component. It is a continuous improvement initiative. To us, that means we will always be working at it—acknowledging shortcomings, making changes. Second, we have learned that we cannot succeed without outside partners—the public, the environmentalists, and the government. And, we cannot succeed without inside partners—all other CMA members, all our employees. Continuous improvement has to remain an important part of our work ethic and should be a part of the work ethic of all business.

How has Responsible Care been received? Chemical Week Magazine *ran a special issue devoted entirely to it in July of 1991, stating on the cover of the issue that:*

> "Responsible Care may prove to be one of the biggest and best things that ever happened to the chemical industry. It represents a total, public commitment to continuous improvement of management and

performance in the arenas of health, safety, and the environment. It is also a commitment to the responsible management of chemical industry products from cradle to grave, from the lab to disposal or destruction. But it is also much, much more. With Responsible Care, the chemical industry has embarked on a journey of profound cultural change, opening its doors to a skeptical public and saying, 'Don't trust us, track us.'"

EPA Administrator William Reilly, quoted in the Chemical Week *issue, states, "I don't think you can legislate or force a cultural change. But constant change is built into Responsible Care...I respect it."*

Others are less sure. Chemical Week *quotes a Greenpeace official as saying "we don't think much of it since I guess we hold the chemical industry responsible for much of the environmental damage we see today. It's like the drug pusher giving people clean needles—it does nothing to wean them of the habit." An NRDC staff member adds "for the industry to say they want to do these things instead of fighting us is good. But I'd like to see them move faster and farther. And people other than the CMA have to make sure they do it."*

Finally, in the same article, Roger Pryor, head of the Coalition for the Environment, and a PAP member, summed it up for many, "I think that Responsible Care holds a lot of hope for improvements in industry's performance, but I'm not convinced yet. It's too early to tell whether companies will be able to make this fairly ambitious program work."

If it does work, Responsible Care can set a splendid example for other industries to follow.

■ ■ ■

Since continued reliance on CFCs in some developing countries could offset the savings made by the Montreal Protocol signatories, and give continuing CFC users an advantage over more responsible firms, it is in the interest of industrialized country companies to supplement World Bank-administered financial aid with technical help in implanting replacement technologies. Thus, the Industry Cooperative for Ozone Layer Protection (ICOLP) *was formed to facilitate technology diffusion, especially to companies in less developed countries, as they address the Montreal Protocol mandate to get rid of CFCs. Here is how ICOLP has been described by the president of the organization:*

Industry Cooperative for Ozone Layer Protection (ICOLP)
(from a 1991 speech by Margaret Kerr, Vice President of Northern Telecom and ICOLP's president)

While much of our work in CFCs was done internally, within Northern Telecom, we have also worked closely with other stakeholders throughout our corporate outreach efforts. We have built solid working relationships on the CFC issue with the Canadian and U.S. governments, the United Nations Environment Programme, environmental groups—even our major competitors.

Our most innovative external CFC activity has been our involvement in the founding of the Industry Cooperative for Ozone Layer Protection, or ICOLP for short, which is a Washington-based association of 17 multinational corporations augmented by governments and industry associations from the United States, Sweden, the Soviet Union, Mexico, and Japan.

ICOLP's mandate is to coordinate the open, worldwide exchange of non-proprietary information on alternative technologies for ozone-depleting solvents in the electronics industry. ICOLP sponsors technology transfer seminars and workshops and has written state-of-the-art technical manuals, published and distributed by the U.S. Environmental Protection Agency.

ICOLP is now offering a new worldwide electronic database called OZONET, which functions as a global bulletin board and information clearinghouse on CFC alternatives. The database—created by Northern Telecom and donated to ICOLP—is accessible from more than 750 cities in 35 countries through the General Electric Information Services Network.

This database is intended to help companies and organizations get access to the latest information—all of which is non-proprietary—on new processes, materials, and technologies that are being used to replace CFCs and other ozone-depleting chemicals.

We anticipate that OZONET will be especially useful in developing countries, where this information may not be readily available.

But ICOLP's most ambitious project yet is a multi-partner technology cooperation project to eliminate CFC solvents from Mexico's electronics industry by the year 2000—that is, on the same timescale as the developed world commitments under the Montreal

Protocol. Northern Telecom has agreed to lead and manage this project. Partners in the project include the Mexican Government Department of Ecology (SEDUE), the Mexican Association of Industries (CANACINTRA), the United States Environmental Protection Agency, Northern Telecom, and ICOLP member companies.

The plan is, over the next eighteen months, to hold a series of workshops throughout the Mexican "maquiladora"* regions. Electronics and metal-cleaning companies are invited by local industry associations and SEDUE to attend an initial workshop in which the problem of ozone depletion and the outline of the project are described. Participants leave with a detailed questionnaire, the results of which will determine their CFC-elimination technology requirements.

After the questionnaire has been completed and analyzed, participants return for an intensive customized three-day workshop in which they become fully acquainted with the technology changes that they can choose to make their plants CFC solvent-free.

If desired, participants will visit ICOLP member company facilities in Mexico and North America, to see firsthand the new technologies and processes in action. The final stage is actual conversion of the Mexican plants to the new technologies. Engineers from Northern Telecom and other ICOLP companies will work with their Mexican counterparts to determine their equipment needs and develop proposals for funding.

SEDUE will then assist Mexican companies in applying to the Multilateral Fund of the Montreal Protocol for the capital to make the necessary investments in CFC alternative technologies and equipment. This extremely important aspect of this project—access to capital for plant conversions from the Multilateral Fund—has facilitated acceptance of the project by all parties: by the Mexican electronics industry on the one hand, which needs to stay competitive while at the same time improving its environmental performance, and by the ICOLP member companies, which will share

---

*"Maquiladora"—originally meaning a fee for processing grain—refers to plants in Mexico that import materials and components from the United States and assemble them into products for export to the United States. Import duties are levied only on the value added in Mexico. Typically, these plants are located along the U.S.-Mexico border.

their knowledge, expertise, and technology but need receptive partners willing to commit and invest in CFC elimination.

We believe that this innovative project is unique in many ways:

- Mexico is the first developing country to commit to a CFC solvent phaseout timetable ten years earlier than that mandated by the Montreal Protocol, which puts it on the same timetable as that for developed nations. This project was the catalyst.
- Once Mexican experts complete the phaseout in Mexico, the plan is to have these experts share their knowledge, expertise, and technology with other developing countries in Latin America. Thus, we will experiment with a ''cascading of technology'' scenario—essential, if we are truly to make the gains required for a sustainable world.
- We believe that this project is an example of how multinational groups can move an environmental agenda forward in a relatively short time. The Government of Mexico, the U.S. EPA, Northern Telecom, and ICOLP were able to reach agreement, design a customized training program, and begin to implement the action plan within nine months.
- In this project, there is a balance between academic and practical components to ensure that the new processes are sustained. Mexican experts will work alongside their ICOLP counterparts to make the technologies suitable for Mexican industry. Through their substantial contributions, we expect this project to be more than a technology transfer or even a technology cooperation between companies; it should result in an evolution of technology.

But it takes more than a compelling idea to achieve such results. We must overcome barriers of language, geographic distances, a poor telecommunications infrastructure in Mexico, and the other complications that arise from working with many partners of different nationalities. The ability to meet frequently in person is one factor that has enabled the project to stay on course and to overcome the operational constraints.

In addition, the historical relationships that had been building between the parties predetermined the potential for success. Other countries and companies wishing to emulate this type of project should appreciate that this is the culmination of several years of developing alliances, respect, and trust between the partners.

The Mexican project is an experiment for all concerned, and, in the broader sense, for the organization ICOLP. We are charting new paths in multi-stakeholder partnerships for environmental protection. There are no "how to" manuals to guide us. We want to assess what we've accomplished to date, document the contribution of ICOLP, and build the business case for future ICOLPs tackling different problems. We want to reach agreement on the next set of ICOLP initiatives, and hands-on technology cooperation will probably be at the core of our future plans.

No effort to reduce the environmental impact of industrial activity can be fully successful until its principles and technologies are diffused worldwide in a fashion that allows developing countries to avoid the older polluting technologies common to the industrialized world's past and present.

Key to this is technology transfer, the process ICOLP is engaging in with Mexico so that the global benefits of CFC elimination can be realized.

[Ed. Note: The term "technology transfer" is being supplanted by "technology cooperation," a description better reflecting the fact that when two parties join in a common effort each is likely to contribute to the other's knowledge base.]

■ ■ ■

The second World Industrial Conference on Environmental Management was held in Rotterdam in April of 1991. A total of 250 companies, 45 of them from North America, were represented as speakers, moderators, or participants in three days of discussion covering such subjects as trade and environment, tools of environmental management, and technology cooperation. Perhaps the most significant specific action of the conference was the adoption of the Business Charter for Sustainable Development, an umbrella code of environmental conduct for business enterprises, developed under the aegis of the International Chamber of Commerce (ICC) with input from numerous corporate members of that organization. As of December 31, 1991, over 500 companies from 35 countries have signed the charter.

Here is how the ICC presented the charter:

International Chamber of Commerce

In its milestone 1987 report, *Our Common Future,* the World Commission on Environment and Development (Brundtland Commission), emphasized the importance of environmental protection in the pursuit of sustainable development.

Sustainable development involves meeting the needs of the present without compromising the ability of future generations to meet their own needs. Economic growth provides the conditions in which protection of the environment can best be achieved, and environmental protection, in balance with other human goals, is necessary to achieve growth that is sustainable.

> We welcome the Business Charter as a very positive and firm step ahead which could encourage companies to move towards sustainable development. Companies' credibility, however, remains to be judged upon the proper implementation of the Charter in the field and their willingness to further enhance the Charter and address in the same context other major issues not included, such as the holding companies' policies, the role of the stock exchange market, the adequacy of the accountability system, and the liability of the producer.
>
> ■ *Michael Scoullos, President*
> *European Environmental Bureau*
> *(from ICC list of endorsements of*
> *the Business Charter, 1991)*

In turn, versatile, dynamic, responsive, and profitable businesses are required as the driving force for sustainable economic development and for providing managerial, technical, and financial resources to contribute to the resolution of environmental challenges. Market economies, characterized by entrepreneurial initiatives, are essential to achieving this.

Business thus shares the view that there should be a common goal, not a conflict, between economic development and environmental protection, both now and for future generations. Making market forces work in this way to protect and improve the quality of the environment—with the help of performance-based standards and judicious use of economic instruments in a harmonious regulatory framework—is one of the greatest challenges that the world faces in the next decade.

So that more businesses join this effort and their environmental performance continues to improve, the International Chamber of Commerce hereby calls upon enterprises and their associations to use the following Principles as a basis for pursuing such improvement and to express publicly their support for them. Individual programs developed to implement these Principles will reflect the wide diversity among enterprises in size and function.

- **Corporate priority:** To recognize environmental management as among the highest corporate priorities and as a key determinant to sustainable development; to establish policies, programs and practices for conducting operations in an environmentally sound manner.
- **Integrated management:** To integrate these policies, programs, and practices fully into each business as an essential element of management in all its functions.
- **Process of improvement:** To continue to improve corporate policies, programs and environmental performance, taking into account technical developments, scientific understanding, consumer needs, and community expectations, with legal regulations as a starting point; and to apply the same environmental criteria internationally.
- **Employee education:** To educate, train, and motivate employees to conduct their activities in an environmentally responsible manner.
- **Prior assessment:** To assess environmental impacts before starting a new activity or project and before decommissioning a facility or leaving a site.
- **Products and services:** To develop and provide products or services that have no undue environmental impact and are safe in their intended use, that are efficient in their consumption of energy and natural resources, and that can be recycled, reused, or disposed of safely.
- **Customer advice:** To advise, and where relevant educate, customers, distributors, and the public in the safe use,

transportation, storage, and disposal of products provided; and to apply similar considerations to the provision of services.

- **Facilities and operations:** To develop, design and operate facilities and conduct activities taking into consideration the efficient use of energy and materials, the sustainable use of renewable resources, the minimization of adverse environmental impact and waste generation, and the safe and responsible disposal of residual wastes.
- **Research:** To conduct or support research on the environmental impacts of raw materials, products, processes, emissions, and wastes associated with the enterprise and on the means of minimizing such adverse impacts.
- **Precautionary approach:** To modify the manufacture, marketing, or use of products or services or the conduct of activities, consistent with scientific and technical understanding, to prevent serious or irreversible environmental degradation.
- **Contractors and suppliers:** To promote the adoption of these principles by contractors active on behalf of the enterprise, encouraging and, where appropriate, requiring improvements in their practices to make them consistent with those of the enterprise; and to encourage the wider adoption of these principles by suppliers.
- **Emergency preparedness:** To develop and maintain, where significant hazards exist, emergency preparedness plans in conjunction with the emergency services, relevant authorities, and the local community, recognizing potential transboundary impacts.
- **Transfer of technology:** To contribute to the transfer of environmentally sound technology and management methods throughout the industrial and public sectors.
- **Contributing to the common effort:** To contribute to the development of public policy and to business, governmental, and intergovernmental programs and educational initiatives that will enhance environmental awareness and protection.
- **Openness to concerns:** To foster openness and dialogue with employees and the public, anticipating and responding to their concerns about the potential hazards and impacts of

operations, products, wastes or services, including those of transboundary or global significance.

- **Compliance and reporting:** To measure environmental performance; to conduct regular environmental audits and assessments of compliance with company requirements, legal requirements, and these principles; and periodically to provide appropriate information to the Board of Directors, shareholders, employees, the authorities and the public.

Because it is intended to serve as an umbrella statement, useful to a wide variety of companies in diverse industries around the world, the ICC statement is much more general—some might say vague—than the preceding examples of Responsible Care and ICOLP.

However, if companies that sign it take it seriously, and from it develop their own more specific codes, they will be led in the direction of greater environmental awareness, and one hopes, become committed to the integration of environmental concerns into corporate plans, continuous improvement, a cautious approach to new products and processes, energy and materials efficiency, education of customers and suppliers, environmental audits, and openness to the public. In short, they will be starting along the path that leads to sustainable development.

Supplementing the Business Charter for Sustainable Development, a similar document, the "Keidanren Global Environment Charter" has been circulated to Japanese industry by the Keidanren, the most influential Japanese business association. (Its members are the parallel in that country to the "Fortune 100" group of companies in the United States.) The Keidanren is itself a signer of the ICC Charter.

■ ■ ■

Cooperative efforts by industry groups have the potential to be especially effective in addressing global environmental concerns. Commitment by all competitors to appropriate world-wide standards lessens the temptation to seek advantage by being irresponsible. The global nature of many industries can make possible the global harmonization of environmental protection measures, and facilitates the diffusion of more benign technologies worldwide. In short, while nation states are constrained by national boundaries and domestic political considerations, multinational companies and global industries are free to establish high world standards of environmental

81

performance. The three examples described above are encouraging examples that they are starting to do so.

The Role of Trade Associations

With the exception of Responsible Care, little attention has been paid by respondents to the potential role of existing industry trade associations in fostering environmental progress. It would seem that many of these can play a major part in helping smaller or more resource-poor companies to move ahead environmentally, in promoting high environmental standards, and in diffusing new and better technology to developing countries. To be effective, however, some trade groups will need to abandon the defensively adversarial mindset that may be left over from years of contentious lobbying against environmental regulation and begin to work cooperatively with environmental groups. Their Boards of Directors will also need to move association standards and attitudes beyond the least common denominator represented by their most recalcitrant member companies. If they can do so, they can be of enormous help in propagating a culture of corporate environmentalism from examples such as those described here to industry at large.

IV.

THE ROOTS OF CORPORATE ENVIRONMENTALISM

Ten years ago, the Continental Group, then a "Fortune 100" company active in several environmentally sensitive areas, commissioned a survey of current public and business attitudes toward the economy and the environment. The report's basic conclusions can be summarized by these words taken from it.

The Continental Group *(from its report "Towards Responsible Growth"—1982)*

Key findings contained in the Continental Group Report point to an emerging consensus: The public desires both economic revitalization and environmental protection, to be attained through a program of responsible growth.

Compared with the 81 percent who believe maintaining a strong economy is a top national priority, only 46 percent feel that maintaining a high rate of economic growth should be an equally important priority. And, similarly, 49 percent say we must accept a slower rate of economic growth in order to protect the environment, as opposed to 24 percent who believe we should relax environmental standards to achieve growth and 24 percent who believe we can achieve both growth and environmental protection. On the more directly personal level, 68 percent of Americans think more stress should be placed on teaching people to live with basic essentials rather than on reaching a higher standard of living.

Such survey results show public desire for growth, moderated by quality-of-life considerations. This desire is echoed by other findings throughout the report.

* * * * * * *

Our firm belief in economic freedom might seem antithetical to a recognition of the need for environmental constraints, but on the contrary, the survey finds that six out of ten Americans (61 percent) think that pollution is one of the most serious problems facing the nation today, and large majorities express agreement with relatively new ideas about man's relationship to his environment:

- Eighty-four percent (84 percent) concur that the balance of nature is very delicate and easily upset by human activities.
- Seventy-six percent (76 percent) agree that the earth is like a spaceship with only limited room and resources.
- Seventy-nine percent (79 percent) believe we must prevent any type of animal from becoming extinct, even if it means sacrificing some things for ourselves.

When it is realized that not long ago such phrases as "spaceship earth" were virtually unheard of, these findings indicate our citizens are truly reassessing the role of the environment in our national vision. This contention is further supported by the surprising discovery that a solid majority of the public (72 percent) agree with the statement, "I feel American beliefs and values have been a basic cause of our environmental problems."

Policy-makers, environmentalists, and business people have been responding in various ways to that decade-old public demand for "responsible growth," or, as it is now called, "sustainable development." And the focus of the debate over economic progress and environmental protection has shifted rapidly from "either/or, take your choice" to "how to achieve both goals." At the roots of corporate environmentalism, as in so many other social phenomena, lies a bed-rock quality of a democratic society—public opinion.

Every company that has changed its approach to the environment has recognized strong reasons to do so—reasons persuasive enough to launch major commitments of management time and corporate assets in order to become a better environmental citizen, to overcome problems of the past and to set a course toward a more benign environmental future.

This chapter presents, in each company's own words, how several came to realize and accept the need for a new corporate environmental ethic, new goals and demonstrably improved corporate performance. In some cases, this new approach built on a history of growing environmental awareness. In others, it represented a sharp change in corporate policy.

Rising public attention to the environmental effects of industry has drawn companies, sometimes reluctantly, to recognize that they cannot operate without public acceptance, and that gaining acceptance requires not only providing products and services of value, and treating employees fairly, but also a concerted effort to reduce the impacts of company activities and products on surrounding populations and the ecosphere itself.

The stimuli that brought on the corporate reactions described below varied from company to company, but generally fell into three categories:

Public Pressure: *Disasters such as Bhopal; continuing high levels of toxic and other emissions; solid waste disposal, community, environmentalist, and other outside complaints; Earth Day; government regulation.*

Economic Concerns: *Material availability; cost savings potential; competitive opportunities; potential risk and liability.*

Corporate Values: *Management's desire that the company be recognized by customers, neighbors, and employees as socially responsible, and to feel proud of how the company conducts its business.*

In one way or another, each environmental problem presents a threat to a company's profitability or even its survival. No respondent company feels environmental issues can be ignored, wished away, or lobbied out of existence. Each indicates its problems must be addressed vigorously. While several clearly believe that a more aggressive attack on environmental problems is "the right thing to do," no company listed this as either its sole motivation or the only important reason for undertaking change.

Thus, the normally cited driving force for change is long-term corporate success, rather than altruism. But, when a new approach to the environment is seen as essential to reaching a company goal, for whatever reasons, the objectives of corporations and their environmentally oriented critics become similar, and the potential exists for cooperative effort to reach consensus on goals and methods.

S.C. Johnson Wax *(from the company's case history)*

In his memoirs, published in 1936, H.F. Johnson Jr. wrote: "Until recent years, American industry has used the raw materials employed in its manufactured products with little regard for future supply. The apparently limitless resources of this country no doubt fostered this practice and it was not until industry found itself embarrassed by actual shortages of raw materials that business began to recognize the need for scientific research at the source of supply of raw materials, or technical research in the laboratory for synthetic materials, to replace those which nature had once provided so bountifully.''

While the foundation of the company's concerns about the environment and its responsibility for the condition of the earth had deep roots, resulting practices were generally provincial. Each of the companies in the corporation dealt with the issues locally rather than on an international basis.

Global attention became directed at the company in 1975 when Samuel C. Johnson, great-grandson of the founder, announced a unilateral decision to voluntarily discontinue the use of chlorofluorocarbons (CFCs) in all its aerosol products worldwide. Fluorocarbons had become suspect in the controversy regarding environmental pollution of the upper atmosphere. Sam Johnson, then Chairman and CEO, stated: "Some scientists feel that the possible impairment of the ozone layer in the upper atmosphere would permit greater penetration of the sun's ultra-violet rays with unforeseen effect on our health. Obviously, this is a very serious concern; our own company scientists confirm that as a scientific hypothesis it may be possible, but conclusive evidence is not available one way or another at this time...

''...We have been reducing our use of fluorocarbon propellants over a long period for a variety of different reasons, including the fact that our unique water-base formulations using other propellants are less expensive...And because we share the concern of our customers and others and since we are technically equipped to do so in [most of] our products we have made this policy decision....

"We at Johnson Wax are taking this action in the interest of our customers and the public in general during a period of uncertainty and scientific inquiry. We are taking this newspaper advertisement and other available means to tell our customers so that they may use our aerosol products with greater confidence...We believe that aerosols are good and useful, or we wouldn't manufacture them. As a result, we will manufacture only those aerosols...that do not contain fluorocarbons.''

This decision took place three years before the U.S. government ban on CFC propellant usage *[for aerosols]* in the United States in 1978 and 12 years before the Montreal Protocol global call to action in 1987.

In his book, *The Essence of a Family Enterprise,* Sam Johnson comments, "We had done some homework on the matter, but when it became apparent that keeping fluorocarbons in some of our products would harm our reserve of consumer trust and loyalty, we made the commitment to removing the propellant within a week. Bang. We quickly made a very significant move for the company."

> ...when we set aside the obvious business benefits of being an environmentally responsible company, we are left with the simple human truth that we cannot lead lives of dignity and worth when the natural resources that sustain us are threatened or destroyed. We must act responsibly and we must act now.
>
> ■ *Samuel C. Johnson, Chairman*
> *S.C. Johnson Wax*

■ ■ ■

Not all managers have the advantages of the concentrated decision-making inherent in a private company and thus the ability to decide to change, "Bang," as Sam Johnson did. And not all have had the foresight or the technology at hand to get ahead of the environmental curve as quickly and find a market advantage in doing so.

For many, the stimulus to change has been catastrophe or public exposure—whether theirs or someone else's—and the public pressure that ensues. Nor has a decision to change come about without considerable internal debate over just how—and how much—to revise long-standing policies. Large organizations, like large ships, are difficult to turn quickly to a new course.

Monsanto *(from the company's case history)*

The event that dramatically changed the way the public thought about the chemical industry, and the way the industry thought about itself, happened in late 1984 when a toxic cloud was released from a Union Carbide chemical plant in Bhopal, India, killing almost 3,000 people and injuring some 25,000 more. If there was any public confidence before this tragedy, it dissipated quickly. The American public wondered, if such a tragic event can happen over there, can it also happen here?

As a result of Bhopal, Title III of the Superfund Amendments and Reauthorization Act (SARA) passed through Congress. Title III required manufacturing companies to report to the government the amount of toxic chemicals kept in inventory each year and the amount they released or emitted to the environment.

Title III was a step-change law in its own right. It was a unique regulation in that it didn't require us to operate any differently. What it did require was public disclosure of chemical wastes released to the environment. The information provided was intended to help emergency responders know what was on site. It was also intended to give the public information about what kinds of chemicals were being released to the environment around them.

The effect it had on industry was mixed. Some companies with limited resources dragged their feet, hoping this law would soon go away. It didn't. Others complied, but by merely submitting the forms to the required agencies where they would sit in stacks of boxes, unorganized and inaccessible for at least a year. Within Monsanto there was a mixed reaction as well. Some believed submission of the forms was enough—why draw added attention to our chemical releases?

In the shadows of the corporation, a new ethic began to emerge. In whispers at first, some in management began asking, "What is the right thing to do? If we truly believe in the public's right-to-know about our operations, as we've demonstrated in the past, shouldn't we make it as easy and accessible as possible for them to get and understand our information? Better yet, shouldn't we take it to the public and explain what the numbers mean?"

After much heated internal debate, it was decided that we would go beyond compliance with the letter of the law; we would embrace the *spirit* of the right-to-know law. This was a major shift from mere compliance toward doing the right thing; toward going beyond compliance with regulations; toward corporate environmental stewardship.

Monsanto brings out the point that the mere public disclosure of emissions, as required by SARA Title III, was enough to stimulate a major shift in company policies, attitudes, and action. The importance of this one government step to increase the visibility of corporate environmental impact is echoed in several succeeding sections of this book. As a tool for environmental improvement, its effect has been profound.

■ ■ ■

One of the nation's oldest environmentally-oriented waste prevention programs was founded on the presumption that much environmental protection could be linked with cost savings.

3M *(from the company's case history)*

3M's Pollution Prevention Pays—3P—Program was initiated in 1975 to prevent pollution at the source—in products and manufacturing processes—rather than removing it after it has been created. While the idea was not new, the concept of applying pollution prevention on a company-wide basis and documenting the results had not been done before.

Dr. Joseph T. Ling, then staff vice president of 3M's Environmental Engineering & Pollution Control Department (EE+PC), suggested to Raymond Herzog, then 3M chief executive officer, that the best way to deal with pollution is not to create it in the first place. If there is no pollution, you don't have to buy expensive add-on devices to control it. Regulatory, and disposal paperwork, and other compliance requirements, as well as potential problems and future liabilities, could be eliminated or minimized.

There was an early recognition that prevention is more environmentally effective, technically sound, and less costly than conventional control procedures. Natural resources, energy, manpower, and money are all used in building conventional pollution control facilities, and more resources are consumed in operating them. Further, conventional pollution-removal equipment constrains but does not eliminate pollution, which is the objective of 3P.

Herzog directed Ling to organize and implement the pollution prevention concept for 3M worldwide. At the same time, the 3M Board of Directors provided vital underpinnings for this pioneering step in environmental management—a corporate policy that mandated pollution prevention at the source.

The 3M case introduces the concept of pollution prevention, brings in the cost savings opportunities inherent in such a program, and points out its ability to lessen future problems and liabilities. Support by the Board of Directors is also noteworthy.

■ ■ ■

Dow had an even earlier insight than 3M into the need for a new preventive approach to environmental problems. Unfortunately for the company, a series of difficult experiences (described in part in Chapter VIII) pushed it into a defensive stance in the face of public attacks on its processes and products. It took more than a decade for the company to realize that to be effective its environmental effort must consider the views of its communities and its critics, as well as its scientists and other employees.

The Dow Chemical Company *(from the company case history)*

In 1966 our chairman of the board, Carl Gerstacker, delivered a landmark speech titled "Management's Role in Pollution Control"—about the importance of a company's commitment to a healthful environment. Gerstacker followed that address with "Profits and Pollution"—a speech outlining ways for pollution control to be a source of profit as well as good corporate citizenship. He proposed three measures for companies:

- sharing knowledge on pollution control,
- reducing waste at the source, and
- enlisting the help of every employee.

In 1969, our Board of Directors voted to form a corporate Ecology Council to accelerate and expand our environmental efforts throughout Dow worldwide.

Early in the 1970s, we made three decisions with significant impact on our environmental performance:

- First, we would treat our own wastes and operate our own landfills.

- Second, we believed burying waste was a bad idea and we would use landfills only as a last resort.
- Third, we would phase out deep-well storage of hazardous liquid wastes.

We were on a critical path toward an environmental policy, a track that could eventually lead to waste elimination, improved productivity, and sustainable growth. However, the mood in Washington grew increasingly regulatory, pushing toward an EPA Superfund for site cleanups. Environmental impact reports became a burdensome chore. Confrontation with outsiders became routine. And the chemical industry became the bad guys in the headlines. We reacted defensively. We thought what we did behind our gates was our business, with trade secrets protected by law.

In the 1980s, the chemical and petrochemical industry were stunned by two disasters of far-reaching proportions—the Bhopal, India incident and the Valdez oil spill. Companies and trade associations began regrouping to improve environmental responsibility and thereby public confidence.

The "time for a change" movement was also coming from within. If a clean environment and a successful economy were to be interdependent, then we needed to open a sincere dialogue with our community, our legislators, our regulators, our environmental critics, and particularly our employees. Proven scientific excellence was not enough to inspire trust. We needed open communication, a campaign to share our corporate ethic, and internal programs to empower our employees to make environmental improvements.

■ ■ ■

Not all environmental problems are a direct threat to human health or the global ecological system. Some, such as solid waste disposal, are more mundane, though just as menacing to the companies whose businesses will be hurt by a failure to address them.

Procter & Gamble *(from the company's case history)*

Public awareness and knowledge that the current ways of managing solid waste are ineffective has been growing rapidly. At the same time, disposal costs started increasing as available landfill space began diminishing and communities began resisting the siting of new landfills within their boundaries.

German consumers, limited to two small waste cans per household each week, were the first to begin exerting pressure on consumer goods companies. In 1987, P&G introduced its Lenor concentrated fabric softener in a refill pouch. Instead of buying a large plastic bottle with each new purchase, consumers would buy a concentrated liquid in a small, flexible plastic pouch, then mix it with water in their original Lenor bottles at home.

This innovation reduced packaging waste by up to 85 percent. German consumers embraced the refill pouch idea, and the new design quickly became the industry standard in Europe. In 1988, Germany's retail grocers named Lenor's refill pouch the invention of the year.

In the United States, the 1987 sailing of the garbage barge "Mobro," with its 3,100 tons of Islip *[Long Island]* garbage, dramatically demonstrated the solid waste problem to the public. At P&G, a team of middle managers provided the impetus internally to develop a solid waste policy statement that would address this emerging environmental issue. It was also clear that corporations had the technical and scientific expertise, as well as the financial and people resources, to serve as leaders in this effort. Corporations, as do citizens and governments, contribute to the solid waste problem; therefore, they are also responsible for helping to find and implement solutions. These managers presented their views to then-chief executive John Smale.

A task force from this middle-management level was formed to develop an environmental quality policy statement, which became the basis for the company's environmental quality efforts as they relate to solid waste. The environmental quality policy is meant to provide clear direction throughout the company of P&G's environmental commitment. The policy is based on realistic expectations and the recognition that all products and packaging have some kind of impact on the environment. In its environmental policy, the company committed itself to the overarching goal of "reducing or preventing the environmental impact of its products and packages in their design, manufacture, distribution, use, and disposal whenever possible."

As a multinational corporation, P&G first encountered the concern over landfill capacity in Germany, where the problem led to drastic reductions on the amount of waste each household was allowed each week. This limitation

92

naturally reflected back into the types of packaging consumers would accept, and it appears to be a key stimulus, along with the "Mobro" incident, to Procter and Gamble's decision to put a team of managers to work developing a policy response to deal with the solid-waste issue.

■ ■ ■

The companies highlighted so far in this chapter have been large multi-nationals. The next is a relatively small firm, located and operating in a sparsely populated Canadian province. As its story describes, it was naturally—and admittedly—provincial in its past outlook. But when its environmental impact became recognized as global, the company used methods to change its corporate culture that are just as sophisticated as those used by any of its larger counterparts. And, so that he could lead in the right direction, the CEO went to extraordinary lengths to enlarge his personal perspective to global dimensions.

TransAlta Utilities *(from the company's case history)*

TransAlta operates in the province of Alberta, where it generates approximately 70 percent of the area's electricity. Some 90 percent of its power comes from coal-fired generating plants.

[Ed. Note: The remainder is from hydro-power, the company's original source of electricity.]

The coal to fuel these plants originates in surface mines that are located in close proximity to the plants. This proximity reinforced the assumption that technology could retain the effect of the emissions from the generating plant within a local area. TransAlta saw itself operating wholly within a limited geographical region.

Public concern surrounding global warming shattered Trans-Alta's view of the world. Technology and processes were not in place to control the emission gasses that were considered to be factors in global warming; it was obvious that the thermal power plants had an effect far beyond their geographic locations. To provide an opening for the organizational and behavioral change required for sustainable development to be "the way it is around here," a major shift in corporate thinking was needed.

93

Corporate paradigms determine our world view. They are those background assumptions that govern our thinking and our corporate behavior. TransAlta's former paradigm encouraged the corporation to consider sustainable development as something outside the company rather than as an integral part of the way it did business. Thus, to reach the goal of being a company that is generative rather than reactionary required that the company change its basic mind-set.

Rethinking the company's view of itself was shaped by several factors. The pace of environmental legislation quickened with the enactment of the Canadian Environmental Protection Act in 1988. The Canadian legislation was the trigger for provincial governments to review their environmental legislation and make revisions. The entire process pointed to strict enforcement of stringent standards for industrial use of the air, the land, and the water. A second impetus was the clear desire by customers, employees and regulators to have TransAlta be environmentally responsible. The third impetus was the realization that the company's comfortable provincial context could no longer address the problem. There was a growing public concern regarding global warming and reliance on technology and process was not supplying a global answer. The corporation could not ignore the global thrust towards sustainability.

With these forces at work, the company began the task of designing a future that would see sustainable development as an integral part of the way it did business. The company had learned that the views of stakeholders are important in creating vision. The decision was made to create an Environmental Advisory Panel, composed of members of the public the company served. They brought with them a wide range of skills and expertise that were used to develop an environmental policy statement that commits the company and the way it conducts its business to sustainable development.

The policy statements created by the Environmental Panel were taken to the company's employees for their input. These are the people who make things happen. An interesting thing occurred at these focus groups—the employees developed statements that were more stringent than those developed by the Panel. Buy-in by employees was not a problem.

The panel was delighted with the response it received. It also provided the company's management with a clear message:

stakeholders wanted their company to be environmentally responsible. There was no ignoring this message. When major stakeholders are clear in their vision, and when employees outline stringent conditions surrounding environmental responsibility, it is incumbent upon management to take their leadership responsibility seriously.

Internally, TransAlta began the process of translating desires into action plans. Work teams were formed and policies were implemented. Externally, new leadership roles were forged. The company's president, Ken McCready, accepted the Chairmanship of Alberta's Round Table on the Environment and the Economy. This group has created a sustainable vision for the province. He also joined the Business Council for Sustainable Development (BCSD), a role that has led to the company gaining more of a global environmental perspective.

[Ed. Note: The BCSD was formed at the request of Maurice Strong, General Secretary of the United Nations Conference on Environment and Development (UNCED), to develop and provide a global industry environmental perspective to the delegates to the UNCED meeting in Rio de Janeiro in June 1992. McCready reports that his membership on the Round Table and the BCSD has provided him with an entirely different view of his and his company's responsibilities for environmental stewardship.]

The BCSD, an international forum of fifty Chief Executive Officers from around the world, is dedicated to harnessing the market to the achievement of sustainable development. The approach is founded on the premise that environmental resources of air, land, and water have a limited carrying capacity. Therefore, they cannot be seen as limitless cost-free receptacles for waste products. The way to ensure that environmental goals are reached efficiently is to harness market forces. Full-cost pricing of products and services—which recognizes and charges for environmental utilization—is the most effective mechanism for reaching those goals.

The essence of this market-based approach is that the polluter pays and thus has a financial incentive to reduce his impact on the environment. This concept will create an entirely different paradigm from which governments, companies, and people will make

95

their consumption decisions, a paradigm that TransAlta enthusiastically endorses.

The company has learned—through trial and error, wins and losses—that to bring about significant change in an organization a new future must be visualized, developed and articulated. In so doing, an innovative approach to inquiry is stimulated. The question is no longer, "how do we solve this problem?" but "how do we invent our own sustainable future?"

The challenge is to create a vision towards which all 2700 employees can make progress, through hundreds of everyday decisions, towards sustainable development. TransAlta intends to become a learning organization, developing and adopting the innovative practices needed to convert this vision into reality.

V.

ENGAGING THE ORGANIZATION

Large organizations are composed not only of many thousands of individuals of varying age, education, experience, and cultural backgrounds, but of numbers of divisions or business units, often in separate industries, that may have come to the parent through acquisitions or otherwise grown up with different organizational values than those of their sister units. Effective modern management, stressing decentralization and individual initiative, usually tolerates and often encourages this diversity and the creativity and self-reliance that it generates. Compared to a military-like hierarchy, directed from the top down, the large modern corporation may be closer to a collection of fiefdoms, responsive more to political leadership from the top than to command.

For these reasons, changing a large company's corporate culture is a difficult and time-consuming task. When change does occur, it is likely to do so in patches, first among a scattering of sympathetic individuals, then among a few units, and finally the inevitable holdouts will disappear only at retirement or termination.

Given this pattern of acceptance, it is unlikely that any of the participating companies, no matter how eager their leaders are to become, and be seen as, environmentally proactive are yet completely so. The fact that the conversion process is not yet complete (and indeed may never be) should not be reason to discount the importance of the metamorphosis under way.

Few corporations change without the initiative, or at least great support, coming from the chief executive. In many cases, the springboard for environmental change has been a strong statement by the CEO, followed by a set of guidelines or principles established as corporate policy and widely disseminated throughout the company and beyond. Changes in a company's approach to a major problem usually require some modification of the organization's structure, both to focus management's skills and attention on finding a solution and to signal the importance of the shift in management's perspective to the whole enterprise. Finally, no change can be fully effective until it becomes part of the basic culture of the company.

> A bit of imagery that I find useful is that of a fish swimming in water. To the fish the water is invisible. The role of the CEO is to make the invisible visible; to bring into focus the changing context in which the corporation is "swimming," making the possibilities and changes needed visible to employees.
>
> ■ *Ken F. McCready, President & CEO,*
> *TransAlta Utilities*
> *Speech at Synergy '92 Conference, 1992*

Here is what some managements are doing to turn their firms in a new direction.

Monsanto *(from the company case history)*

On January 30, 1990, Chairman and CEO Richard Mahoney summed up the new philosophy of environmental stewardship. He announced the Monsanto Pledge, our environmental vision:
It is our Pledge to:

- Reduce all toxic hazardous releases and emissions, working toward an ultimate goal of zero effect;
- Ensure that no Monsanto operation poses any undue risk to our employees and our communities;
- Work to achieve sustainable agriculture through new technology and practices;
- Ensure groundwater safety;
- Keep our plants open to our communities and involve the community in plant operations;
- Manage all corporate real estate, including plant sites, to benefit nature; and
- Search worldwide for technology to reduce and eliminate waste from our operations, with top priority being not making it in the first place.

The Pledge was set forth as a public target against which to measure the progress of our environmental programs. Through the Monsanto Pledge, the company publicly committed itself to a new way of environmental thinking—that of environmental stewardship.

The environmentalism embodied in the Pledge is far more than compliance. We believe:

- It is the right thing to do.
- It will help us take a more comprehensive and cost-effective approach to solving environmental problems as we process raw materials into products more efficiently with less waste and strive for products that can be reused or recycled at the end of their productive lives.
- It is good business—good for all our stakeholders, including our customers, employees, shareholders, and others. Improved environmental performance will result in greater manufacturing efficiencies and higher product quality.
- We are committed to continuous environmental improvement and are publicly accountable for our actions.

Employees responded enthusiastically to the Pledge. Many added their signatures alongside the chairman's to prove their personal commitment. Mr. Mahoney claims he received more positive employee mail on the Pledge than on any other subject. He recalls one letter from a group of employees that read:

"The new thinking, refreshing and revolutionary, has brought the right to operate, profitability, empowerment and environmental responsibility together into one elegant possibility. We offer our support and our goodwill and our faith that the journey will result in clean air, clean water and clean land, and that the causes for which Monsanto is in business will be advanced and secured."

The Monsanto Pledge has the virtues of directness and brevity. It signaled a sharp change of approach, and was welcomed by many employees for stepping out ahead of the regulatory requirements in order to "do the right thing." While "zero effect" may be an idealistic goal, setting anything less as the ultimate challenge implies acceptance of some imperfect standard.

To implement the change, Monsanto chose to form a committee of both line and staff managers, chaired by the executive vice president of

99

environment, safety, health, and manufacturing (who reports to the chair-
man), to carry the message down through the organization. And the new
committee's name stresses the environment, though it also handles health
and safety matters.

To ensure our environmental commitments were met, a new
Environmental Policy Committee was created in 1990 to replace the
company's Environmental, Safety, and Health Committee. The new
committee has environmental experts just as did its predecessor,
but also has business representation from the company's operating units and divisions worldwide.

The committee's role is to keep the company focused on its
environmental goals and delivering on its commitments. It coor-
dinates elements of the Monsanto Pledge and finds ways to appropriately reward exemplary environmental stewardship. The
committee also looks at current policies and continuously updates
them to keep them fresh and on the leading edge. Tasks of some
of the subcommittees include: examining product life-cycle issues,
following a product from raw material through disposal of the end
product; tracking progress on elements of the Pledge; and encouraging employee participation in environmental improvements.

Each of the operating units is also organized to fulfill environmental goals, which are incorporated into each strategic group's
long-range business plans. This makes the environmental goals
truly grassroots based—ideas for pollution-reduction projects and
the funding for those projects that come from the business units
where wastes are generated.

More than 1,200 Monsanto employees are now involved full-
time in environmental safety and health issues, an increase of 12
percent from 1987 levels.

[Ed. Note: To enlist the entire organization, Monsanto stressed face-to-
face interaction, including conferences, as a supplement to conventional
communication.]

To keep Monsanto's 40,000 employees going along the same
path, employee communication is very important. The most effective communication takes place face to face, within each department both in staff and operating groups, in plants and at the general

offices. Policies are posted on bulletin boards throughout the company. New ideas are encouraged and discussed in department and quality team meetings.

Company employee publications include regular environmental stories. Features highlight the many successful projects being accomplished throughout the company and the employees who made them possible. Environmental achievement stories and reduction data are communicated to employees first before release to the media.

Another internal communication vehicle has been a worldwide environmental conference for employees with primary responsibilities in the environmental field. Although environmentalism is the job of all employees, some are on the front lines dealing with new technologies, a wary public, ever-changing regulations, and tougher corporate standards that require environmental improvement without sacrificing safety, quality, or financial performance. To deal with common problems and concerns, this bi-annual conference, first held in 1968, brings together Monsanto people from across the globe.

Conference highlights have included talks by high-ranking EPA officials, national environmental group representatives, community advisory panel members, as well as our own executives and experts. Breakouts and round table discussions allow time for common issues and concerns to surface and for participants to brainstorm together, learn from each other, and try to come up with creative solutions.

■ ■ ■

In the late 1980s, Chevron recognized the need for greater attention to the environment. Chevron's management gave the responsibility for developing a new approach to a diversified group of middle managers drawn from a variety of sources within the organization. While this process lacks speed and possibly management focus, it has the great benefit of building equity in and commitment to the concept through the company, even as the policy itself is being formulated.

Chevron

As former Chevron Chairman George Keller outlined in a speech in late 1987: "Today, we are in a very real sense a society of environmentalists. We all want clean water and pure air and wilderness and wildlife. I don't know anyone who's against these things. Most people in industry, like most people in general, place a high value on a wholesome environment. At Chevron, we're very proud of a corporate environmental policy that says we comply fully with the letter and the spirit of all laws affecting our operation. But as long as our environmental philosophy is framed by the concept of compliance, we won't get much credit for our positive actions. Compliance means that the moral initiative lies elsewhere—outside of industry." The time had come, he added, for the industry to move beyond compliance.

The seeds and strategy for a new policy came from a highly informal, cross-functional study team. The team had no specific mandate—other than to look at Chevron's internal environmental policies—no timetable and didn't even give itself a name. The group's principal asset was the leadership and encouragement of then-vice chairman Ken Derr, now Chevron's chairman, who initiated the team effort.

"A key lesson in forming and implementing any new policy is that the message must come from the top," says Dave O'Reilly [then-Senior Vice President of Chevron Chemical and a team member]. "Senior management must act to support the policies if employees are to believe in them." As is also true of any new corporate program, the substance, guts, and working parts of it must in turn be generated from below, at the front lines of the company's business.

At the front, the team found considerable confusion over Chevron's policy of complying with the "spirit and letter" of the law, observes Darry Callahan, [vice president of Chevron Chemical and also a team member]. "People interpreted it in vastly different ways, from zero risk to business-based decision-making. There was internal confusion and all this outside regulatory pressure. One of our facilities replaced all the no-slip treads on stairways, even though the treads were in good shape and prevented slipping. But they were placed an eighth of an inch away from the placement the OSHA requires."

What emerged from the informal study team were thoughts formalized in what Chevron calls Policy 530, a proactive guide to corporate responsibility. It demands compliance with all safety, fire, health and environmental regulations, without regard to the degree of enforcement. It calls on employees to participate with government agencies in forming cost effective and useful regulations. It demands the conservation of resources and the reduction of waste. Perhaps most important, it introduced the concept of "risk management" into all Chevron operations.

Risk management is a balance of economics and good engineering practices in the design and siting of new facilities and modifications to existing ones. In practice, what it has meant at Chevron is that employees and managers are rewarded for identifying and fixing potential environmental hazards, rather than squeezing the last dollar of profit out of an aging piece of equipment. It's the heart of a proactive program and the mechanism to take Chevron ahead of mere compliance. Risk management is also good business.

"Consider our Tank Integrity Program, in which all the old underground gasoline tanks at service stations were replaced with double-walled fiberglass tanks," reflects Callahan. "At the time, such tanks were not required. But making right contamination from a leaking tank could cost the company $250,000 or more. If such a liability can be prevented with an expenditure of $25,000 to $50,000, then it's well worth it."

Initial drafts of Policy 530 were not, however, met with universal favor within Chevron. The very subject, in fact, sparked spirited and even rancorous debates, and over some extremely legitimate points that weighed on the side of caution. For one thing, the suggestion of going "beyond compliance" can be interpreted by outside parties—read, litigious environmental groups—as promising perfection.

For another thing, uniform regulations and compliance within an industry mean that competitors are on a level playing field. A company that builds a squeaky clean plant that costs twice as much to operate as a competitor's polluting plant may go out of business—unless that competitor is forced to be equally clean.

"Being proactive is a competitive issue," adds Callahan. "Some of our competitors don't comply with the law, whether out of ignorance or a willingness to take their chances." But Policy 530 urges Chevron's people to get involved in the regulatory process; when the corporation can help establish the standards, when it can take a leadership role, then it has a head start on others. In fact, it can even profit by licensing proprietary pollution-control technology.

103

And, of course, it can prevent some whopping liabilities. "How much," asks Callahan, "do you think Exxon might have been willing to spend if it had foreseen the Valdez accident?"

In a pair of 1991 public opinion surveys, Chevron asked 600 of its people and 1,600 members of the general public about how strongly they identified with the label "environmentalist." Respondents were asked to rank themselves on a scale of 1 to 10, with 1 meaning "don't identify at all" and 10 meaning "strongly identify." Fully 85 percent of Chevron's people identified themselves as 5 or above. Only 3 percent labeled themselves as a 1. Most significantly, 37 percent put themselves in the 8 to 10 category, which could be taken to mean environmentalist of the ardent stripe. The numbers in the Chevron employee survey were almost identical to those in the general public study.

Unlike the general public, however, oil company employees have a greater opportunity than most to actually do something about the environment. A single Chevron worker with an inspired idea is in a position to make a concrete, large, and enduring cut in pollution. Moreover, management consultants suggest that workers whose jobs or organization gives them something to believe in—or allows them to take action on those beliefs—are more motivated than if profits are the sole or dominant motive for their work.

There is another environmental policy factor that any CEO worth his or her corner office ought to consider. Chevron discovered this in a 1989 survey of its individual stockholders, which revealed that 88 percent of them felt that the company's "commitment to the environment is a sound business investment."

At its 1991 Annual Meeting, Chevron's stockholders voted to endorse Policy 530 by a 99.1 to .9 percent margin. Says Chevron Public Affairs Vice President, Rod Hartung: "If there's a CEO anywhere who is sitting on the fence about putting his or her company onto an environmental track, this overwhelming example of stockholder support ought to convince them to get on board."

The approaches described by Monsanto and Chevron are major efforts to institutionalize change, and their ingredients are similar. They include:

- *Leadership by the chief executive officer*
- *A new corporate environmental policy*

- *Changes in the organization structure*
- *Internal communications efforts to spread the word*
- *Involving the middle management and rank-and-file workers in implementation of the new corporate policies, including rewards for outstanding contributors*
- *Training in environmental matters*
- *Relating the environment to established corporate values, such as health and safety*
- *Recognizing the positive gains to be made through risk reduction, shareholder support, and enhancement of competitive position.*

■ ■ ■

The Xerox approach builds on another established corporate value—quality—which has been a long-time preoccupation at Xerox.

Xerox *(from the company case history)*

In December of 1984, the world was shocked by the catastrophe in Bhopal, India, which caused several thousand deaths with over a hundred thousand injuries reported. David Kearns, then CEO of Xerox Corporation concluded that Xerox must act quickly and thoroughly to ensure that such environmental mishaps would not be possible anywhere in Xerox.

This focus on prevention was in line with the company's increasing focus on quality. In 1984, Kearns and senior Xerox management launched the Leadership Through Quality process, which led to Xerox Business Products and Systems winning the Malcolm Baldrige National Quality Award in 1989. This process, a major cultural change for Xerox, embraced quality principles, management action and behavior, and the use of quality tools.

Error-free work is the most cost-effective way to improve quality, and employee involvement is essential. It was, therefore, natural to apply the quality process to environmental management as part of a total quality program.

In January of 1985, Mr. Kearns charged Jim MacKenzie *[Director, Corporate Environmental Health & Safety]* with ferreting out and eliminating all potential environmental hazards in the company, anywhere in the world. The worst potential outcome of any hazard was assumed. Chemical storage was minimized, and hazardous

105

chemicals were eliminated from processes wherever possible. Safe building evacuation standards that are routinely applied in the United States were required at all locations worldwide. A program was begun to eliminate, or in a few cases secondarily contain, all underground storage tanks.

In August of 1985, the company discovered that solvents had leaked into groundwater at Xerox's largest manufacturing site in Webster, New York, and migrated, contaminating a neighbor's well. The solvents had apparently come from an old containment vessel that had been removed some time before the problem was discovered.

Xerox then focused on searching for any other environmental impacts at other locations worldwide. The company surveyed locations at which industrial solvents had been used at any time in the past. This survey focused on possible groundwater contamination or soil deposits of such solvents either adjacent to or underneath each facility. Where such deposits were found, action was taken immediately to prevent the material from migrating, appropriate government agencies were notified, and remedial plans were developed and implemented with the consent of the agencies. At locations not covered by environmental laws, Xerox took voluntary remedial action, applying the same policy everywhere. The company also replaced solvents with non-toxic machine-cleaning agents wherever possible.

As a cornerstone of quality, a prevention program was implemented to protect the environment, and it is ongoing at all operations. This included institutionalizing procedures for reviewing all processes and process changes from an environmental standpoint. Systematic environmental audits are conducted at least annually at all manufacturing facilities. In addition to looking for potential hazards, auditors make sure that all practices meet the higher standards established for the corporation. These standards greatly exceed the local requirements in many of the countries with Xerox operations. In cases where environmental impacts are suspected, or found to have taken place, an extensive investigation and remediation effort is undertaken. Work of this nature is admittedly costly. But failure to remedy environmental problems early can be orders of magnitude more costly. Ultimately, it can subject a business to potentially huge fines and generate public ill will that can seriously hurt the business.

106

[Ed Note: The Webster leak haunted Xerox for some time, as these extracts from a March 22, 1989 Washington Post *article show:*

"Rochester, N.Y., March 21—Sen. Daniel Patrick Moynihan (D-N.Y.) and New York state health officials today sharply criticized a court-approved secret settlement involving a toxic spill at a Xerox manufacturing plant near here, citing the case as an example of how such legal secrecy can inhibit scientific and medical inquiry into questions of health and safety.

. . . "There is something unseemly about public health information, environmental health information, not being available in any circumstance," Moynihan said.

. . . "As a result of the secret settlement, Xerox agreed to pay $4.75 million to two families who had alleged that discharges from Xerox's plant in Webster, N.Y., had damaged their health. Xerox also relocated the families and bought their houses, which are now vacant. The judge sealed all records in the case, and prohibited the parties from discussing the matter."

At the congressional hearing that was the subject of the Post article, Xerox general counsel, Richard S. Paul testified:

"I think the purpose and scope of our confidentiality agreements have been misinterpreted and I would like to lay to rest any concerns that you or the community may have with how our company has handled this matter. . . .

"It is true that the parties and their lawyers agreed to keep the terms and conditions of the settlements of these two lawsuits confidential. This means that, for example, the parties cannot divulge the amount that Xerox paid the various plaintiffs in settlement. However, nothing prevents the members of the families from sharing their medical records with the public, if they choose to do so. Concerned public health officials are free to inquire of the families about their health problems and any causal relationship which they may believe exists."

Mr. Paul went on to point out that the court had ordered certain records of one of the cases sealed because minors were involved. He then added:

"Despite this, if this Committee or a legitimate public health authority were to move the Court to unseal the children's medical reports for viewing by public health authorities, I can assure you that Xerox would support the motion."

The lesson here is that when public health is involved, any form of corporate secrecy, no matter how proper, is likely to prove an irresistible target for journalists and politicians.] The Xerox story now continues:

Even with strong corporate direction, the task was difficult in the mid-80s since the environment was not a top priority for most managers. Xerox was facing stiff domestic competition at the high-end, and the Japanese at the low-end of the copier and printer market. The additional expenses mandated by higher corporate standards and corporate policy (environmental clean-up costs are the responsibility of the business divisions) were seen as unnecessary by many managers. There was little tangible or immediate payback for them. In retrospect, with the increased focus on the environment and the ensuing stricter regulations, Xerox managers are glad to have made these investments.

[Ed. Note: Xerox's experience points out that environmental remediation can be initially expensive and that cost-conscious managers may resist spending money on it unless provided with resources—including budget relief—that avoid a short-term drain on their operations and the yearly financial results on which they are normally judged.

As it continues, the Xerox story uses revealing words about employee participation—"empowerment," and "cultural change"—and points out that environmental projects generate a special enthusiasm. The company also refers to "environmental intensification" as a desired result to which employees contribute significantly.]

The cultural change took place over several years. The changes cascaded from the top down in direct support of the expanding environmental leadership program, as well as product design, manufacturing, and marketing activities. Empowered through the quality process, employees started a number of initiatives, from local grassroots recycling efforts to worldwide, all-plant programs.

Under the quality program, management encourages employee involvement and the formation of cross-functional teams to focus on quality-improvement projects. In many cases, these Quality Improvement Teams (QITs) focus on environmental issues, and they have discovered that they can help business and the environment at the same time. Employee enthusiasm for projects that include environmental benefits is significantly higher than for other types of projects.

Another aspect of the quality process is reward and recognition for team excellence and individual excellence. Five environmentally oriented QITs won the 1990 Xerox Team Excellence awards. The projects undertaken by these teams included improved environmentally sound packaging ($2 million/year savings), reuse of pallets and packaging (10,000 tons of waste avoided, and $15 million/year saving), marketing recycled paper for Xerox copiers and printers, and waste reduction and recycling at the sites. Added public recognition and environmental awards were provided to the teams to encourage increased focus on environmental excellence. Individual top-level awards were given for energy conservation, initiating the National Office Paper Recycling Project, and a patented two-phase vacuum-extraction clean-up process.

The second phase of environmental intensification at Xerox was aided by the increased awareness and enthusiasm from employees and customers stimulated by Earth Day 1990. As a result of his involvement with Earth Day, the manager of Standards and Systems Engineering approached Xerox management about providing increased focus and communication on environmental concerns.

As a result, in October of 1990, the Xerox Environmental Leadership Program was formally approved by senior corporate management, and communicated to all managers and employees by Paul Allaire, the CEO of Xerox. This action brought increased focus on reduction of non-hazardous wastes and the growing recognition among management that the profit motive and concern for the environment are two sides of the same coin. Protecting the environment by "doing the right thing" is the safest and surest way to long-term profitability.

A senior management Environmental Leadership Steering Committee was formed to guide the environmental programs. This steering committee has representation from the heads of Manufacturing,

Engineering, Supplies, Research, Quality, Real Estate/General Services, Marketing, the Worldwide Operating Companies, and the Environmental Health and Safety department. The steering committee has been meeting quarterly to provide added focus and resolve program content and funding issues. Quarterly reporting on the program to the CEO and his staff provides measurements of progress towards the established goals: to coordinate and help improve the environmental initiatives company-wide, to facilitate communication to employees, customers, and the public about such initiatives, and to benchmark the progress of other companies in order to provide a yardstick for Xerox's efforts.

■ ■ ■

At Southern California Edison, a company whose operations lie in the heart of the Los Angeles Basin, an in-coming chief executive with an environmental background articulated a new approach that called for the company to be both a role model and a community leader in solving the area's huge environmental dilemmas.

Southern California Edison *(from the company's case history)*

With the October 1990 change in Edison's top management, a new vision has been created calling for the company to be Southern California's corporate leader in helping solve regional environmental problems. The decade of the 1990s may see increasingly sharp debate in California over whether environmental concerns should be balanced and tempered with more concern for economic growth. What makes most sense for the region and Edison is to work toward a balance between concern for the economy and protection of the environment. Hence, Edison's role must be to help build a consensus for "sustainable development." To achieve this vision, we believe we must:

- Be a model for our customers of an environmentally responsible corporation. By demonstrating that it is possible to comply with environmental regulations and benefit by taking environmental initiatives, we can set the foundation for consensus.
- Take the lead in helping to solve regional environmental problems. Continued regional economic growth depends on

preserving and enhancing the quality of life of our customers. If we demonstrate that critical environmental concerns such as air quality, waste disposal, and urban growth can be managed, we will establish the mechanism for an environmental consensus.

- Help promulgate cost-effective, risk-based environmental laws. To promote consensus, it is critical to reach agreement on the magnitude of environmental health and ecological risks facing us. By engaging key decision-makers, environmentalists, and customers in a dialogue on the nature and scope of environmental risks, we may be able to lessen the amplitude of debate and discover consensus.

As a consequence of this vision, Edison has identified the need for five key functions in its environmental organization.

- The role of Environmental Research is to chart the course for the environmental organization by applying sound science to environmental issues, devising new approaches to resolving environmental problems, and providing sound science as a base for forming Edison's legislative and regulatory policy.
- The role of Environmental Policy & Regulation is to integrate the financial and operational needs of the company with scientific, engineering, legal, and regulatory information to develop company policy on proposed environmental initiatives. This function also provides the interface with outside entities, such as legislative and regulatory bodies and environmental action groups.
- The role of Environmental Compliance & Services is to implement environmental laws and regulations within the company and to provide environmental engineering and natural/environmental science expertise to various Edison departments. Key new functions supported by this area of the environmental organization are a revised environmental auditing program and coordination of expanded training and education functions as an adjunct to the auditing process.
- A new Environmental Planning activity is being designed to be the "early warning" function for the company on environmental matters. It will involve environmental issue scanning

drawing, for example, on scientific literature, opinion surveys, and media coverage to identify and track environmental issues of potential importance to the company, and then the preparation of appropriate issue response plans. It is envisioned that this Environmental Planning process will lead to the preparation of an annual Integrated Environmental Plan for the company that will be presented to the corporate management committee.

- Another new direction intended to deal with critical strategic issues is to assign an Issue Manager to direct specific action with total responsibility for managing the issue and the resources necessary to address it, reporting directly to the manager of the environmental organization for the entire time needed to resolve the issue.

Of particular interest in the Southern California Edison report is the degree of detail in which the company describes the five elements of its evolving environmental organization structure and the responsibilities of each. Also worth noting is the inclusion of "Issue Managers" as part of the structure.

■ ■ ■

The Bank of America approach summarizes much of what the previous cases cover and adds a few twists of its own.

The research of the past 20 years has made it clear that protecting our environment is an economic imperative. If we abuse the natural resources that support our economy, we are literally polluting our future.

■ *Richard Rosenberg, Chairman*
Bank of America

Bank of America *(from a May 1991 speech by Richard Morrison, senior vice president)*

First and most important, we have the personal leadership and participation of our chairman, Dick Rosenberg. Both in reality and perception, the chairman has been the main driver behind our environmental principles. This element is absolutely essential.

Second, many people at various levels were involved with developing our environmental principles. All of the senior management council was deeply involved. That meant that by the time the principles were announced, the opinion leaders in the bank had all had their say and were with the program. It was the Japanese method of long decision making and short implementation. With the opinion leaders on board, and enthusiastic employees voicing support at all levels of the company, I don't think it occurred to anyone to resist—the job was to design the best program.

Third, we have an "environmental team" to oversee implementation. It is made up of 14 senior officers, all of whom remain in their functional and geographic organizations. This means environmentalism at Bank of America is not a central staff function. It is the responsibility of the major line and staff departments. We come together as a team only about every two months.

Fourth, we created a full-time unit, staffed with three people and dedicated solely to ensuring that the environmental principles are properly implemented, to act as catalyst and coordinator. The team makes it happen, but we [the staff group] keep it rolling in a cohesive direction.

Fifth, we clearly separated what was required for sound banking practices or to comply with laws and regulations from what is voluntary and desirable. On the required side, we have our environmental services unit, set up after passage of the Superfund legislation that assigned environmental clean up liability to current property owners, including banks that foreclose. All banks have that function, and all do it well, out of self-interest. The voluntary side has to do with our principles. I think this distinction has made our program more understandable and given it credibility because we are not mixing up what we *have* to do with what we *choose* to do.

And, sixth, we mounted a well-orchestrated employee communications blitz during the first several months of the program, which included a special employee newsletter, frequent articles in a variety of other employee publications, and speeches to various bank units. Consequently, there was a pretty high awareness level among staff by the time they were asked to do something—such as participate in recycling.

In addition, we went after our employee social clubs, which exist almost everywhere we have a branch or operation. These clubs have historically focused on social activities, such as Disneyland trips or ball games; we are now trying to get them interested in taking on environmentally beneficial projects as group activities.

Last, we created awareness by launching what we called "Green Ideas in Action" to solicit employee suggestions on improving BOFA's environmental performance. This was a special enhancement of our employee-suggestion program. We dubbed March "Green Ideas Month" and got several hundred environmental ideas from line and staff. We will publish the adopted ideas in employee publications and implement those with operational implications. All adopted ideas will win cash awards.

Environmentalism in our organization is a program where individual ideas and effort are what will yield the results, with lots of individuals doing what they can in their own specialized areas. We have been fortunate in having a particularly receptive employee audience and particularly effective employee participants.

■ ■ ■

These examples of how companies involve employees describe both "top down" communication efforts and "bottom-up" participation in developing programs and providing feedback for improvement. Perhaps the ideal method would incorporate both. In any event, engaging the entire organization to a point where environmental thinking becomes a way of life, a part of the corporate culture, is an essential basis for widespread persistent efforts to improve environmental performance.

In most cases, organizational change brought the senior environmental officer greater status and direct access to the chief executive. Often, a senior line manager was appointed to head up the expanded environmental effort, further stressing its importance to operating elements of the company. In most cases, it was noted that results depended on enlisting the support and involvement of the entire organization, often despite lingering skepticism or outright opposition among some managers.

Several companies found a connection between safety, health, and quality—values already institutionalized and accepted—and the emerging concern with the environment. And in each case, if it was not already so ranked, the late 1980s saw the environment promoted to equal or superior status in that hierarchy of corporate concerns. As a further plus, committed and involved employees become enthusiastic external mission-aries for the company, while those that are given cause to doubt the company's sincerity or determination will fail to engage in its programs and remain counter-productive cynics.

Participating companies varied in their reported emphasis on staff-directed environmental efforts (as opposed to charging line executives with prime responsibility). Possibly, that difference is only a reflection of the job held by the writer of the particular case history. More likely, it is a function of corporate style and the degree that the environmental ethic has taken root in the company. In the early stages of change, a committed CEO will need a strong central staff leader empowered to spread the word, direct change, and report on progress. As care for the environment begins to take root in the corporate culture, it becomes more logical to shift the prime environmental burden to operating officials in the same way that they are held accountable for profit, safety, quality, and employee relations, with central staff withdrawing to a support-and-audit role.

As the modern corporation shifts from relying on top-down autocratic command to instead depending on collective and collegial participation of all its members, the innovative skills and efforts of the entire workforce become critical to its success. In this type of company, appropriate organization structures, company policies, and administration procedures all have their place. But management leadership and enthusiastic employee response become the essential ingredients in making the changes in corporate culture that the new environmental challenges demand.

A good summary of the process of organizational change is contained in the words of Robert F. Daniell, Chairman of United Technologies, reprinted from an article in the Summer, 1991 edition of the magazine Directors & Boards.

United Technologies *(from Mr. Daniell's article "Remolding the Environmental Organization")*

Federal environmental regulations today total some 35,000 pages, and Corporate America must comply with every subsection and semicolon on those multitudinous pages. As a leader or as a follower, every company that operates in the United States must deal with environmental protection issues that are growing in volume and complexity. At the same time, we are seeing hopeful signs of industry's increasing concern and responsibility for its own environmental actions.

That is the case at United Technologies Corporation, where we are motivated not only by the tangible rewards of good environmental citizenship, but also by the threat of serious penalties that can be levied by various federal, state, and local environmental enforcement agencies.

I do not pretend to be an expert in the field, nor to hold up United Technologies as a shining example of a company that has achieved perfect environmental compliance. But, I hope, by describing the process we've gone through, some of the landmarks and milestones along the way, and, particularly, how we have structured and restructured our environmental organization in the past few years to cope with changing needs, we may offer some helpful lessons to other companies.

A decade or so ago, our corporate environmental staff of half a dozen people was a part of our Government Affairs function. Theirs was mainly a service role: performing some training for our operating units, doing some regulatory monitoring, and, in general, reacting to problems.

In the mid-1980s, the environmental function began reporting to Human Resources. And, in 1988, environment and safety—historically separate—were integrated under one director of Human and Natural Resource Protection. This was done to eliminate redundancy, to recognize the fact that much of the legislation and regulation dealt with concerns that involved both the environment and safety staffs, and to apply the safety function's long history of experience and practice to the relatively new field of environmental protection.

But as regulations proliferated (at an average of two major pieces of legislation a year since the Clean Air Act of 1972) and as enforcement intensified, we realized that a few organizational changes at the corporate level just weren't enough to make a difference in how we were attacking the problem as a corporation. And there was no consistency across the company as to how environmental issues were being handled. Even so simple an issue as the reception of federal inspectors was inconsistent. At some of our manufacturing plants, federal inspectors were met with open arms; at other locations, with—almost literally—locked doors.

From these and other mixed signals they received, the regulators perceived that United Technologies, as a corporation, just wasn't giving enough attention to environmental issues. The regional Environmental Protection Agency (EPA) administrator, in announcing environmental violations at several of our Connecticut locations, said, ''There have been violations in the past. They haven't set in motion a process to make sure there is continual compliance. So, we have to assume that they have not taken their corporate environmental responsibilities very seriously.'' Those are not words a board member, or an employee, or a resident of our plant communities wants to hear. And they most certainly were not the words I, as CEO, wanted to hear. But such comments—and the fines and warning that accompanied them—spurred us to redouble our environmental efforts.

We strengthened the role of the corporate environmental staff in working with their counterparts in operating units. We reviewed and revised the environmental standards for the corporation and, as part of that, in 1989, developed a new corporate policy and set of accompanying principles dealing with human and natural resource protection. Dissemination of that policy let our employees know that we would treat environmental issues as the core business issues they are.

We launched more training in environmental issues—not only for professionals in the field but also for our plant management and labor who, in most cases, are directly responsible for such issues as proper handling and disposal of potentially polluting or hazardous substances. And we began corporate-led environmental audits—a formal method of measuring compliance and the effectiveness of our environmental and safety management systems. These audits involved plant management as well as environmental and safety professionals.

All this was good progress, and we had elevated the recognition of environmental issues. But our pronouncements about the importance of environmental compliance weren't matched by the role we had given it on the organization chart—the function was still two levels away from the CEO's office, reporting to Human Resources—or by the resources we had allocated to it. It was time to walk our talk.

Therefore, in 1990, we elected Frank W. McAbee, a highly regarded veteran United Technologies executive, as senior vice president responsible for environmental and business practices. He

117

has direct access to the CEO, which underscores the importance of the function. In surveys of peer companies, we discovered that companies with environmental leadership credentials have this type of high-level post for environmental management.

We also established similar environmental executive posts at each of our operating units, with a solid-line reporting relationship to our corporate environmental senior vice president, as well as direct access to their own business unit presidents. These environmental executives throughout the company make up our Environmental Council, which meets monthly to review current issues. This group helps to set company-wide environmental policies, standards, and strategies, while operation of day-to-day environmental programs remains the responsibility of each business unit.

Under the direction of our new environmental senior vice president, we have announced expanded environmental initiatives that will help us achieve our goals. This expanded program was announced early this year [1991] in a televised conference broadcast to audiences of United Technologies executives at 15 locations across the U.S. and Canada. There are five primary elements:

> **Training**—We selected training programs to provide an increased level of environmental awareness and responsibility at all levels of management—beginning with top management. Other training programs provide detailed compliance instructions for every employee directly involved in satisfying regulatory requirements to make sure they understand the process and procedures—and, most important, the attitude—needed to meet those requirements.

> **Assessment and Auditing**—We are reviewing procedures and standards established by our corporate staff to audit and assess environmental performance at each of our operations. Audits will be conducted regularly by each business unit, as well as by an assessment team led by the Corporate Office.

> **Environmental Electronic Data Base Development**—We are developing a process and format for collection of environmental data from all United Technologies facilities. The data-management systems will be able to give operating

units the information they need to monitor their environmental performance and to meet regulatory reporting requirements. At the corporate level, the data will be used to define our overall performance and to give us early warning of trends.

Waste Minimization—Our waste-minimization effort is being built on the base already established by our business units, our corporate Research Center, and our manufacturing and technical councils. This is a major initiative in our expanded program and it covers the full spectrum of environmental issues: air, water, and hazardous waste. We are looking both inside the company and industry-wide to identify materials, processes, and techniques that can be adopted or adapted by us to reduce the amount of waste and pollutants we produce through better design, manufacture, and use of our products.

Legislative and Regulatory Proactivity—In what is a key step for all industries, we are expanding our participation in the legislative and regulatory processes at the federal, state, and local levels. We intend to take a more active role in the evolution of environmental laws, policies, and regulations that affect our operations. We have not worked actively enough in the past—on our own and with the trade groups that represent us—to participate in the early stages of the regulatory process.

We have made good progress, in a short time, to increase our awareness and strengthen our environmental organization. As I told my managers at our televised conference, not only are we going to comply with the letter of the law, but we're also going to make environmental sensitivity a way of life in everything we do at United Technologies.

■ ■ ■

It is worth noting that, as described in the last two chapters, the rising corporate awareness of environmental issues and the decisions to become more active in addressing them are generally of recent vintage, though the seeds have existed for a long time in some companies. In the stories

119

they submitted, essentially all of the participants cited major new environ-mental commitments and organizational changes between 1987 and 1990. Since these companies were selected because they had shown themselves to be leaders, it is clear that this present level of corporate environmental-ism is new and not yet well diffused throughout industry. We are en-couraged that the leading companies now practicing it see many benefits. Its merits can only become more widely recognized as the new decade unfolds.

VI.

GOALS, MEASUREMENT, AND ACCOUNTABILITY

Environmental issues are of great importance to this company. Through the Monsanto Pledge, we've committed ourselves to serious, reportable improvement aimed at an appropriate long-term target of zero environmental effect.

> ■ *Richard J. Mahoney, Chairman and Chief Executive Officer Monsanto Company*
> *—from 1990 Annual Report*

The truism "if you don't know where you are going, any road will take you there" is as valid for environmental improvement as for any other activity. So it is not surprising that most participating companies make at least passing reference to goal-setting in their stories, each at least envisioning a company whose processes and products will tread more lightly on the natural world.

The most compelling goal-setting efforts, however, supplement philosophical generalities with hard, quantifiable and measurable targets, to be achieved by dates certain, and fully incorporated into the company's strategic and operating plans.

S.C. Johnson Wax

One of the immediate results of the [*environmental*] policy was that its principles were developed into objectives with measurable goals and made part of the long-range strategies of the company. The establishment of these goals was a recognition that environmental

121

responsibility has become as integral a strategic element of the business as product performance and cost effectiveness.

Jane Hutterly *[Director of Environmental Actions-Worldwide]* commented, "historically, environmental actions taken by industry have focused on the control of pollutants as required by regulation rather than the prevention of pollution before it occurs. Like most members of industry, S.C. Johnson Wax has largely practiced pollution control, which essentially results in a transfer of our pollutants to somewhere else—moving them around rather than preventing them in the first place. Conversely, pollution prevention is a philosophy gaining acceptance with environmental leaders and is an outgrowth of the cradle-to-grave analysis evolving throughout industry."

The objectives and strategies in the 1991 plan, with 1990 as the benchmark year, focus on both product changes for pollution prevention, and manufacturing controls.

The *first objective* calls for an improvement in the environmental value of products in their formulation, packaging, application, and disposal. Goals here include reduction of volatile organic compound (VOC) ratio to total raw materials by 25 percent by the end of 1995; minimizing adding to landfills by reducing packaging components by 25 percent by the end of 1993, and phasing in the use of recycled materials to 50 percent of total package content by the end of 1995 in the regions of the world where recycling has taken hold.

The *second objective* is to reduce air, water and solid waste discharges in manufacturing operations by 50 percent by the end of 1995. Raw materials used, as well as the processes employed, are targeted for careful analysis to assure achievement of this goal.

The *third objective* laid out the company's commitment to recycle virtually all paper, cardboard, plastic, glass, and steel materials in its manufacturing and office facilities by the end of 1995 in recycling countries.

■ ■ ■

Dramatic goals, announced before their means of accomplishment are at hand, have the advantage of galvanizing attention, stimulating debate, and harnessing innovative skills to find answers. And, if they are bold enough, stating them publicly can have a ripple effect far beyond the company's boundaries.

Monsanto—The "90 Percent" Goal *(from the company case history)*

Two short weeks before the *[SARA]* Title III announcement, while PR teams completed press releases and communication plans, the environmental staff finished compiling the *[emissions]* data. The numbers were expected to be large, but no one was prepared for just how large they turned out to be. Chairman and CEO, Richard J. Mahoney, when presented with the totals, reacted with shock. "The air emission numbers aren't acceptable," Mahoney said. "They're not acceptable to me and they won't be acceptable to the public." After a brief silence, Mr. Mahoney announced what the company would do. "We're setting a goal of reducing toxic air emissions by 90 percent by the end of 1992. Then we'll work toward the ultimate goal of zero." He said, "This is what the public expects and we should expect no less of ourselves."

While our plant managers were grateful to have some good news to deliver to the public along with the pollution statistics, they had no idea how they were going to achieve that goal. Financial targets weren't relaxed. Much of the technology needed to make the reductions was not even developed. People questioned the wisdom of "reducing emissions for the sake of reducing emissions." Nicholas L. Reding, then the head of Monsanto's agricultural products division recalls declaring, "You want us to do *what*? By *when? How?"*

The 90-percent program marked a turning point in the company's environmental culture. Those who were questioning the wisdom of reducing emissions are now talking about the manufacturing plant of the future—one with little or no emissions. And the executive that questioned how this could be accomplished is now executive vice president of environment, safety, health, and manufacturing, charged with successfully implementing this and other environmental goals.

The 90-percent commitment was unprecedented. Not only did it surprise Monsanto employees, it also sent shock waves throughout the industrial community. Environmental groups moved quickly to urge other companies and other industries to "take the Monsanto Pledge" and reduce their emissions by 90 percent.

The 90-percent goal is an interim target as we pursue the ultimate goal of zero effect. Although many eyebrows were raised, zero is the only standard we should be judging ourselves against. Technically, it may be impossible, but in safety we strive for zero injuries, and in quality we strive for zero defects. Our intention is to continue to earn the right to operate; therefore, zero effect is the only acceptable standard to strive toward.

The 90-percent commitment was praised by politicians, reporters, and even environmental groups. Other companies such as 3M, Du Pont, General Electric, Union Carbide, Merck, and IBM announced environmental commitments of their own. Pre-and post-announcement research showed that, of the people who had heard about Monsanto's commitment, opinion of the company significantly improved. This positive perception even spilled over to attitudes toward some of our non-chemical products.

Once management moved from protest to acceptance, the focus quickly turned to meeting the goal. Research dollars and people were applied to making the commitment a reality. Environmental operations managers scrutinized each and every process to assess where reductions might be possible. Employees were encouraged to identify and submit ideas for waste-reducing projects. So far, over 400 employee-identified waste-reduction projects involving air, water, and land releases are being implemented.

Today, all projects to meet the goal are mapped out. Some have already been installed, and dramatic reductions have been achieved. We have already reduced air emissions of SARA Title III chemicals by 58 percent in the United States, and, by the end of 1992, we will be operating at a rate that is 90 percent lower than where we were in 1987.

By taking the initiative in voluntarily announcing the 90-percent goal, we are able to reduce emissions our way, applying technologies and making changes that arrive at the desired end—ways that make sense for us—rather than reacting to prescriptive regulations that can result in inefficiencies and unnecessarily burdensome costs. In fact, regulators are studying our programs and incorporating certain aspects into new regulations. For example, the 1990 Clean Air Act amendments provides a six-year extension in complying with emission-control technology standards for companies which voluntarily reduce air emissions by 90 percent.

The 90-percent goal was only a beginning. It set a tone for our people. It demanded that getting out of the waste business be a high priority, led by Monsanto's chemical unit, which established a goal to reduce [all] hazardous waste released to the environment by 70 percent by the end of 1995.

[Ed. Note: The 90% figure stated earlier applies to air emissions only].

Other operating units developed similar commitments. This has now become the company's waste-reduction goal.

In short, specific measurable goals to provide the groundwork for solid environmental improvement if progress is regularly measured and these goals are upgraded as appropriate. If concerned outsiders have a role in developing the goals, and an opportunity to measure progress towards them, so much the better.

AT&T *(from the company case history)*

Truly worthwhile goals require stretching to achieve. And they must be measurable and monitored. Therefore, as part of AT&T's quality measurements, the company set aggressive goals for its environmental and safety performance, as well as the means to measure progress.

AT&T's environmental goals are *tough:* tougher than any national or international body requires. They can be measured. They can be monitored. Our environmental goals are:

- **Phaseout CFC Emissions From Our Manufacturing Operations**
  50 percent by year end 1991
  100 percent by year end 1994
- **Eliminate Total Toxic Air Emissions**
  50 percent by year end 1991
  95 percent by year end 1995
  Striving for 100 percent by year end 2000
- **Decrease Total Manufacturing Process Waste Disposal**
  25 percent by year end 1994
- **Recycle Paper**
  35 percent of paper by year end 1994

125

- **Decrease Paper Use**
  15 percent by year end 1994
- **Improve Safety**
  Ensure that 100 percent of AT&T eligible manufacturing facilities gain acceptance into the OSHA Voluntary Protection
  Program/AT&T Equivalent Program by year end 1995 and ensure that 50 percent gain STAR status.

Bob Allen, Chairman of AT&T, made these goals public at the
April, 1990, shareowner's meeting. He pledged AT&T's commitment to these goals. "AT&T takes its environmental responsibility
seriously," he said. Quality management provides tools to trans-
late good intentions into measurable progress towards the company's goals. Each year, the Corporate Environmental Engineering Group gathers SARA III emissions data from AT&T factories,
accumulates and graphs the data, and is thus able to track progress towards the company's ambitious goals.

AT&T's environmental & safety goals are benchmarked against
the best companies in its class. AT&T intends to be the best, and
won't settle for a static standard of excellence. Continuous improvement is the way to success.

AT&T takes three fundamental approaches towards its goals:

- First, applying quality principles to all operations: Handling
  materials more efficiently and minimizing waste in all
  operations.
- Second, applying technology to environmental problems: Using new manufacturing technologies and exploring new applications of information technology.
- Third, accelerating existing programs, such as recycling and
  innovative packaging for AT&T products.

■ ■ ■

*To be realistic, environmental goals must be integrated with other objec-
tives if a company is to develop a coherent strategy for its future. New
England Electric System (a group of companies collectively referred to as
NEES) has meshed its environmental and business goals into its newest
corporate plan, which it calls NEESPLAN 3.*

126

New England Electric System *(from NEESPLAN 3)*

The companies of the New England Electric System are pledged to provide their customers the highest possible value in electric service. In resource planning, this pledge requires constant attention to environmental improvement, to cost control, and to reliability of service.

In the 1990s, NEES intends:

GOAL 1: To continuously reduce the environmental impact of its electric service by:
- reducing *[weighted]* net air emissions (including greenhouse gases) from its operations by an estimated 45 percent;
- Continuing the nation's leading energy-conservation program; and
- Purchasing renewable energy and emission offsets.

GOAL 2: To maintain the competitiveness of its electricity prices by:
- Restoring real price stability; and
- Keeping its rates among the lowest in New England.

GOAL 3: To enhance its diverse and competitively procured power supply by:
- Increasing its non-utility generation to at least 900 MW;
- Repowering its Manchester Street plant and fueling its Brayton Point Unit 4 with natural gas; and
- Exploring and fostering new technologies for the future.

During the 1980s, NEES made substantial commitments to competitively procured energy from non-utility generators (NUGs)* and from Hydro-Quebec. While these purchases have added to short-term costs, they help to provide a secure energy supply for the 1990s.

---

*The term Non-utility Generator (NUG) applies to power plants that sell electricity on a wholesale basis, but are not regulated as traditional electric utilities.

127

NEES must now confront new challenges:

- Growing environmental concerns, including issues such as global warming that are not currently addressed by regulations;
- Increasing cost pressures at a time of stagnant demand for electricity and a regional recession; and
- Expanding competition with electric utilities (including those in other states), with NUGs, and with other energy suppliers, such as natural gas distributors.

NEESPLAN 3 responds to these challenges. It has evolved from the quality management process that NEES began in 1990 with a comprehensive service commitment:

The NEES companies pledge to provide our customers the highest possible value by continuously improving electric service, managing costs, and reducing adverse environmental impacts.

NEESPLAN 3 incorporates this vision into resource planning. For the first time, this plan sets forth a corporate commitment to continuous, measurable environmental improvement in all areas of operation. As the leading demonstration of this commitment, NEES plans to reduce its [weighted] net air emissions, including greenhouse gasses, by 45 percent from 1990 to 2000, without sacrificing the diversity, reliability, or economy of our energy supply.

Goal-setting is also referred to in the stories of a number of companies quoted elsewhere. The preceding four, however, cover goal-setting as a specific activity and so provide the most comprehensive examples of how leaders can use goals to stimulate environmental improvement.

■ ■ ■

Xerox describes how, by applying the quality process of benchmarking, demanding goals can be established and then ratcheted up as initial targets are met. As in the quality program, continuous improvement is the intended result.

Xerox Corporation *(from the company's case history)*

Benchmarking is an important element in the quality process. It involves identifying the industry leaders in each area of business practice, including environmental improvement, then studying their methods, noting their results, and identifying their goals. Xerox's goals and practices are then based in part on what is learned from these leading companies. In addition, a benchmark review is performed on the internal operations to study the leading organizations within Xerox. This process provides increased insight and motivation to the teams working on quality improvement projects, and ensures that higher, realistic, and achievable goals are set.

One of the important themes of the quality process is continuous improvement. This builds upon benchmarking, measurement and monitoring, and the tracking of goals that are raised as improvements are made. As an example, when the goals for site recycling were first set in early 1990, they called for a 50-percent waste reduction and recycling by the end of 1992. At the time, this seemed to be a really uphill task. By early 1991, many of the larger manufacturing sites were already exceeding the 50-percent goal. The goal was then revised to call for continuous improvement quarter after quarter, and year after year. By mid-1991, quite a few sites had reached 60 percent and the Xerox manufacturing site in Venray, Netherlands exceeded 80 percent. The initial Xerox goal of 50 percent by 1992 was based on industry benchmarking. While overall it may still be a reasonable goal, internal benchmarking showed that this was not a high enough goal for individual sites, which can aspire to 90 percent by the end of 1992. Benchmarking not only looks at overall goals and performance, but also goals for specific operations, and the methods employed in achieving the goals for each category of waste material.

As a prime example of these new initiatives, Xerox has adopted a "cradle-to-grave" requirement for product design architectures that addresses environmental concerns throughout a product's life. Environmental concerns at every phase of a product's life-cycle have been addressed to minimize environmental impacts and provide savings through enhanced parts recovery, remanufacturing, and recycling. The key objective in the Xerox "Asset Management"

129

program is to design into our products and systems all the elements of environmental quality at the outset. Thus, design will consider the total life strategy for the product—not only form, fit, and functions, but also disassembly, remanufacture, reuse, recycling, and final disposition. Environmental requirements are now being incorporated into design specifications, architecture standards, and long-range plans. Enforcement is achieved via periodic reviews built into the Product Delivery Process.

Decision-making based on life-cycle costs is not easy since many of the tools and techniques are not fully developed. Even more difficult is taking into account the full environmental costs of a product or a process. However, Xerox has long tracked the life-cycle cost of its products, and a good beginning has been made in considering the environmental life-cycle costs, leading to decisions that facilitate economical remanufacturing and result in significant environmental and cost savings.

■ ■ ■

There is increasing pressure from outside—from environmentalists, politicians, consumer organizations—for information about what we are doing and how it might affect them. We have as it were a requisition from society to communicate with them about the impact of our activities and to fulfill certain requirements to gain acceptance. The generation of relevant data and its interpretation cost money and effort. It's a sort of license fee to do business—no bad thing, in my view.

■ *Freek Rijkels, Head of Health, Safety and Environment Division, Royal Dutch/Shell Group of Companies (from Shell World, Aug/Sept '86)*

Accountability—the public reporting and independent validation of the details of environmental problems and progress—is a difficult issue for many companies and one that citizens' groups most insistently demand that industry address. In its simplest terms, the issue appears to revolve around two once seemingly irreconcilable points of view. On the one hand, observers say, in effect, "Tell us exactly what your problems are, what risks they entail, what you are doing about it, and prove to us that the results you say you are obtaining are in fact being achieved." These concerns have arisen because corporate doors were long closed, because many fear exposure to involuntary risks of unknown severity, and because of a natural skepticism that promises may not be followed by action.

Companies, on the other hand, often feel that it is the role of government, not private groups, to assess hazard and judge compliance. Further, some are concerned that, if disclosed, scientific data will be misrepresented by poorly informed or hostile communicators, distorting the public's perceptions of risk. And, finally, there is the pervasive fear that any imperfection—even in an imperfectible process—can lead to litigation ultimately decided not on that basis of actual harm done or scientific fact but on emotional grounds, fear, and compassion for the presumed victims.

Despite corporate reluctance to open doors, the public's right to know about matters that may affect it seems unchallengeable. The company eager to be seen as a good citizen will need to find ways to disclose what it is doing so that it may be judged on its actions.

In establishing quantifiable goals and dates for their attainment, companies do establish standards by which their performance can be measured and evaluated. But, as Xerox points out, satisfactory techniques for determining the full environmental costs of a product over its life-cycle are not yet available. Internalizing these costs so that they can enter a company's economic calculations is still an embryonic and empirical practice. In this regard, the New England Electric example described in Chapter II is the most sophisticated approach reported by any participating company.

Some environmental measurements simply cannot be refined to the precision of financial statements; nor are there generally accepted environmental standards (other than regulatory compliance) comparable to the generally accepted accounting practices (GAAP) on which corporate profit-and-loss calculations and balance sheets are based. And it is very difficult to convert environmental costs into dollars. Thus environmental accounting is in its infancy, and it is not yet possible to audit all aspects of a company's environmental program in the same fashion as its books of account are verified, though the environmental audits mentioned by a number of companies represent a helpful start. They can be carried out by inside teams or outside consultants. They can assess:

- *Compliance with regulations,*
- *Effectiveness of company procedures for environmental improvement,*
- *Performance against established quantitative goals, and*
- *Standards and procedures compared to those of other companies.*

Even though they lack some of the precision of financial audits, environmental audits are useful to managements eager to assure compliance with company policies and government regulations, and to measure progress toward goals. They can also add reliability to managements' reports that describe environmental problems and progress to interested outsiders, though their language is not yet sufficiently standard to make overall comparisons between one company and another easy.

In this connection, a number of corporations now issue periodic environmental reports to shareholders and other interested groups. Many now include a section on the environment in their Annual Reports. Others discuss the specific results of individual programs with local citizens or environmentally interested observers. And, of course, all report their SARA III emissions to the government, figures that are then available to the public. Thus, a framework for corporate environmental accountability is beginning to be established.

The credibility the public gives to company efforts at improvement will depend in part on how quickly and effectively this process is developed and refined and its messages disseminated. Setting goals in collaboration with outside stakeholders will give them confidence and equity in the process. Measurable improvements, independently verified, will add substance to company claims. Ongoing dialogue with critics, based on a willingness to listen, can lead to continuing improvement. An important and commendable beginning is being made, but there is a distance to go.

One of the most developed environmental surveillance programs is that of Allied-Signal, as described by Jonathan Plaut, its Director of Environmental Compliance.

Allied-Signal, Inc. *(from an article by Jonathan Plaut of Allied-Signal)*

"The Uninspected Inevitably Deteriorates."

■ *Dwight D. Eisenhower*

This article will focus primarily on Allied-Signal's (1) corporate-wide Environmental Audit Program, (2) Environmental Assurance Reviews, and (3) its Annual Environmental Assurance Letter Program.

Some of the programs were undoubtedly created, at least in part, in response to the Kepone incident in the mid-1970s.

[Ed. Note: An Allied Chemical* licensee and supplier discharged the toxic chemical Kepone into the James River of Virginia, an incident for which Allied was held accountable.]

The corporation was a target of unfriendly private and government actions at the time, including an SEC complaint and Consent Order. The ill-wind Kepone, however, may have blown some good, and not only on Allied. Hopefully, others can learn from the experiences of Allied Chemical.

The Corporation's Health, Safety and Environmental Policy is fairly succinct. The key elements of the Corporation's commitment are that it will:

- ''. . .design, manufacture, and distribute all products and handle and dispose of all materials safely and without creating unacceptable risks to health, safety, or the environment.
- "Establish and maintain programs to assure that laws and regulations. . .are known and obeyed."
- "Adopt its own standards where laws or regulations may not be adequately protective.
- "Every employee is expected to adhere to the spirit as well as the letter of this policy. Managers have a special obligation to keep informed. . .and to advise higher management promptly of any adverse situation. . .''

The real secret to compliance is not the lawyer. Rather, the secret lies in the active involvement with line and business operations of a sufficient number of competent multidisciplinary environmental professionals. These folks should be primarily at the plant level, but with a sufficient number on staff to develop, implement, and monitor the various environmental programs.

---

*Allied Chemical was the previous name of Allied-Signal, Inc.

In a financial context, the term "audit" is accepted and understood. Environmental "auditing," on the other hand, is a relatively embryonic science.

This Environmental Audit Program was adopted in 1978, after a gestation period of over a year. Its objective is to provide top management and the Board of Directors with an independent verification that our operations are in compliance with Allied-Signal's health, safety, and environmental (HS&E) policy and procedures, as well as HS&E laws and regulations.

The program is headed by the Corporate Director, Audit (a senior member of the Corporate HS&E Department). It provides an historical snapshot showing through factual observations where a facility stands with respect to current laws/regulations and corporate and plant policy and procedures. Deficiencies are noted for follow-up and correction, but it is not the function of the audit review to make recommendations to change or modify programs to improve the overall programs from a future risk-management perspective. The latter is the primary function of the Environmental Assurance Reviews.

Audits cover six HS&E disciplines or areas: water pollution control and spill prevention, air pollution control, solid and hazardous waste, safety and the prevention of loss, occupational health and medical, and product safety and integrity.

In 1991, approximately 80 manufacturing facilities were reviewed—out of 200-plus worldwide.

Each facility is given advance notice of a pending audit. In addition, as part of its advance preparation, it receives a copy of the then-applicable review protocols. We are not policemen; the reviews are intended to be constructive and, at least for the most part, are perceived in that light by those reviewed.

One inspector is always the Audit Director or a member of his staff; another may be from an outside environmental consulting firm, with the remainder, if any, from the HS&E staff who possess expertise in the discipline being reviewed. Allied-Signal may review one or more disciplines per visit. Audits include establishing progress on program elements, as well as including, for example, the ASAP program (Allied-Signal Against Pollution) or emergency preparedness under "Responsible Care."

At the conclusion of the review, a complete detailed oral exit interview (along with written lists of findings) is held with the plant or business manager. In addition, before the final report is issued, the plant or business manager gets an opportunity to comment on the draft report.

Shortly thereafter, a formal written report goes to the sector president with a request for a written reply indicating corrective action taken or anticipated in response to each finding of deficiency noted. Having the president in the loop helps ensure top management involvement and commitment, including assurance that sufficient funds will be appropriated to accomplish the corrective action in a timely way.

These formal reports are always written by the Audit Director or a member of his staff. They set forth factual observations (no conclusions) measured against (a) federal-state-local regulatory standards, (b) corporate policies and procedures, and (c) local control systems. Twice a year an overview report is made to the Corporate Responsibility Committee of the Board of Directors. A representative of the outside consultant (A.D. Little of Cambridge, Mass.) is present, and at the conclusion of the meeting, inside personnel (including the CEO) are excused and the outside directors have a chance to privately chat with the outside representative.

Some people fear that the reports generated by reviews will inevitably create a "smoking gun" and prove too dangerous in the long run. To accomplish their purpose, these reports must be accurate and complete; they must communicate in a meaningful way. Since they highlight deficiencies, *if left unattended* in the files, they could indeed be a "smoking gun" that shoots.

But in Allied-Signal's judgment, the benefits far outweigh the risks. Initially, we take great care in drafting the reports—facts, not conclusions. There is only one set of working papers—retained three years—and all rough notes and draft reports are supposed to be destroyed as soon as the action plan prepared in response to the formal report is received.

One step we deliberately did not take, however, was to run the program through the Law Department to impart "attorney work product" or "attorney-client privilege." If the whole program were run through the Law Department, that might not only prove to be a bottleneck, but, of even greater concern, we might also lose the very protection we sought by overreaching or abusing the privilege.

Of most critical importance, however, is the exacting system in place to assure that every finding in the audit is corrected or otherwise dealt with. To fix deficiencies is the greatest protection and evidence of diligence. Follow-up inspections assure that the system is working.

Environmental Assurance Reviews

These reviews are thorough, in-depth inspections by the professionals in the four basic HS&E disciplines (pollution control, safety and loss prevention, product safety and integrity, occupational health and medicine) which make up the core group of professionals in the Corporate HS&E Department. The output of an assurance review will ultimately be an action plan to implement the agreed-upon corrective steps.

Annual Environmental Assurance Letter Program

This is perhaps the most effective program of all, in that it vividly demonstrates top-management's insistence on environmental compliance and dramatically raises the level of environmental consciousness down to the corporate grassroots. Action programs of compliance with laws, regulations, and company standards worldwide in health, safety, and the environment are carried out every day by the operations. In addition, each year the CEO formally requests each operating sector president to go on the line that he/she understands the corporate HS&E policy (remember—spirit as well as letter) and has taken steps to bring that policy to the attention of employees in that sector. He/she states that control systems are in place—or explains why they aren't—to assure compliance or adherence to the law and regulations, as well as corporate HS&E policy and procedures; that the sector has satisfied its responsibilities with respect to permits, notifications, and other actions required by law; that significant violations/deviations have been reported to the corporate HS&E Department; and that he/she knows of no matters that could have a materially adverse future impact on any of the sector's business areas.

This last is key—in a company the size of Allied-Signal, few environmental problems would have a material adverse impact in the Securities and Exchange Commission sense. By breaking it down to separate business areas, the CEO's letter helps to ensure that problem areas on a smaller scale "bubble-up" and thus can be promptly corrected or otherwise handled.

Executives right down the line to the plant manager and beyond execute similar letters, and those flow back up the line with action plans and schedules and with target compliance dates until the sector president has what he/she deems adequate to enable him/her to sign an environmental assurance letter to the CEO. The same type of diligent follow-up system attaches to this assurance process and action plan as previously described.

All key executives develop annual action plans that detail the steps needed to accomplish selected objectives. Some goals are financial, but about 40 percent of an executive's incentive compensation depends on meeting nonfinancial objectives. A nonfinancial goal for many operating executives is environmental and safety program compliance.

In short, environmental excellence pays in many ways. The proactive programs described may not be appropriate for all manufacturing companies, but they work pretty well for Allied-Signal.

The discipline of Allied's surveillance, review, and certification process gives management assurance that the good intentions of the company's environmental policy statement are being realized in its day-to-day operations and that the risk of unpleasant surprises is reduced. Recording unsatisfactory situations may create a paper trail that prosecutors could follow later—Allied calls it a "Smoking Gun"—but that very threat also provides strong pressure to correct unsatisfactory situations promptly. The annual compliance letter chain forces each manager to go on record—to put his or her reputation on the line—that the company's environmental policies are indeed being carried out, a technique used successfully elsewhere in industry in such areas as anti-trust compliance.

Despite their increasing use, most environmental measurement and surveillance or audit programs fall short of the full public accountability on which trust will ultimately be based. Until public disclosure and independent validation of environmental performance is a regular practice (as Dow is urging in the case of Responsible Care), critics are likely to remain skeptical of corporate claims, no matter how justified they may seem to

management. In a future of sustainable development, a corporation's environmental books are likely to be scrutinized just as carefully as its financial reports are today.

VII.

FINDING PEOPLE TO MAKE IT HAPPEN

No longer is it sufficient for major corporations to relegate an environmental agenda to lawyers and engineers. Environmental concerns are a strategic part of today's business decisions. From raw materials to marketing, today's marketplace is intertwined with the environment. To integrate them, environmental education must become a part of the business curriculum both in our universities and in our offices.

> ■ *Jay Hair, President, The National Wildlife Federation (from "Environmental Education: A Statement for Business Management," 1991*

Earlier chapters have emphasized the role of the Chief Executive in turning a company in an environmentally progressive direction and the need for organizational changes and individuals committed to environmental improvement to carry out the new policies. But where do these people come from? How are they trained? And what message does the management send to the organization as it defines qualifications for and career potential of newly appointed environmental leaders?

Although no participating company reports that its senior environmental officer was trained academically in environmental management, the field is expanding rapidly in size and stature as environmental concerns become integrated into business analyses and decisions.

Several companies indicated the desirability of blending line management and environmental experience in executives' career paths.

The background of a number of recently appointed senior environmental executives is in operations. Lloyd Elkins, who heads up Chevron's Health, Environment, and Loss Prevention Group, until recently the company's youngest corporate vice president, was previously vice president of production for Chevron U.S.A. At Dow, the new job of Vice President, Environment, Health and Safety was given to David Buzzelli, who had established an outstanding track record as president of Dow Canada. Jane Hutterly was appointed Director of Environmental Affairs-Worldwide at S.C. Johnson Wax after a successful career as a marketing executive. Other companies found the best qualified candidates, such as medical doctor Bruce Karrh of Du Pont, and engineer and attorney Jonathan Plaut of Allied-Signal, within their senior professional ranks.

The implicit message seems to be that if the CEO wants to elevate the level of environmental awareness within the company, one way to do it is to give the top environmental assignment to a widely respected and well known executive from within the company. Here is how one such person approached his new job as the company's top environmental officer:

Monsanto *(as told by Nicholas L. Reding, Executive Vice President for Environment, Safety, Health and Manufacturing)*

Before I took on my current responsibility, I spent 34 years working in Monsanto's agricultural businesses—in technical service, marketing, product management, and division management. I wasn't oblivious to environmental issues, but my experience with environmentalism was limited to specific product applications. These typically emphasized the toxicology and public acceptability of new and existing agricultural products. My organization and people were often focused on the narrow world of regulation and arcane jargon—parts per billion, quantitative and qualitative risk assessment, residue studies, environmental fate studies, and all the rest. Our goal was to ensure compliance with all federal, state, and international laws.

In 1988, when Richard J. Mahoney, Monsanto's chairman and chief executive officer, announced the company's goal to reduce toxic air emissions by 90 percent by the end of 1992, my reaction was surprise, tinged with a little shock. Why did we have to do more than what was required by law? Why spend tens of millions of dollars when our studies showed that our air emissions posed no risk to anyone? If there were no benefits to public health, what was the point?

Those questions, which reflected a business concern with issues like cost, capital, and investment, were legitimate questions. The answer was equally legitimate: because we earn our right to operate from the public; and because we earn that right every day, we must respond to the public's concern and judgement.

In 1990, when I accepted my current position, it was immediately clear that, not only did we have to find ways to sustain our drive to environmental stewardship, we also had to do more. We had to find ways to add value—the value of our environmental goals and programs—to our products and businesses. We had to find ways to bring "corporate environmentalism" to critical mass within the company, to the point where the environment became the responsibility of both Monsanto's regulatory experts and the individual businesses in their day-to-day operations. In my experience, most business managers consider the environment a cost of doing business, so we had to convince these managers that the environment wasn't a cost of doing business; instead, it *was* their business.

That effort continues. We are making good progress, but we haven't yet reached perfection. We've made changes in Monsanto's environmental policy staff that enhance the traditional focus on compliance but that also bring a new focus to adding value. That business perspective is absolutely critical.

We've now begun a program that exposes our business managers to the challenges of the environment. We are increasingly involving our customers and their concerns in our environmental programs. And we've made a number of environmental converts who are, in turn, continuing to spread the message, increasing the flow of creative juices, creating a new environmental ethic—one that incorporates environmental stewardship as a competitive edge in business operations.

We're just beginning to have fun.

Nick Reding, a chemical engineer by education, brought a wealth of technical and management experience, as well as a detailed knowledge of his company's operations, to his new post. The challenge he met was to redefine the company's environmental problems, to recognize that they stretched beyond technology, risk evaluation, and cost to include social values and

141

*the company's right to operate and then to diffuse that new way of think-
ing throughout the company and beyond.*

■ ■ ■

*Another company's case history covered the background, talents, and
aspirations of some members of its environmental team, in the process demonstrating the importance of personal commitment to environmental issues.*

Chevron *(from the company case history)*

Many Chevron employees consider themselves as part of an
"environmental workforce," and in truth environmental matters
are a growing component of thousands of jobs. In addition, environmental problem-solving has generated full-time work and career opportunities.

An electrical engineer by training, Bill Mulligan, for example,
figured to spend much of his work life in refinery operations. Starting in 1967, he applied his skills to plant engineering and, after
14 years, found himself the maintenance superintendent at
Chevron's Philadelphia Refinery. But as times evolved, so did Mulligan. Radically. As the manager of Environmental Affairs in
Chevron's Health, Environment & Loss Prevention (HE&LP)
Group, Mulligan holds a job that 25 years ago did not exist.

Norm Zeiser developed an inkling of what might be coming
during Earth Day in 1970. While doing graduate work in occupational health science at Temple University, the event and its atten-
dant publicity reaffirmed his leanings toward a career that in some
way involved the environment. Seven years later, when he joined
Chevron, Zeiser recognized that "the oil industry was at the point
of many environmental concerns. Here was a chance," he says,
"to use my education and experience in an industry that was under more pressure than most to do a better job on the environment.
I could push from the inside."

Originally in the industrial hygiene field—a precursor, of sorts,
to environmental affairs—Zeiser is today HE&LP's coordinator for
water quality issues. At a Chevron conference Zeiser organized in
Houston a few years ago, participants from throughout the company shared experiences and forward-looking ideas on wastewater
treatment technology.

142

Growing up in the San Francisco Bay Area, Tom Booze couldn't avoid an awareness of the burgeoning environmental movement, even if he'd wanted to. But it was a segment on the CBS program *60 Minutes* that finally pushed him toward a career in toxicology. "It was a story about a pesticide and its manufacturer's employees who didn't know about the hazards of the chemical they were handling," he explains. "They had it on their clothes and on their food. I wanted to do something to help out." Earning an undergraduate degree from the University of California at Davis and his toxicology doctorate at Kansas State, Booze joined Chevron five years ago.

With Chevron's Environmental Health Center in Richmond, he's part of a multi-disciplinary team that studies potentially contaminated sites and assesses whether they pose significant health risks. "A lot of problems are a result of past practices," he says, "But we're trying to turn things around. This environmental work is certainly a growing field."

Whether by choice or chance, the career paths of Mulligan, Zeiser, and Booze are part of what's now in the mainstream of corporate concerns. Chevron has approximately 500 full-time environmental affairs specialists, in jobs that demand various backgrounds. Sixty-seven percent come from the chemical, mechanical, and civil engineering disciplines. Chemistry and geology backgrounds are behind about 12 percent of the formal environmental workforce. The rest come from toxicology, microbiology, and other sciences, and there are also those with legal and business training.

However, putting a precise number on the total magnitude and range of the environmental workforce is virtually impossible. That's because there are refinery operators, attorneys, miners, government affairs reps, office assistants, and many others who spend part and even much of their time on environmental work. In fact, by the nature of the petrochemical industry—and Chevron's land, coal, and mineral operations—environmental concerns have become incorporated into literally thousands, if not tens of thousands, of jobs.

Not long ago, vice president Lloyd Elkins conducted an informal survey. "It wasn't a precise analysis, but I asked various work groups across the company—not the environmental professionals—but the supervisors, the roustabouts, operators, service workers,

143

and the like, to estimate how much time they spent in their daily jobs only on environment, safety and health affairs," he explains. Typical responses were in the range of 20 to 30 percent."

"Environment is not just a staff activity," says chairman Ken Derr. "It's also a principal responsibility for operating people." And protecting the environment has become a credible career unto itself.

"If you go back 20 years to that first Earth Day," says Bill Mulligan, "you've got to recognize that there were few environmental statutes. Many of today's regulations didn't come into existence until the late 1970s. But we all were starting to recognize the pollution of the post-war period, through the classic touchstone examples of Los Angeles smog and the Cuyohoga River catching fire."

Industry initially reacted to the regulations by digging in and questioning changes, fearing the costs. "Command and control" regulations issued by federal, state, and local governments were met, but often with little enthusiasm. Industrial firms and their employees were on new ground. "Our very first environmental workers were naturally drawn from other areas of the company," says Mulligan, "people who had minimal training on either the technical aspects of the environment or the increasingly complex regulations themselves." Their main function, he adds, "was to try to keep the company out of trouble." As these regulations grew more complex and expensive, health and safety specialists "bridged" into environmental affairs.

"At one time, employees shunned these jobs, fearing that they were dead ends," Mulligan continues. "Now, environmental affairs is a company priority and draws strongly motivated employees who want to work in the field. We have Ph.D.'s ranging from biology to zoology, with sterling professional credentials, which are needed if they and the company are to have credibility with the outside world."

"We're the eyes and ears of the refinery," says Karen Means, an Environmental Shift Coordinator (ESC) at the El Segundo, California refinery. The ESCs juggle their hours so that the refinery has 24-hour coverage. "We've gotten our senses educated so we know the typical sights, sounds, and odors of the operation," she explains. "We recognize anything atypical very quickly and feel that we've not done our job if we don't correct something before there is a complaint. Dealing with the public is hard, mainly because people get only bits and pieces of information from the media. When we get calls, it's tough to explain something when they already believe something different.''

A former air quality specialist, Means has developed still other abilities; she trained with the International Bird Rescue organization in Berkeley, CA. During the recent Huntington Beach oil spill, she was part of a team of nearly 20 El Segundo employees who helped clean birds on the team's off-hours.

''What were simple compliance programs have evolved into proactive programs to avoid the costs associated with pollution,'' Mulligan notes. ''To do this, we need professionals and others with specialized training in wastewater, air, or what have you, and a knowledge of complex regulation. We also needed management with a greater understanding of the regulatory process. In the future, I don't think anyone will reach senior management without in-depth exposure and an appreciation for safety, health, and environmental issues.''

The academic backgrounds and experience of the senior environmental officers listed at the start of this chapter, and the Monsanto and Chevron stories, illustrate the scarcity of executives and professionals with specific training in ecology and environmental sciences. The corporate answer to this rapidly growing need has usually been to take competent individuals with compatible scientific training—engineers, medical doctors, and toxicologists for example—and expose them on the job and through conferences and seminars to the breadth of skills and knowledge needed to address environmental matters successfully.

This lack of specific training for an emerging field is not unusual— few senior managers understood computers a generation ago—but it does highlight the need for prompt effort by universities, whether in the undergraduate, graduate, or mid-career courses, to give the environment a significant place in the curriculum.

■ ■ ■

The need for trained professionals who can combine environmental and business thinking has not been lost on Allied-Signal. One of their answers has been to help Tufts University establish courses of study that will prepare prospective leaders to be environmentally sensitive as well.

145

It is especially noteworthy that this "seed-corn" funding came not from government or a private foundation, but from a concerned corporation.

Tufts University and Allied-Signal, Inc.

If we are to preserve the environment and at the same time continue to enjoy the benefits of advanced technology, we must educate tomorrow's leaders to think in new ways about protecting the environment. It is gratifying that a new educational initiative at the university level has received support from a federal agency and private industry, and perhaps surprising to some that the initiative was provided by the latter. But attitudes in corporate America are changing.

■ *Edward L. Hennessy,*
Chief Executive Officer
Allied-Signal, Inc.

Here is a summary of the new program at Tufts University, adapted from comments by its Dean, Anthony Cortese.

Tufts University has embarked on an ambitious program to develop the intellectual capital needed to meet human needs and many of our wants in an environmentally sustainable manner in the future. This program seeks to have all graduates of Tufts University—in the college of liberal arts and engineering, the schools of medicine, veterinary medicine, dentistry and nutrition, the Fletcher School of Law and Diplomacy and the graduate school of arts and sciences—be environmentally literate and responsible citizens. Through broad, continuing, and repetitive exposure to environmental issues throughout the educational experience at Tufts, we will strive to develop a fundamental awareness and understanding of how we can protect the environment as we live and have a sense of stewardship for the planet.

To achieve these goals, environmental issues are being incorporated into the curriculum of all major disciplines taught in Tufts. This requires the development of a faculty capable of teaching about environmental issues in the context of their disciplines. In April 1990, Tufts President Jean Mayer announced the formation of The Environmental Literacy Institute (TELI) to help faculty develop this capability.

TELI is carrying out a series of programs to develop the capability of 150 faculty members at Tufts. The first TELI program, a faculty workshop involving 31 Tufts faculty members, was held in May 1990. During the summer, faculty members worked to revise their course curricula to incorporate environmental issues and concerns. The program is being repeated with new faculty each year. They offered the new or revised courses in the 1991–1992 academic year. Similar training is being made available to faculty at other universities. TELI is, to our knowledge, the nation's first program attempting to integrate environmental issues into undergraduate, graduate, and professional school curricula across a variety of disciplines.

Our goal is to provide Tufts graduates with a fundamental awareness and understanding of the importance of the natural environment to life, of how all human activities affect the environment, and of an ethic for responsible stewardship of the planet's resources. To achieve this goal, TELI holds a series of workshops, seminars, and other programs to develop and augment the environmental knowledge and skills of the Tufts faculty, as well as to help them revise their curricula to include environmental issues. In this way, students receive broad, continuing, and repeated exposure to environmental issues throughout their academic experience. The institute facilitates the process of faculty development by providing financial and intellectual support, as well as access to resources, information, and environmental experts.

TELI was established by a two-year grant from Allied-Signal, Inc.—an advanced technology company based in Morris Township, New Jersey. Tufts has also received grants of $75,000 from the U.S. Environmental Protection Agency (EPA) and $20,000 from Union Carbide for the 1991–92 year. Additional funding is being sought to ensure that 150 Tufts faculty members will receive training over the next five years and to expand TELI programs to other universities and high schools, including those in developing countries (a process which has already begun).

147

> It is quite obvious that to educate undergraduates we must provide a solid multidisciplinary education so that students understand the methodologies of their fields and can sort facts from hypothesis, fantasy or propaganda. We also need to foster learning through multidisciplinary projects. There is no way to bring about environmental literacy without all elements of the university working together.
>
> ■ *Jean Mayer,* President,
> *Tufts University*
> —from TELI *Executive Summary; 1990.*

What should informed citizens and professionals know about the world we live in and how human activities affect the world? In short, what does it mean to be environmentally literate? TELI believes that fundamental knowledge, skills, and attitudes are necessary for an environmentally literate society.

This educational approach is built on the premise that such fundamental shifts in awareness and understanding will come only with a broad, continuing, and repetitive program throughout the educational experience. The integration of these concepts through a broad array of courses and experiences with an emphasis on expansion of curriculum in existing courses is the best method of achieving the goal of environmental literacy. The limited value of a specialized course for all students, combined with the extraordinary pressures for new curriculum requirements during a time of limited resources, argue strongly for the former approach. TELI is committed to developing this educational approach.

The results to date have been very encouraging. In its first year, TELI developed the capability for 25 Tufts faculty members to incorporate the teaching of environmental issues into such diverse curricula as mechanical engineering, economics, history, international diplomacy, drama, sociology, and chemistry. This year [1991], 45 faculty members from Tufts and 10 other universities, including universities in Brazil and Canada, participated in the program. A member of the Supreme Soviet, a Korean development economist, an Indian university president, and a Brazilian university faculty member joined Tufts environmental specialists in conducting the program. As a result, between 5,000 and 8,000 students have been, or will be, exposed to environmental issues and perspectives in non-environmental courses in 1991 and 1992.

For example, an engineering professor has redesigned the freshman course in Engineering Design involving 200 students. Using the university itself as a case study, students identified ways to reduce the use of fuel, electricity, water, and solid materials and the production of pollution and wastes in three major Tufts buildings. An economics professor developed a course in Environmental Economics and Policy which involved executing a major project in cost/benefit and life-cycle cost analysis on products used by Tufts dining services, water conservation, fertilizer use, transportation, and composting. A language professor has revised all six major courses required for a major in Spanish to include environmental reading from Spain and Latin America and to make environmental issues and controversies the subject of paper topics and debates.

Our long-term goal is to have TELI serve faculty from high schools and other universities in the Northeastern United States and universities in developing countries. By developing the capability of 500 faculty members from Tufts and other universities over the next 5 years, 75,000 to 100,000 students will receive broad, continuing and repeated exposure to environmental issues in the context of their regular disciplinary studies.

It will be some time before the results of this and similar programs are felt in the industrial world, for investments in education have a long gestation period. But without managers who have a holistic view of the environment as a vital element of economic life, there will continue to be temptations to regard it as only the concern of scientists and special interest groups. If preservation of the global ecosystem is to assume its proper central place in the world's future, it must also have a central place in the minds of the world's future leaders.

VIII.
BEYOND
CORPORATE WALLS

Individual companies and industries are inextricably woven into the web of economic, social, political, and environmental forces shaping human experience today. Thus, any change in their approach to environmental matters quickly affects others outside the corporate community. The response of outsiders to new corporate initiatives can, in turn, affect future corporate attitudes, behavior, success, or even continued existence. This chapter explores how some companies are reaching out beyond their boundaries to various other constituencies.

Communicating with the Public

In the final analysis, corporations depend on public acceptance for their right to do business. And so, as several observed earlier, it is not only important to do the right thing environmentally, but also to be perceived as doing so. Effective communication starts with knowing what is expected of you and how the public feels about what you are doing. Surveys are one way of listening to that public.

S.C. Johnson Wax *(from the company case history)*

In July 1990, the company commissioned a poll by the Roper Organization to determine public attitudes and identify individual behavior toward the environment. The poll revealed that public environmental concern was consistently high, but that people's environmental actions seldom reflected that concern. In fact, the diversity of environmental behavior enabled Roper to segment respondents into five distinct groups, from the most active "True-Blue Greens" (11 percent) to the "Basic Browns" (28 percent). Other key findings of the study are:

- Improving the environment ranked fourth on the list of national priorities, after solving the problem of crime and drugs, finding a cure for AIDS, and containing health-care costs.
- Since 1987, public concern about the environment has grown faster than concern for any other national problem.
- The public perceptions as to the true causes of many environmental problems are inaccurate. For instance, most people think disposable diapers, plastic packaging, plastic bottles, and aerosol containers are the primary contributors to landfills, when, in actuality, combined they account for about 10 percent of solid waste. The public ranked paper and grass clippings (44 percent of contribution to landfills) as the least important cause of the solid waste problem.
- The most serious environmental problems are thought to be water pollution from manufacturing plants, oil spills, chemical waste, industrial air pollution, destruction of the ozone layer, contaminated drinking water, and nuclear waste, all cited by two-thirds or more of the public.
- Business receives most of the blame for causing pollution problems because of its manufacturing operations and the products it uses. And most believe that government action would be the only impetus for industry to solve the problems it had caused.

On the whole, Roper showed that Americans don't care about how industry is improving its environmental practices and fail to see their individual roles in effecting positive environmental change. They just want business to fix it.

■ ■ ■

Unfortunately, while citizens are calling on business to "fix it," they are also unlikely to believe what business tells them it is doing (Fig. 6). Thus, corporate environmental communications programs have a huge credibility gap to overcome in a society conditioned to disbelieve most of what all of its institutions are telling it.

Many participating companies report that they are increasing their communications with stakeholders on environmental matters, listening more intently to critics, and seeking greater public understanding of their operations. To do this candidly and effectively has required a considerable

Figure 6. Who Do Americans Believe?

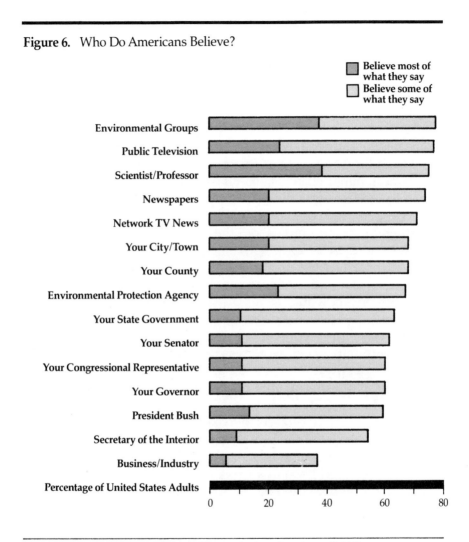

Source: Environment U.S.A., Golin/Harris Communications, Inc., Angus Reid Group

change in traditional corporate practices—broadening the cadre of corporate spokesmen from the headquarters team of chief executive and public affairs officer to include location managers, technical specialists, and marketers as well.

Many companies are finding that these new spokespeople need to learn to listen first and then to speak, not in the jargon of the company, but in language easily understood by their audiences. In doing so, they need

153

to go beyond scientific facts and marketing glitz to establish a bond of shared understanding and concern for the community and for the future.

Monsanto *(from the company case history)*

A great deal of preparation was necessary before we could talk publicly about our waste numbers. While the environmental operations people learned how to collect the data using actual measurements and EPA-approved estimation procedures, employees from the medical, public relations, manufacturing, and other departments began to discuss what the public would want to know about the data. We prepared communication materials to educate employees first, then the community, about the Title III law, its requirements, and the intention behind them.

Confronted for the first time with numbers that were expected to be large, first and foremost people would want to know what the health impact would be for them and their families. The company health experts collected fenceline data *[data on emissions as they leave the company property]* on key chemicals and calculated the risk to the community. Their work was reviewed by a panel of outside scientists to verify the conclusions.

A logical question would follow: "what are you planning to do about the waste?" Some plants had already completed waste-reduction projects, or projects to make their operation safer. Others had some projects on the drawing board. Very few were impressive, but we were glad to have any little example of waste reduction. We produced layman's versions of our material safety data sheets so the public could better understand what kind of chemicals we were using and emitting from the plants.

We conducted focus group research first with a group of employees, then with members of the public to see if the information we were going to communicate could be easily understood. The results told us which explanations were useful, and which caused confusion and even outrage.

We worked closely with a risk communication consultant, Dr. Peter Sandman of Rutgers University in New Jersey, to help point us in the right direction. The kind of risk comparison that people in industry made at the time, particularly in the chemical industry, was, for example: the risk of cancer from this chemical is the same as smoking 1.6 cigarettes per day, or as living in Denver for three months. We learned that comparing voluntary and involuntary risks only served to anger the public. They have control over their own actions, but want to hear what industry is going to do about its actions. The more appropriate comparisons became: This is how much we are emitting now and this is how much we are going to reduce it by when.

Because it would not be comfortable for a plant manager to get up in front of his or her neighbors and discuss pollution statistics, we held risk communication training for plant managers and their staffs to help prepare them for the kinds of issues that could arise and to help them communicate the information for best understanding. We also assisted other companies, making numerous speeches to trade associations and others in the field, sharing our materials and plans to help them prepare as well.

As the first disclosure date (July 1, 1988) approached, we prepared to go public. Employee, community, and media communication materials were prepared. The plan was to hold meetings with employees first, then community leaders and neighbors. We wanted them to hear the information first so no one was blindsided. The media would receive the information last. Media materials were prepared for a press conference to be held in St. Louis. Most plant locations would deliver their information to local press themselves.

[Ed. Note: Later in its report, Monsanto returned to the subject of communications with the citizens of its plant communities, as described below.]

According to consultant Dr. Peter Sandman, many chemical plants and communities don't understand each other because they are talking different languages and don't take the time to listen to each other's concerns. The public doesn't want to know about parts of chemicals per cubic centimeter, it wants to know how will your emissions and discharges affect me and my family. Conversely, many scientists throw up their hands after a lengthy discussion with the public about exposure effects and are met with blank stares.

So we could better understand the questions and concerns of the public, a number of community advisory panels have been established in our plant communities. Advisory panels have as members a cross section of the public that might include teachers, firefighters, housewives, businessmen, and local politicians. They set the agenda for discussion, and the plant responds. Sometimes the plant will make a presentation updating the group on environmental progress or issues of potential concern, but for the most part, the panels are the plant's ear to the community and the plant is best served when it listens. So far, 12 community advisory panels are now functioning at Monsanto plants, ten in the U.S., and two in Europe.

[Ed. Note: Supplementing the Company's case history, Monsanto's Plant Manager at Chocolate Bayou, Louisiana, supplied a set of "do's and don'ts" identified by successful community advisory councils (CACs), that were developed by Monsanto people and printed in their publication "MCC Commentary" in December, 1991. They are:]

- Don't preach. The best CACs focus on the community's interests, not on establishing a platform for industry or company propaganda.
- Be willing to hear unpleasant comments and discuss uncomfortable issues truthfully. Accept—and encourage—constructive criticism without becoming defensive.
- Recruit participants who can be objective. Don't stack the council with people who are predisposed to a favorable view of the company or industry.
- Encourage council members to be full participants in the process. Let the committee set the agenda. Create an atmosphere in which no subject is off-limits.
- Listen, and trust the process. The worst mistake is to raise expectations—to invite community members to voice their opinions and ask for information—and then to ignore their input. This scenario can be more damaging than not initiating the community partnership at all.

[The Monsanto case history continues:]

Monsanto employees and retirees at some locations have started an "ambassadors" program to help reach out to the community. At the Pensacola, Florida plant, employee and retiree volunteers give speeches to civic groups, conduct classroom demonstrations, and get involved in community events on behalf of Monsanto. This allows the plant to get the word out about the plant's environmental improvement activities and also allows it to better understand community concerns and priorities so we can be better neighbors.

Because grassroots communication is so important, another communication outreach tool being developed is a kit to help plant managers communicate Monsanto's environmental commitments. Environmental improvement is part of each plant manager's job. However, given limited resources, it can become difficult to find the time necessary to communicate all the things the company is doing locally. The communication kit will assist plant managers in this effort and make it easier for them to get the word out. The kit will contain slide shows and scripts for use in describing Monsanto's environmental efforts to local groups, brochures on environmental efforts that can be handed out to interested parties, backgrounders on environmental programs, and ads that can be placed locally. The materials can be personalized to discuss not only what Monsanto is doing globally, but also what the plant is accomplishing in its community.

According to Monsanto, the communications training and the plant manager's kit have been very helpful in making plant managers much more comfortable in dealing with the outside community, and thus more forthcoming and effective in doing so.

■ ■ ■

Few companies have had a longer or more agonizing experience with an environmentally condemned by-product than Dow has had with dioxin. Its experience provides numerous lessons in the uncertainties of science, the dangers of corporate self-righteousness, and the difficulty in overcoming long-held feelings of hostility in elements of the public.

Dow itself has long had trouble deciding how to respond to these problems. In the July/August 1991 issue of the magazine Garbage, *an article entitled "The Three Faces of Dow," by Art Kleiner examined the problem and concluded that over the years Dow had been* traditional *("collegial, close-knit, and egalitarian"),* antagonistic *("The Dow of napalm and Agent Orange"), and* learning *("the Company with a change of heart about environmentalism"). At times, all three Dows co-existed, Kleiner added.*

157

It is the learning Dow that now struggles with the legacies of its past incarnations.

The Dow Chemical Company *(from the company case history)*

In the late 1940s, Dow began making and selling 2,4,5-T a chlorinated phenol herbicide developed for broad leaf weed control. It became a successful agricultural product that increased food production for American farmers. In 1964, we ran into difficulties with an impurity in the process that seemed to cause some employees working with the product to develop an inexplicable skin condition. We shut down the plant and began a research program to learn more. We found that 2,3,7,8-tetrachlorodibenxo-p-dioxin ("dioxin")—a trace impurity resulting from the herbicide-production process—was causing the condition known as chloracne. With the problem identified, we redesigned the plant and started producing again in 1966, with the impurity at a level (less than one part per million) considered safe. This analytical research was the beginning of toxicology and epidemiological studies of the effects of dioxin that continue to challenge scientists everywhere to this day.

By 1970, independent studies, testing the product at the high impurity level of 27 parts per million, reported deformities in mice and rats, bringing the concern into the spotlight again. What followed was a decade of push and pull within the scientific community and heightened reaction by the popular media. And although we felt we were on the right environmental track, our scientists, management, and employees soon became caught up in a whirl of science and emotion.

By the mid-70s, the internal Dow mood had become one of frustration over what seemed to be a growing proliferation of regulation. At one point, Dow was suing the EPA for hiring a pilot to take aerial photographs of the Midland* plant site. There was a genuine internal belief that we were within our legal right to protect our proprietary business interests. Right or wrong, it was a belief that would not serve us well by the decade's end.

---

*Dow's Headquarters and a major plant are located in Midland, Michigan.

A form of the herbicide (2,4,5-T) also became a component of Agent Orange, the defoliant the U.S. military had used as a tactical weapon in the Vietnam war. Media accounts began to focus on the potential hazards of dioxin to returning Vietnam veterans who had been exposed to Agent Orange. Some of the vets became convinced that a large number of their health problems were the result of that exposure. And since Dow was one of the companies that produced Agent Orange for the government, public opinion began to turn against us.

[Ed. Note: As Art Kleiner reports: "The antagonistic Dow began to feel the effects of the ill will in the late 1970s. Cancer complaints from exposure to herbicides—particularly 2,4,5-T and 2,4,-D, as well as Agent Orange, which is a mixture of both of them—began to hit the courts and newspapers."

Speaking of that period in its January 2, 1985 issue, The New York Times *said: "Through it all, Dow seemed impervious to criticism, taking hard-nosed positions on specific issues and insisting that the critics did not know what they were talking about." The Dow story continues:]*

In the spring of 1977, Dow scientists found and reported traces of dioxin in the fish from the Tittabawasse River that flows alongside our Midland plant. The Department of Natural Resources soon began checking local health statistics. Others soon joined the controversy. Epidemiology studies were later (February, 1991) to find no abnormal illness rates.

In September of 1978, the day before we were to hold a major press conference in Midland, we talked to our employees. Our Michigan Division general manager, a division environmental manager, and a Dow scientist spoke to employees through our internal television network. They told them what we had discovered about the sources of dioxin and what we were going to do. We also sent videotapes of similar information to hundreds of our customers.

The next day we welcomed reporters and camera people to a first-hand examination of our plants and labs, with access to our employees and scientists. We gave all media visitors a packet filled with information, including detailed summaries of dioxin studies from the American Medical Association and various scientific institutions in Sweden, Italy, Germany, and the United States. Later that day, those who had planned the press conference manned telephones to take media calls.

By 1979, the EPA had banned 2,4,5-T for most agricultural uses. And, while dioxin research continued, a class action lawsuit was filed on behalf of Vietnam veterans against several companies including Dow.

Gradually, the media coverage of dioxin began to fade. By that point, technology was enabling scientists to measure threshold amounts of emissions in parts per trillion. Yet, throughout the 1980s, the dioxin issue, like a brushfire, continued to spark up here and there around the world.

Michigan environmental groups were calling for a full investigation to determine the effects of dioxin pollution on the environmental health of the air, land, and water. We announced we would participate in joint studies with the EPA and independent scientific organizations. The studies would examine dioxin levels from locations within the plant site and the community.

Soon the EPA and Dow seemed at loggerheads over who was reporting what.

[Ed. Note: Mr. Kleiner continues: "In 1982, an EPA staffer leaked the fact that Dow had critiqued an EPA report before publication.· This triggered a Congressional investigation. TV cameras descended on Midland.

"It was a remarkably frustrating series of events for both sides. I've talked to seven or eight Dow executives, including some speaking off the record, who say dioxin was a technical non-issue; they had studied their own workers' cancer rates and found them lower than in the general population; and if that were true, how could the public be at greater risk? Nor did local department of health records show an increase in cancer."

But, as a January 2, 1985 New York Times *article reported: "The [1983 congressional] hearings thrust Dow into the white hot glare of attention by Congress, news outlets, and the public."]*

The Dow story continues:

The company we all knew was not the company that was portrayed on the nightly news. And we began to understand that we needed to do a much better job of listening to our critics and of communicating what our studies were finding out about dioxin in ways they could relate to. Just professing good science was no longer enough. Our employees also began to have unsettled feelings. And they expressed them in mixed opinions about how to communicate with the public and the scientific community. Another media tour of our Midland facilities in 1983 was followed by a period of quiet from the public.

Here and there in the company, people pressed for a re-evaluation of their company's attitude and approach. "Perception Is Reality" signs went up on bulletin boards. Our top executives began participating in roundtable conferences, sitting down with people from the public and private sectors, including environmental groups. And our management began making environmentally focused speeches.

[Ed. Note: Dow chairman Robert W. Lundeen was quoted by the New York Times *as saying: "All those awful things said about Dow and dioxin, stuff I never even heard of. You've heard of how you get the attention of a mule by hitting it on the head with a two-by-four? Well, those hearings were the two-by-four that hit Dow over the head.*

"We found that if we were perceived as not running our business in the public interest, the public will get back at us with restrictive regulations and laws. That is not good for business."]

Employees began grassroots recycling programs in their offices and plants. Waste reduction programs began to save money as well as emissions. The changing attitude became endemic. Yet the dioxin question persists, even though Dow ceased production of chemicals containing it in the 1970s.

What has Dow learned from these years and experiences?

We have learned that, whatever the level of scientific concerns regarding the human toxicity effects of dioxin, when an issue involves public exposure to an involuntary risk, we cannot over-respond to a sensitive and concerned public. The reality is that people don't really care how much you know, until they know how much you care.

The debate over dioxin's toxicity goes on.

At its heart is a dispute over whether tests showing high incidences of cancer in dioxin-exposed laboratory animals indicate equally harmful

161

effects in humans, since some epidemiological studies seemed to show little effect in people exposed to dioxin at relatively low levels. The question, then, is: does dioxin react radically differently in one species than in another?
The Multinational Monitor, *in its October 1991 issue, stated (in part):*

> *The National Chamber Foundation, a group affiliated with the U.S. Chamber of Commerce, issued a report declaring that new studies reveal that cancer risks from exposure to dioxin are greatly exaggerated.*

> *A high-ranking public health official is one of the key proponents of this industry message. Dr. Vernon Houk, director of the Center for Environmental Health and Injury Control at the CDC [Center for Disease Control], recently announced that he believes dioxin is less dangerous and carcinogenic than he had previously thought.*

> *"I think the consensus is that low-dose exposure to dioxin causes very little in the way of human health effects," Houk told* Multinational Monitor. *"If it is a carcinogen, it's a relatively weak one, only at extremely high doses." Representative Ted Weiss, D-New York, strongly criticized Houk's position on dioxin. Noting that Houk's dioxin claims "run counter to the stated...policy position of the three federal agencies that have taken a position on dioxin, that is, EPA, FDA (the Food and Drug Administration) and CDC itself," Weiss said he found Houk's efforts "distressing" and "nothing short of arrogant."*

Scientific disputes are unlikely to be resolved satisfactorily in the newspapers or in Congress. For a businessperson, the lessons of Dow's experiences include at least these:

- *Listen, acknowledge error, communicate, respond candidly to public concerns.*
- *Be sure your science is good, be open in sharing it, but do not depend on it alone to make your case.*
- *Recognize that often scientific conclusions are tentative, and later knowledge may alter them for better or for worse.*
- *Try to avoid the politicization of scientific arguments by being open in your thinking and prompt and factual in your reporting.*

To make most effective use of resources, the costs of actions to improve the environment have to be weighed against the risks of not taking them—a concept not easy to sell when the public is already critical or frightened. For this and other messages, Chevron has relied on America's most used medium, television, not without some pain in the process.

Chevron

Chevron has been fairly successful in communicating its emerging environmental policy, past achievements, and goals. The qualifier, "fairly," stems from the fact that large corporations—and Big Oil in particular—face a public that has already called two strikes against the organization's credibility. Indeed, there are folks who will dismiss some of what you say some of the time, and there are some who will dismiss all of what you say all of the time. Still, what Chevron finds heartening is that many—from the media to legislators and the general public—seem willing to listen. So long as the company is open, direct, and credible, and its people are willing to speak frankly about events good and bad, trust can build. That's what makes the communications element of environmental policy worthwhile.

Communicating about energy issues is by no means easy. Oil is a terrifically complex and often misunderstood industry. During the 1970s, public opinion of oil companies often hinged on the price and availability of gasoline. When gasoline was expensive and in short supply, Big Oil was hated by many. When the price fell and supplies were plentiful, hostility persisted and Big Oil remained far from being admired. Even though the price of gasoline in 1990 and 1991 was—when adjusted for inflation—as low as at any time since before the Second World War, the public still responded with ire at even the smallest of market-induced price increases.

A recent opinion survey asked adult Americans to estimate the amount of profit per dollar that oil companies make after costs and taxes. Their answers averaged out to 41 cents on the dollar. They were then asked to state what they thought was appropriate and responded, saying an average of 24 cents per dollar. In reality, the actual 1990 profit per dollar of sales for Fortune 500 petroleum refiners was but 4 cents.

163

[Ed. Note: Some observers have speculated that the unflattering public image of the oil industry stems from the dependence of consumers on their automobiles, and thus their helplessness in the face of gasoline shortages or price increases. Others believe the roots lie in arrogant industry behavior, past or present. And surveys show that an industry's reputation tracks that of its least admired member, all of which poses a major public perception problem for oil companies trying to move up on the scales of social performance and respect. More recently, as Chevron notes below, environmental problems have added to industry woes.]

During the latter half of the 1980s and into this decade, however, the environmental liabilities of the petroleum business began to supersede price and supply as the major public opinion issue. High visibility accidents—such as oil spills at sea—form lasting, negative impressions. Just as insidious are fears that the petrochemical business produces cancer-causing emissions and substances, and the consequent beliefs that the purported dangers of the substances far outweigh the benefits of their use. The latter generally receive little attention; yet, it's a fundamental in the science of risk assessment.

One of Chevron's outreach efforts involved funding a major PBS [Public Broadcasting System] series on the subject of risk and the public's perceptions of it. "Living Against The Odds" discussed how everyone takes risks, whether it's while rock climbing, taking a bath, or eating peanut butter. The program demonstrated that some risks, including most pesticide contamination scares, are overrated. Others, most notably driving, are underrated.

[Ed. Note: Earlier in this chapter, Monsanto noted that no matter how accurate the calculations of relative risk may be, the public is angered by comparing risks they take voluntarily with those that are imposed on them involuntarily. If Monsanto's conclusion is correct, the Chevron approach, while statistically interesting and scientifically correct, may prove less successful as a communications effort with people already disposed to believe the worst of a company.]

Chevron's best known outreach effort, however, may well be its "People Do" series of television and print advertising. Created in 1985, "People Do" focuses on what are typically small efforts by employees to do the right thing environmentally, protecting nesting areas of barn owls and donating marshlands near a refinery for a National Environmental Center. "People Do" has clearly and measurably improved perceptions of Chevron. Public opinion research shows that in areas where the commercials run, the company's environmental reputation is good and is getting better. It has stayed the same or even declined where "People Do" has not appeared.

The series of ads has generated some controversy. Critics have argued that a few of the ads depict actions that were required by government regulations. Others claim that the examples are mere fluff, and that the company is spending millions advertising relatively minor good deeds instead of spending that money on more significant environmental efforts.

[Ed. Note: The annual cost of "People Do" is about $8 million. In 1990 Chevron spent about $750 million on projects and activities aimed at improving its environmental performance.]

The fact is that eight of the 13 examples were not required by regulation, explains Chevron advertising specialist Ralph Wooton. "Besides, we have no problem with reminding the public that we comply with the law. What's more important is how we comply. We often go beyond compliance with innovative solutions, and we're proud of that." The format of the ads also recognizes that public perceptions aren't usually formed through intense and detailed analysis of long, fact-filled reports. In an era where attention spans for wars, revolutions and major natural disasters are down to a week or two, any institution trying to get its message across must do so succinctly.

That's the advertising element of "People Do." More fundamentally—in terms of truth, legality, and the moral imperative—"People Do" must be, and is, a reflection of Chevron's much larger and much more complex environmental efforts. The reality is there to back up the impressions conveyed in the ads. It has to be. In the 1990s, no company can get by for long trying to fake environmentally responsible performance. The public will ultimately smell a rat, and the regulators will trap the rodent. Communication must be built upon a foundation of substance. It is the only way a company can take that moral initiative.

165

Chevron's experience seems to confirm the findings of Monsanto. It is essential to communicate honestly, based on factual data, and avoid any overstatement or "feel-good" images. Risk assessment has a necessary place in setting priorities for environmental investment. But the public may be less interested in these matters than in feeling that the company is sympathetic with—in fact, shares—its concerns for the hazards and uncertainties of life and is willing to discuss them candidly and openly.

■ ■ ■

In November, 1990 Dr. Peter M. Sandman offered some cogent thoughts about corporate communications on environmental subjects. The following paragraphs, extracted from the much longer paper, speak directly to the frustrations over communications evident in some of the preceding company stories.

Dr. Peter Sandman *(extracted from his 1990 pamphlet "Addressing Skepticism About Responsible Care")*

In some of my own speaking and writing, I have distinguished two different definitions of risk. The technical definition—expected annual mortality, for example—I relabeled *hazard*. The public's definition, though, is much more influenced by the factors I have collectively called *outrage*: trust, fairness, control, dread, etc. Reframed in this terminology, the core communication problem of industry is that you need to reduce the outrage, not just the hazard. To reduce the outrage, of course, you need to listen to people, not just talk to them.

* * * * * * *

Too many advertising campaigns are aimed more at the client than at the customer. Maybe companies need that kind of moral support. But it's expensive, not just in dollars but in credibility as well. At the risk of bruising industry egos, I suggest a focus on industry *publics* instead.

No communication campaign, however shrewd, is going to overcome the past quickly, or protect you from backlash if the future doesn't add up to real improvement. Even if you live up to your promises, it will take people a long time to believe you.

* * * * * * *

The bulk of the American public "knows" (whether we are right or not) that your track record is poor. For those in industry who think your record is excellent, the temptation is understandably enormous to say so, early and often. Without taking a stand on whether the record is as good as you think it is or as bad as the public thinks it is—I suspect it is neither—it's a great handicap to begin a communication campaign by telling people they're wrong.

Any claim to future responsibility works best if you ground it in acknowledgments of past irresponsibility. This is partly a matter of credibility; how can we believe you are turning over a new leaf if you keep claiming there was nothing wrong with the old leaf?

But it's also a matter of forgiveness. How can we accept your apology for your past if you keep insisting you have nothing to apologize for?

* * * * * * *

It is understandably appealing to industry to claim the moral high road, but depicting change as a business necessity has several powerful advantages. First of all, it's closer to the truth (always an advantage). At industry meeting after industry meeting, the message is the same: "This is what the public demands. Our license to operate is at stake." What you say to each other is precisely what you should be saying to the public. If you tell us you are cleaning up because you care so deeply about the environment, those of us who question the depth of your environmental commitment are bound to question the truth of your clean-up claims.

* * * * * * *

Your management may feel better pretending that its change of heart is voluntary, not a response to pressure. But for those who spent years applying the pressure, the pretense is offensive... and makes it harder to notice that the change is real.

* * * * * * *

When trust is low, asking to be trusted is always unwise. The paradox of trust is that it builds faster when it isn't demanded.

For the foreseeable future, I think *all* industry claims should lean very lightly on the public's trust. Preparing to prove your Title

167

III emissions reductions, for example, is far superior to simply asserting them. An independent environmental audit is no more insulting to your corporate integrity than an independent financial audit. The essence of dialogue is learning to put up with questions and suggestions from interfering outsiders—learning to be accountable.

■ ■ ■

A leading environmentalist recently had some constructive thoughts to offer on the subject of "green" advertising.

National Wildlife Federation *(by Jay D. Hair, President)*

The environmental community tries to be vigilant about alerting the public to corporate advertising that tells only half-truths or disingenuously glosses over a company's overall impact on the environment. Yet, it is difficult, if not impossible, to find examples of corporate environmental advertising that environmentalists support and encourage.

Perhaps the reason for this stems from the character of "green" advertising itself. After all, "green image" advertising is, by its nature, misleading. No thirty-second soundbite can adequately convey a company's overall impact on the environment. Thus, as many environmentalists see it, too many ads leave viewers ill-informed and somewhat deceived about a company's true environmental commitment. Some corporations, on the other hand, complain that environmentalists are too quick to condemn all environmental advertising as "greenwashing." Such companies claim that indiscriminate criticism places them in a "Catch 22" where there is no reward for environmental improvement.

Unfortunately, it is too often true that companies instituting positive environmental initiatives—and advertising that fact—frequently open themselves up to just as much criticism from environmentalists as companies that maintain business as usual. This is at odds with our goal of moving companies toward environmentally sustainable practices.

If we in the environmental field are sincere about wanting to help industry improve its relationship to the environment, then we must ask ourselves how corporations may—without criticism or assertions of falsehood—take public credit for making positive, fundamental changes in the way they do business.

Perhaps the answer to this question lies in redefining corporate advertising. Environmentalists want consumers to have enough information to make well-informed purchasing decisions. At the same time, corporations have an interest in improving their environmental records and avoiding lawsuits and negative press.

A new corporate advertising approach may address both sets of interests. Consider the following three suggestions:

- craft future advertisements to emphasize the merits of a particular environmental initiative without implying that the company as a whole has eliminated all its environmental impacts;
- devote more time to explaining the cause-and-effect relationship between an environmental problem and the company initiative addressing that problem (e.g., oil spills and double-hulled tankers); and
- promote consumer education by providing a way for the customer to get additional information about the company's activities.

A company using these approaches would make its environmental successes more believable and would give environmentalists less cause to cry foul.

Dr. Hair's prescription for green advertising makes sense, but the proposal he offers may be hard to accommodate in a short television commercial, by far the most powerful tool companies have to reach the general public. Perhaps the answer lies in a two-pronged approach—sophisticated in-depth communication with knowledgeable critics, and substance-based, but briefer and simpler, TV messages for the broader audience. The trick will be to coordinate the two efforts so that they reinforce each other, and that the brevity—and thus incompleteness—of the TV spots does not work against the longer, more complete presentation. For environmentally proactive companies, this is an important subject for which the best formula is not yet apparent.

Involving Suppliers, Customers, and Consumers

The environmental impact of a product is the sum of the impact of each input that goes into its making, use, and disposal. Thus, it is logical for the proactive company to look not only at its own processes, but up and down the chain of materials sourcing, production, distribution, and use—a concept known as product stewardship.

S.C. Johnson Wax *(from the company case history)*

In February 1991, S.C. Johnson hosted an environmental symposium in Racine, Wisconsin for almost 100 representatives from 57 of its largest worldwide business suppliers. The conference, titled "Partners Working for A Better World," was designed to initiate joint efforts between supplier and company to reach the company's announced worldwide environmental goals. The Partners symposium provided a common ground forum for open, direct dialogue among all participants—company and supplier alike—from which three key issues were identified as possible roadblocks to progress toward S.C. Johnson's environmental goals: environmental illiteracy, inconsistent scientific opinion, and stalled environmental technology advancement.

Richard M. Carpenter, S.C. Johnson president and chief executive officer, in his keynote speech, outlined the company's specific worldwide objectives: to improve the environmental value of products in formulation, packaging, application, and disposal; to reduce manufacturing emissions; and to recycle virtually all recyclable at plants and facilities in recycling regions* of the world. He called on suppliers to join the company's active environmental commitment by advancing technologies for sustainable environmental solutions, citing the possibility of applying recognized good environmental technology to other products or processes.

The suppliers' response during and after the symposium was extremely positive and supportive. Importantly, the meetings

---

*S.C. Johnson Wax defines "recycling region" as a location in which the infrastructure exists to collect and reuse recyclable materials—at present including principally North America and Europe.

revealed an overall desire to not just find solutions, but to find the right solutions—those that meet today's needs without impairing the ability of future generations to meet theirs.

To maintain the momentum of the meeting, a semi-annual newsletter will highlight worldwide supplier/company partnerships contributing to progress against the environmental goals. Also, some S.C. Johnson subsidiaries are planning similar localized meetings with their suppliers in the coming year.

Addressing the symposium were such noted persons from the environmental and governmental communities as Dr. Jay D. Hair, President and CEO of the National Wildlife Federation; Gaylord Nelson, former U.S. Senator and Counselor of the Wilderness Society; and, William J. Stibravy, International Chamber of Commerce representative to the United Nations. Each speaker reinforced his constituency's expectation of progress, not necessarily perfection, from industry—an important bridge-building message, especially when coming from perceived industry detractors. A transcript of the symposium was prepared and distributed to attendees as well as other interested parties.

[Ed. Note: Another interesting Johnson initiative involves consumers— enabling them to create a fund to help support environmental innovation. "Couponing" that might otherwise have merely been "cents off" in the consumer's pocket instead directs the money saved to environmental innovation.]

In 1990, Johnson's U.S. Consumer Products Division initiated a major program entitled "We Care For America." It enabled customers and consumers who bought S.C. Johnson products to contribute directly to the development of new environmental technologies. Consumers who purchased S.C. Johnson products using special coupons decided whether 10 cents from each purchase would be donated by S.C. Johnson to benefit clean earth, clean air, or clean water. Trade customers similarly directed a percentage of their S.C. Johnson product orders to one of the three designated areas.

In just two years, the "We Care For America" program has raised $1 million in donations for innovative efforts designed to identify sustainable environmental solutions. The "We Care For

America'' fund is administered by World Wildlife Fund, which in 1990 and 1991 awarded research grants of up to $50,000 each to 23 new environmental technology research projects that met specific criteria of practicality and replication, as well as to 18 community-based environmental action efforts. Proposals submitted by numerous universities, government agencies, and environmental groups were reviewed by an independent panel of environmental experts convened by the World Wildlife Fund.

The "We Care For America" concept was adopted by the S.C. Johnson Canadian company, which in 1991 donated $100,000 to protect precious species and spaces through a "We Care For Canada" coupon effort. Such cross-border efforts to increase individual positive environmental actions underscore the fact that environmental problems are not restricted by geographic boundaries so efforts to solve them should not be similarly constrained either.

In 1992, both the U.S. and Canadian companies will be mounting "We Care" programs based on the overwhelmingly positive trade support and strong consumer response as measured by coupon redemption. The environmental challenges we face will require people everywhere in all walks of life to make an individual commitment and take positive environmental action. It's this individual action in the aggregate, which "We Care" promotes, that will bring about meaningful environmental change.

Through these programs, S.C. Johnson Wax is moving its environmental thinking up and down the chain of production and end use, and educating and enlisting potential allies in environmental improvement.

■ ■ ■

Perhaps a bit more risky than urging suppliers to change their ways is to take the same stance with customers:

Bank of America

As a first step in practicing what we preach, we are now deeply involved in developing environmental credit policy guidelines to be used by account officers and credit administrators, as one element in making relationship and transaction decisions. Our new commercial credit policy states that we will "weigh the degree of environmental responsibility displayed by potential borrowers and their affiliates as a significant part of our decision on whether or not to grant credit.'' This means both trying harder to make an environmentally beneficial deal bankable and denying credit to borrowers who show a blatant disregard for the environment.

The beneficial side is relatively easy, because people like to try harder where there are socially positive outcomes. We are already working on a couple of unusual deals that will have environmental benefits. It is more difficult to figure out when to deny credit. There are a lot of hard questions and a few dilemmas; for example:

- In determining whether a potential borrower is environmentally responsible, our expectation is that they will follow the ''normal environmental practices of the industry.'' We don't want to finance companies that are well outside that norm. That creates some questions:
  —How do we determine an industry norm?
  —Are we talking about the industry norm in the United States? Europe? Korea? Indonesia?
  —Is the norm always acceptable?
  —Even if we figure out where the norm is, how far off the norm does a credit-taker have to be to be declined credit?
- Second, we know we want to use our loan policies to benefit the environment. But how far should we try to go?
  —Just disassociate ourselves from environmentally damaging businesses?
  —Try to encourage and cajole individual borrowers to move closer to the mainstream?
  —Try to move whole industries closer to accommodation with responsible environmentalists? or, another angle:
- Do we base a credit decision on the company's current condition or on how hard it is trying to become environmentally responsible? How do we distinguish between public relations and actual operations?
- Do we look only at the activity of potential financing, or should we also consider environmental impacts upstream or downstream in the process—for example, implications of raw material acquisitions, or impact from special energy or water requirements?

173

A lot of questions. No answers today, though we are getting close on many. We are definitely learning as we go along in this program.

One way to make sure that new policies take root is to break the implementation phase down into individual components, assign responsibility for each to a specific individual, set deadlines for accomplishment, and publish periodic control reports noting progress or delay.

The Bank of America has broken its program down and follows up on it in just such a fashion. A copy of its 1991 Midyear Report is included as Appendix 3. This document reveals the many detailed steps inherent in any overall environmental improvement program, and in designing a company follow-up procedure.

■ ■ ■

While the application of environmental standards to the granting of bank credit might seem to have an element of the ''stick'' philosophy, there is also an opportunity to use ''carrots'' to encourage customers to upgrade their environmental performance by using the supplier's products properly.

The Dow Chemical Company *(from the company case history)*

Cradle to grave. This somber sounding philosophy grew out of the realization that no matter how safe our products are when they leave our plants, they can become unsafe in other hands. Smaller more specialized companies buying our materials may, understandably, lack the years of safety data we have accumulated or the extensive lab facilities we maintain. Yet, if they have an environmental problem, involving a Dow product, so do we. Hence, our prudent philosophy. If it's our product, and in the eyes of some from the day we make it until the day someone else discards it, we had better be ready with some preventive customer and user support before it becomes anybody's problem. And if we can develop that support into a competitive edge, we have a win-win proposition for our business, for our customers, for the environment.

That's essentially why, in 1985, we launched ChemAware+, a Dow product-stewardship program that originated in our Chemicals and Metals Department. Under the ChemAware umbrella, we provide free to customers various services, including regulatory updates, Material Safety Data Sheets, safety and handling information, facilities surveys, vapor monitoring, plant visits, quality management exchanges, analytical services, product literature, audio/visual presentations, and regional environmental seminars. Our ChemAware services are now only an 800-number phone call away for a Dow customer, a number that we also advertise in leading trade publications.

One such call came from Parker Pen U.S.A. Ltd., as it completed its 1988 SARA Title III, Section 313 report. This venerable producer of writing instruments had noted increased emissions and needed ways to reduce solvent consumption. First, the company's own Voluntary Improvement Process (VIP) set a problem-solving team in motion. Then, a call was placed to a Dow Technical Service and Development specialist for technical assistance and hands-on-training. The specialist had trained Parker employees before in the safe handling of chlorinated solvents. He seemed the obvious choice for advice.

The VIP team helped target needs for improvement and our specialist made recommendations and led them through techniques that reduced emissions by 39 to 47 percent right away. Because Parker employees were involved in the decision-making and understood the reasons for change, they stayed committed to the process, shift-by-shift. As a result, Parker reduced chlorinated solvent consumption more than 40 percent in 1990. The company now expects to exceed its long-term goal of reducing solvent consumption by 50 percent, while maintaining a cost-effective operation in the face of Clean Air Act's tougher regulations and OSHA workplace standards. And Dow's position as Parker's supplier of choice remains strong.

Today, catching up with Dow technical specialists, many of our scientists in Environment, Health, and Safety say they spend more than half their time with customers. Ten years ago, most of them remember spending less than 20 percent of their time on customer service.

What have we learned from the ChemAware initiative? Our products are always our products. Therefore, a product-stewardship policy that incorporates a face-to-face customer relationship keeps us focused on our customers' success, establishes our position as a value-added supplier. Cradle-to-grave becomes not a threat but a competitive advantage.

■ ■ ■

Not everyone would instantly think of labeling as a vehicle for companies to communicate with consumers about environmental matters. Yet, the use of packaging and product labels is among the most cost-effective ways to reach concerned audiences.

Procter & Gamble *(from the company case history)*

There has long been a commitment by P&G to use labeling to inform consumers so that they can make educated choices as they shop. P&G uses strict guidelines to insure that the labeling is clear and informative. The Company believes in using descriptive language instead of seal programs and other shortcuts to information. The company was part of an industry group of more than 35 major trade associations, encompassing thousands of companies, that developed voluntary guidelines for environmental communication. These guidelines have been presented to the Federal Trade Commission (FTC) in the hopes that it will adopt national guidelines to:

- provide national, uniform guidance for manufacturers and advertisers in making accurate and responsible claims;
- build consumer confidence in environmental information and claims from industry; and
- help protect consumers in every state from false or misleading claims.

P&G believes that labeling guidelines will be most effective if they educate consumers; are consistent and relevant; are fairly administered and provide national uniformity; and provide incentives for innovation. Including these considerations in any environmental labeling program will assure that environmental issues are moved toward solution. Consumers will then be able to play a meaningful role, and it will be easier to gain industry participation.

Procter & Gamble's caution regarding ''seal programs'' is worth noting. As product studies have progressed, it has become obvious that it is difficult, in many cases, to trace and then compare on a value judgment basis the environmental impact of various products, product ingredients, or packaging alternatives. Procter & Gamble seems wise to adopt a cautious— though positive—approach to the matter.

Cooperation with Environmental and other Citizen Groups

A number of companies have stressed the importance of talking with and listening to critics and concerned citizens. The next logical step is to engage them formally in a collaborative effort to help companies find paths that lead to sustainable development. Here are the stories from three companies that have taken this approach.

The Dow Chemical Company *(extracted from the company's press release)*

WASHINGTON, D.C., October 15, 1991—Citing the importance of greater public involvement in the company's environmental activities, The Dow Chemical Company today announced the formation of a Corporate Environmental Advisory Council, an external group of global policy and opinion leaders to advise the company on environmental, health, and safety issues.

David T. Buzzelli, Dow's vice president and corporate director of Environmental, Health and Safety, named the group's first seven members at a Washington, D.C., news conference. Ultimately, he said, the panel will consist of 10 to 14 members and meet three to four times a year... The first seven members are:

- The Dean of Environmental Programs, Tufts University.
- A former Premier of Quebec.
- A former deputy director of the Pollution Prevention Directorate of the French Ministry of the Environment.
- A professor of Environmental Sciences, University of East Anglia, Norwich, England.
- The executive publisher of *Greenwire.*
- A former administrator of the U.S. Environmental Protection Agency.
- The president of INFORM, an environmental research organization.

"I'm especially pleased that the group reflects such a broad geographic diversity," Buzzelli added. "Dow is a global company, with just over half of our sales outside of the United States, so operations or products have the potential to impact environmental, health, or safety considerations internationally." Buzzelli said

177

that the remaining three to seven panel members will be selected in the months ahead, with input from the initial group. He added that panel members are serving not as official representatives of any organization, but as individuals.

Frank Popoff, Dow's president and CEO, said the formation of the advisory council is in keeping with the company's philosophy of being accountable to the public and willing to listen to divergent viewpoints. He said the company already has in place community advisory panels at several plant locations. These panels meet regularly with Dow representatives to discuss issues of local concern. "We recognize that the public has a right to know what we're doing and a right to contribute to our decision-making processes," said Popoff. "Over the years, we have learned the importance of opening our doors, seeking new ideas, and gaining the support of our neighbors."

Other than Buzzelli, who will be the panel's chairman, Dow will not have a seat on the council. However, one or more senior-level company executives will attend each meeting to provide input and hear the group's views. Buzzelli said panel members will be asked to serve for a 24 to 36 months. "We recognize that to keep the panel fresh, members should rotate off of the council—at the mutual discretion of the member and Dow," he said. "Through this panel, we hope to broaden our perspective, become more responsive to public concerns, and most assuredly, elevate our environmental, health and safety performance," said Buzzelli.

The Washington Post *article reporting Dow's move contained an interesting paragraph describing an environmentalist's reaction to the announcement. It went as follows:*

> *"I think that any initiative like that is to be welcomed," said Brent Blackwelder, acting president of Friends of the Earth, an environmental group—"The key thing is to make sure that there is sufficient representation to make sure critical environmental issues will be raised and discussed—not just the so-called safe issues."*
>
> *Dow's appointees to its council are "thoroughly knowledgeable about the issues," he said. "Some of them, I have confidence, will raise key issues, but ultimately it is management that is going to make the calls as to whether to accept the recommendations."*

Procter and Gamble's emphasis on partnerships can have a positive effect in generating constructive dialogue among industry, government officials, and citizens with a wide variety of interests. Here are a few of the partnerships the company reported:

Procter & Gamble *(from the company case history)*

Sharing knowledge and influencing public policy help advance solutions to managing environmental issues. P&G has been working closely with selected industry associations and has developed private/public partnerships to maximize its environmental efforts, especially in the area of solid waste infrastructure. These partnerships have been developed primarily to help support recycling and composting programs.

P&G helped initiate "Closing the Loop" a public-private demonstration project in the Washington D.C., Maryland, and Northern Virginia regions that was designed to build consumer awareness of regional recycling programs. The "Closing the Loop" partnership is a group of industry, environmental, and community organizations who have banded together to support closed loop recycling. In addition to creating televised public service announcements, the partnership works with local schools and community groups to provide educational materials on recycling. A key element of the program is that recycled plastic bottles get made into containers for P&G detergents, fabric softeners, and household cleaning products.

In Newcastle, England, P&G joined with the City Council to establish a recycling collection infrastructure. After a successful pilot project, the company continues to collect plastic bottles from laundry detergents and household cleaners, using them to make 25-percent recycled plastic bottles for Lenor concentrate fabric softener.

P&G also was active in the creation of the Solid Waste Composting Council (SWCC). This is a diverse coalition whose members include compost producers and users, consumer product companies, academic institutions, public officials, waste management firms, and nonprofit organizations. "The Council's primary objective is to encourage the production of high quality, waste-derived compost that will meet the demands of an emerging market and

179

to seek the support of government officials for municipal solid waste composting.'' The Council also seeks to develop compost quality standards, increase awareness of composting benefits, and serve as an information clearinghouse.

In 1991, P&G announced its sponsorship of the U.S. Conference of Mayor's National Composting Program. This program is a major collaboration among the Conference of Mayors, the SWCC, and P&G. The program is designed to help local governments bring municipal solid waste composting to their communities by providing them with direct access to the latest technical and economic information on composting. It will also serve as a clearinghouse for updates as future technology and regulatory standards evolve.

Since 1990, P&G and KAB [Keep America Beautiful] have joined with the General Federation of Women's clubs (GFWC) to sponsor an educational program on solid waste management. The GFWC includes over 380,000 women with a tradition of community service and environmental concern.

In the United States, P&G has established toll-free ''800'' numbers so consumers can call in to speak with representatives who can provide information about the environmental impact of packaging and products. Also, consumers can obtain the addresses of recycling collection sites and composting facilities. Often, the dialogue that takes place can help the Company learn more about consumer understanding and preferences, and callers sometimes present suggestions that can help improve P&G's environmental effort.

Some environmentalists are reluctant to serve on advisory groups organized by business, feeling that doing so may undermine their objectivity and credibility as environmental advocates. Roger Pryor of the Coalition for the Environment was quoted by Chemical Week *as having a different and perhaps novel view.*

> *''I don't see a conflict. I can serve on the panel and then walk down the hall and argue for the upcoming RCRA (Resource Conservation and Recovery Act) reauthorization. If Responsible Care gives the industry more credibility and makes them a more powerful adversary, that's fine, especially if they really improve their act. On the other hand, I'm learning a lot about the industry,*

*and, frankly, to buy that kind of insight would cost a fortune.
I feel it is also making me a more powerful person.''*

■ ■ ■

*Not all cooperative efforts are instant successes. An early attempt,
using the good offices of Robert Redford and his Institute of Research
Management (IRM), entailed a lot of work but in the end did not fully
reach its goals. The experience, though, as described by one of the industry participants, exposes some pitfalls to be avoided.*

*As the following piece points out, the conclusions of self-selected groups
that do not include all interested parties at interest are likely to lack the
support of those excluded, if not arouse their outright opposition. And,
as the author also notices, bureaucracies guard their "turf" with the ferocity
of a mother bear protecting her cubs. These are lessons well learned.*

Chevron *(as told by its Vice President and Director, William E. Crain)*

On March 5, 1985, three industry representatives, including my-
self, and three environmental leaders (from the Environmental Policy
Institute; The Conservation Law Foundation, New England; and
NRDC) met with Congressman Phil Sharp and Institute of Resource
Management (IRM) officials to explore undertaking a mediation ef-
fort in resolving conflicts on the Outer Continental Shelf (OCS).

As a result, in May, senior executives of 12 oil companies, com-
prising both large and small companies, and leaders of 12 environmental groups, including the Sierra Club and NRDC, met in Morro
Bay for two days under IRM guidance to determine if there was
common ground for resolving conflicts over offshore oil exploration and development.

At this meeting, it became apparent through open discussion
that industry was not interested in exploring all the offshore sub-
merged lands, and the environmentalists were not interested in
protecting all such lands from exploration. Prior to this, industry
felt that all lands should be put up for bid and they would lease
only a small portion, and the environmentalists felt they must protect everything because they could not know beforehand what industry would lease. We, therefore, agreed to conduct an experiment in the Bering Sea to determine how much of that area was
actually in conflict.

181

Price Waterhouse *[an accounting firm]* was hired by the industry to conduct a confidential survey among 20 oil companies, which would prioritize their areas of interest. Fourteen companies responded. The environmental members surveyed their interests, as well as those of the Alaskan natives and fishing interests.

At a subsequent meeting in November, the group determined that priority areas described by the environmental coalition and industry did not greatly overlap. Following this, a long negotiation period took place, with all the parties agreeing that offshore oil activities could occur in most of the Bering Sea area, including the most attractive potential oil areas of the Norton Basin, St. George Basin, and Navarin Basin, provided certain limited areas were excluded and certain stipulations could be worked out by all parties that, however expensive, would not render oil development uneconomic. Parties agreed to give these recommendations on both the areas to lease and the conceptual stipulations to the Secretary of the Interior. Subsequently, several meetings took place and the parties worked on stipulations.

On May 8, 1986, recommendations for leasing and stipulations were made to the Secretary of the Interior, and a press conference followed. The recommendations were ultimately contained in the draft environmental impact statement as one of several alternative programs. That this proposal was not the main proposal was disappointing, considering the effort that both the industry and environmental groups had put into this process. It appeared from our view that the recommendations might have been better received had we included the Department of the Interior in our process much earlier. It might also have been better received if State of Alaska officials had been involved earlier as well. Even our trade associations viewed these efforts dimly, as a special group of environmentalists and industry leaders had worked on a process that to some degree belonged to them.

I still remain a believer in the conflict mediation process. Robert Redford has since left the IRM, and it has been renamed CRM (Center for Resource Management). I have remained in close contact with this center and recently have begun to explore a new conflict-resolution process wherein industry and the environmental community sit down together and work on some large-scale project such as jointly developing an urban transportation program in some specific major metropolitan area in the United States. Industry would obviously fund this program. Its value would be not only in project results, but in the alliances and understanding that would be developed between key environmental and industry leaders.

The silver lining is that Chevron feels the effort was still worthwhile and wants to give cooperative efforts another try. Cooperative agreements among business, environmentalists, and citizen groups have a good chance of succeeding if the parties to them have the power to implement them. If, after reaching agreement, they must then depend on a third party (such as government), success is much less likely if the proposed program gores any constituent's ox.

Although it may make life initially more complicated, it seems important to bring all the players who will eventually be affected into the discussions from the start and to make sure that their views are considered and that all are committed to seeking a constructive outcome in the public interest.

■ ■ ■

The effectiveness of these attempts at outreach is as yet uncertain. As Chevron pointed out earlier, many companies must start by dealing with a negative public image, no matter how unjustified they feel it to be. And, with their new environmental attitudes just that—new—there is often not yet much to report in the way of positive results. Having something good—and verifiable—can make all the difference in a communications campaign. So will a willingness to admit mistakes and imperfections. Increased scientific understanding of environmental matters seems to disclose new problems at least as fast as old ones are addressed and cleaned up. As a result, it appears to much of the public that on balance, things are getting worse.

Finally, the normal marketing-communication channel from a corporation to the general public—television—seems better suited to selling products the consumer already is in a mood to buy than it is to explaining a company's environmental efforts to skeptical viewers. Evaluating the attractiveness of automobiles or brands of beer, companies and consumers are on common ground. Dealing with the complexities of the environment, they are separated by both an emotional and a knowledge gap that 30-second sound bites and advertising agency "hype" are unlikely to close.

In both the business and environmental communities years of mutual suspicion and hostility have left their mark on many of the players. Listening, though necessary, is often very difficult for either side. To some in each group any accommodation with the other can be seen as an abandonment of basic principles. Lack of empathy can also exist when companies are concentrating on fixing the present and potential future difficulties while communities and governments are dealing with past messes. Failure to address both types of problem can result in continued misunderstanding of each other's motives and good faith. Despite these difficulties, those companies that are concentrating on listening to outsiders, and the environmentalists and other citizens that join them at the conference table, seem to be starting on a hopeful road to better understanding and cooperative effort.

IX.

PUTTING
IT ALL
TOGETHER

So far this book has addressed its subject, chapter by chapter, using extracts from corporate case histories and other material provided by participating companies. At this point one comprehensive case history, written by the company's CEO, can serve to summarize the preceding material. Selecting Du Pont for this purpose is logical for a number of reasons.

- *Du Pont is a major player in two industries of critical concern—chemicals and petroleum.*
- *Despite the long record of environmental concern it reports, Du Pont has been identified as the emitter of more SARA Title III substances than any other company.*
- *Du Pont thus has a great opportunity, on its own initiative, to make a major reduction in its emissions and environmental impact.*
- *Ed Woolard, its Chairman since 1989, describes himself as Du Pont's "chief environmental officer," and has personally led the internal attack on the company's environmental problems.*

Here, then, is how a major diversified international company chief executive views his company's environmental situation and responsibilities.

Du Pont *(as submitted by its chairman and CEO, Edgar S. Woolard, Jr.)*

Du Pont has been involved in environmental management in one form or another for over a half a century.

In the late 1930s, the company hired its first "pollution engineer." In the late 1940s, Du Pont and Dr. Ruth Patrick of the Academy of Natural Sciences in Philadelphia established environmental baselines at sites where company plants were to be built. Known for her pioneering studies in limnology, Dr. Patrick and her team refined this approach into pre- and post-operation environmental inventories. Du Pont was, in effect, doing environmental impact studies long before this term was part of our everyday vocabulary or a legal requirement. We are not a newcomer to environmental affairs.

Needless to say, the great surge of environmentalism in the late 1960s and 1970s—and the major environmental legislation of that period—also had a profound effect on the company's policies and practices. As with other companies that had large businesses in the chemical industry, we learned to adjust to continually changing laws and regulations, and we made substantial investments to keep pace with legal requirements.

The most telling experience in the recent environmental affairs of the company was the decision to phase out chlorofluorocarbons (CFCs), a decision we made in 1988. Concern over the impact of CFCs on the ozone layer had been first expressed in the 1970s. Evidence continued to accumulate, and studies completed in 1988 suggested that if the theories linking CFCs to destruction of the ozone layer are correct, the potential environmental impact would be severe if use of these compounds continued at current rates. That is why we went beyond the Montreal Protocol and elected to phase out CFCs completely, rather than simply cut back. Our decision to phase out CFCs by the end of the century was generally applauded. However, some observers, notably Greenpeace, argue that we were doing too little too late, and continue to agitate for immediate cessation of all CFC production. We maintain that, on balance, an orderly withdrawal from this business will prevent economic dislocation and hardship in many economies around the world.

By the time I became Du Pont's chairman in 1989, we already had substantial environmental affairs management behind us. However, my impression at that time was that good as we were in terms of legal compliance and a general willingness to do the right things environmentally, management was not looking at environmental concerns with the same rigor as other concerns.

It was clear that a growing segment of the public subscribes to the view that good environmental performance requires more than obeying the law. While our examples of a long and sincere concern for environmental protection were undeniable, we were not engaged in progressive programs that would enable us to keep pace with accelerating societal expectations, let alone get out ahead of them and actually be a force for leadership.

Perhaps the most telling concern we faced was our status with regard to the U.S. EPA's Toxic Release Inventory (TRI). According to the published data, Du Pont releases more listed substances into the environment each year than any other company in the United States. All of these emissions are legal, and more than half actually are wastes properly disposed of using EPA-approved underground injection technology. Nevertheless, they are recorded in the inventory. I believed that given the tenor of the times and the mood of the public, these emissions would not be tolerated indefinitely. Indeed, in the last two years, the data from the TRI has been used at different times and to varying degrees of effectiveness by activist groups in order to criticize companies publicly.

We concluded that the commitment to position us in the forefront of industrial environmental leadership had to come from within and that the changes necessary to make good on such a commitment had to be first of all attitudinal, not technical. Good as we were at compliance, environmental excellence in and of itself was not a deeply held value of the corporation. The tendency was for us to evaluate environmental issues against technical and legal criteria only. Environmental protection was not as vigorously promoted as safety, for example, which has been an ethic of distinction and absolute commitment throughout the history of Du Pont.

The time was right to raise environmental affairs at Du Pont to a new level of conscious concern, to adopt a proactive means for dealing with environmental issues, and to evolve this new environmental stance into a source of competitive advantage for the company. This initiative would have to be led by executive action. The month after I took office as chairman, I used my first opportunity for a public address to announce this new approach. In an address to the American Chamber of Commerce in London, I spoke only of environmental issues and called both for a change in corporate attitude and for the achievement of specific environmental goals. I identified myself as Du Pont's "chief environmental officer" and called for an ethic of "corporate environmentalism," which I defined as an attitude and a performance commitment that place corporate environmental stewardship fully in line with public desires and expectations.

187

In this and several other subsequent speeches, I did not hesitate to describe what we saw as the shortcomings of industry's historic approach to environmental issues. We also indicated that improved performance was the only way that industry could hope to earn and keep public good will on environmental matters. We set challenge goals for Du Pont to accomplish in the decade of the 1990s. These goals were in such areas as waste minimization, pollution prevention, product stewardship, wildlife habitat protection and development, stakeholder dialogue, and management compensation. They were intended to be broad and to touch all employees in the company in one way or another. Addressing all the components of environmental stewardship would be necessary if deep change was to be accomplished and if the effort was to be effective.

Judging from the press coverage and other reactions that followed the London speech, we succeeded in ratcheting up Du Pont's visibility on this issue several notches. A lot of this was no doubt based on surprise that a large chemical company was declaring a "sea change" in its environmental stance. But nowhere was the surprise greater than within Du Pont itself, and because the goals we set were determined with only limited assistance from the full organization, a period of definition and buy-in followed. Leadership groups within the company had an opportunity to hear from me directly and to assist in defining the specific terms of several of the corporate goals.

We also determined that a senior policy-setting body was needed to build momentum for corporate environmentalism inside Du Pont and to develop this new ethic for the company in terms that the rest of the organization could follow. We accomplished this by creating, in addition to our existing Environmental Quality Committee, a new higher level organization we call our Environmental Leadership Council (ELC). This Council consists of senior vice presidents representing key manufacturing, staff functions, and international sectors. The ELC determines policies and guidelines and reviews compliance within the corporation. The ELC is counseled by the professional environmental staff of the company to assure the technical content of its work is of the highest caliber; but conversely, it also gives the environmental staff immediate access to the highest levels of the company. The ELC made environmental performance the responsibility of operating management, and this has resulted in rapid implementation of our goals and objectives.

Performance Goals

Those goals and objectives themselves turned out to be a sound basis for developing environmental awareness and improving environmental performance. Knowing that we cannot easily show improvements in what we cannot measure, the specific corporate environmental objectives we instituted tend to be quantifiable and are pegged to timetables. These goals are to be met by 2000 or before, unless a stricter time frame is indicated below:

- Reduce hazardous waste by 35 percent compared to 1990 levels.
- Reduce toxic air emissions by 60 percent compared to 1987 levels (by 1993).
- Reduce carcinogenic air emissions by 90 percent compared to 1987 levels.
- Phase out of CFC manufacture by 2000 at the latest, and replace CFCs with safe alternatives.
- Provide for the management of 1000 square miles of wildlife habitat with special emphasis on wetlands.
- Eliminate, or render non-hazardous, all toxic discharges to the ground or surface waters.
- Eliminate the use of heavy metal pigments in polymers.
- Take greater responsibility for the disposition of plastic wastes.
- Include local communities in safety and environmental planning at all our plant sites.
- Build only double-hulled oil tankers (by Du Pont's energy subsidiary Conoco).
- Install double-walled storage tanks at Conoco gasoline outlets.
- Intensify research and development of clean fuels.

In the two years since these goals were announced, we have made quantifiable progress. Based on data Du Pont reported to EPA for 1990, total toxic air emissions were 15 percent below those reported in 1987. Hazardous materials disposed of by EPA-approved underground injection technology (accounting for more than two-thirds of Du Pont's total reportable releases) have been cut by 33 percent. Overall, total reportable releases have been reduced by 30 percent. More than 250 square miles of corporate land is being managed for habitat. Two commercial plants have been started to recycle post-consumer plastic waste. CFC production is down to 45 percent below the allowable limit of the Montreal Protocol. Conoco recently announced that it would provide clean-burning propane at its service stations for customers who have had their cars modified to accept that fuel. And construction has begun on four double-hulled tankers that will be placed in service by Conoco over the next two years.

This progress toward our specific objectives is encouraging, and many are on track toward completion by the stated times. Several of the operating businesses have accepted the challenge and set even more stringent goals for themselves or additional goals related to their specific business. To keep the company abreast of developing environmental issues, the corporate environmental affairs division, in addition to compliance and regulatory tracking, has been charged to follow issues. This has allowed for the development of proactive policies, guidelines, and actions in the area of global climate change, for example. There remains much work to be done, and it is still too soon to feel comfortable that we will achieve all we've set out to do. Our progress thus far, though, reflects a wide variety of approaches and some genuine innovation—technologically, procedurally, and conceptually—on the part of people throughout our company. Some specific cases illustrate the variety and imagination with which our goals have been approached.

Waste Minimization

Our single most outstanding example to date is work we accomplished at our Beaumont plant in Texas. We manufacture acrylonitrile there, which is a key intermediate for making engineering plastics and fibers. Ammonium sulfate waste from the acrylonitrile process, according to the figures we reported to the EPA, was totalling more than 110 million pounds annually. Beaumont's waste is disposed of by EPA-approved deepwell injection. But it's still waste that gets recorded as an "emission" in EPA's toxic release inventory. Because of our deepwell waste, Du Pont has topped that list for several years. Beaumont alone accounted for one third of Du Pont's total emissions of listed substances. So our engineers set about modifying reactor conditions to reduce the amount of ammonium sulfate generated from the process.

We historically ran the process to maximize yields, and models suggested that modifying the process would result in a cost penalty—which I'm pleased to say the plant was readily prepared to accept in exchange for less waste. But what we discovered was that the process modifications resulted in better yields, while cutting generation of ammonium sulfate waste. As a result, the process change intended to minimize waste nets a savings of almost a million dollars a year, due partly to reduced raw material consumption and partly to reduced hazardous waste disposal taxes. Next year, when EPA's 1990 inventory is published, Du Pont will show, overall, a 30-percent reduction in toxic emissions, much of which comes from the minimization work at Beaumont.

Not all our efforts have been so large in scale. Consider another example, smaller, but just as important. In New Jersey, we manufacture fluorelastomers. This production unit recently projected the need for an incinerator to reduce about 200,000 pounds per year of air emissions. The incinerator would have cost $2 million to purchase and $1 million per year to operate.

By rethinking the fundamental engineering of the process, a better solution was found. It turned out that simple engineering changes that cost a mere $3,000 cut the air emissions by **50 percent** and saved $400,000 in annual costs. A second phase of engineering changes that cost $250,000 will reduce emissions by an additional 30 percent. The result is a total air emission reduction of **80 percent** within one year. Our investment of just over $250,000 results in annual savings of $400,000—instead of a $2-million investment for an incinerator that would have cost an additional $1 million annually to maintain and operate.

These examples, just two among dozens in Du Pont, point out something else that we've learned: Running environmentally cleaner often means running smarter and running cheaper.

Habitat

Local plant managers have been encouraged to support employees in wildlife habitat projects on or about their sites and to work with local groups to assist in this end. In the United States,

Du Pont helped form the Wildlife Habitat Enhancement Council, bringing together other major companies with conservationists. Some examples of our programs in this regard include:

- Kinston plant, southeast of Raleigh, North Carolina has 650 acres of land, 450 acres of which are open to use by wildlife. Mown lawn has been converted to habitat by planting shrubs and establishing foodplots. Woodlands are managed for wildlife and a one-acre stocked pond was created and boxes for wood ducks and eastern bluebirds were set out.
- At the 2,500-acre Fayetteville Works, 60 miles south of Raleigh, food plots have been established for waterfowl and wild turkeys, areas have been reforested, and shrubs have been planted for food and cover.
- At Seaford, Delaware nylon plant, 500 of the 750 acres have been reviewed for wildlife habitat. The programs under development will focus on promoting and protecting diverse native ecosystems.
- In 1990, the Martinsville, Virginia nylon plant was the site of the first observed nesting of Canada geese in south-central Virginia. A plan has since been developed to encourage Canada geese, bobwhite quail, rabbits, deer, and songbirds. The program includes planting of winter wheat, white clover, and lespedeza for food and providing nesting structures for Canada geese, wood ducks, and eastern bluebirds. Grassy fields are being maintained for cover.

One of the corollary benefits of the habitat program has been a growing awareness of the need to minimize the impact on wildlife habitat of all our operations. A remarkable example of this commitment to protecting habitat has been the manner in which Conoco, Du Pont's petroleum company, has reduced the environmental impact of petroleum exploration and development activities on habitat, notably environmentally sensitive areas of the tropics. An approach to oil field development that relies on involvement of indigenous peoples, government officials, and third parties has resulted in several innovative plans:

- A Conoco project in Bintuni Bay was the first to be held under Indonesia's new (1986) environmental impact assessment regulations. Because the authorities had no practical experience in translating these regulations into action, it fell to the Conoco engineer to assist. Under his supervision, a committee of academic specialists in ecology were assembled who conducted a baseline study and estimated the project impacts on the wetlands, on the indigenous population, and on the local fishing industry. The resulting recommendations were unbiased and took into account the interest in protecting the environment, as well as the need for the project.

- Along the Congo, Conoco applied the principle of "no net environmental impact" during an oil-exploration project. Prior to drilling, environmental professionals identified flora and fauna and made recommendations to Conoco for their conservation and protection. During exploration, portable mats formed temporary roads; no new roads were built. Work crews were transported by helicopter and boat. Development was achieved in a sensitive wetland area using a novel floating drilling platform that not only avoided major ecological disturbances, but also saved several million dollars in capital costs over traditional measures. Wastes were burned, buried, or transported out and camps restored to their original condition. Wildlife was protected by prohibiting the purchase of bushmeat from indigenous hunters.

Another project planned by Conoco represented a novel and sophisticated plan for developing petroleum reserves in Ecuador's Yasuni National Park, a rainforest area of major biological diversity and the location of an indigenous tribe, the Waorani. Conoco's projected development of this area would have included the use of cluster well sites and horizontal drilling techniques to minimize the amount of surface area disturbed. Botanists and anthropologists were consulted. The pipeline leading out of the oil field would avoid areas of special biological character. A scientific research station was planned to conduct ongoing studies of the area.

Nevertheless, this project ran into substantial opposition from environmental groups. Objections included the desire to keep a national park immune from development; the concern that building of a road to the oil field would result in colonization; and the fear that contact with outsiders would threaten the Waorani.

193

After several years of planning, Conoco elected in 1991 not to proceed with the project in the light of projected financial returns and changing allocations. (Other companies participating in the project are continuing.) This was done with some reluctance, however, because our engineers and planners were confident that they could safeguard the environment and the native people while creating a model for developments in other environmentally sensitive areas where much of the world's remaining oil is likely to be found.

[Ed. Note: Since the development in Ecuador is being pursued by other companies, perhaps less environmentally conscious, Du Pont's departure may prove to be an environmental negative.]

Inclusion of Environmental Performance in Compensation

Having provided conceptual and specific guidance for our businesses to improve environmental performance, as well as the tools to make good on these commitments, we also believed it was necessary to put in place an assurance mechanism. We informed managers that their compensation will now be affected by the environmental performance of the areas they manage. Performance is judged on the basis of compliance with company policy and legal responsibilities, achievement of corporate goals, and the impact of self-initiated programs.

In addition to the reinforcement within management that compensation actions provide, a recognition process was developed to acknowledge employees at any level who make an outstanding contribution to environmental affairs. A corporate initiative, developed at the suggestion of a foreman at one of our plants, was designed to recognize individuals, groups, and businesses that have displayed superior environmental stewardship. A screening committee composed of Du Pont employees and non-Du Pont environmental advocates selects the annual winners, who are publicly recognized. The winners are also given cash grants, which they can designate to the environmental organization of their choice.

A New Corporate Ethic

The degree to which our environmental commitments have helped instill an ethic of corporate environmentalism in our corporate culture can also be seen by examining how the corporation is taking a "precautionary approach" to environmentally related decisions. This approach derives not just from environmental concern, but also from involvement in the scientific process as issues develop. For example, when the U.S. Environmental Protection Agency came forward with a plan to seek voluntary reductions in the emissions of certain toxic air pollutants, we were able to join the program quickly because we had already made a broader and more substantial commitment of our own.

[Ed. Note: This is a reference to EPA's 33/50 program described in Chapter XII.]

Similarly, through our awareness of and participation in the scientific discussions surrounding the global warming process, we were prepared to announce plans to eliminate nitrous oxide emissions from nylon manufacturing, even as studies were being published indicating that these emissions were an important greenhouse gas. In addition, Du Pont offered the technology for eliminating these emissions to any other company who wished or needed it.

We see further examples of innovation continuing. Former wastes are now being marketed in place of intentionally manufactured products, thereby satisfying markets with essentially waste-free products. In several cases, we have been so successful that we now must produce these second-line products intentionally. We have also found that our experience in handling our own wastes can help customers handle their wastes. In some cases, we are recycling these materials for customers, as in our imaging businesses. In addition, we now offer environmental consulting and remediation services to non-Du Pont customers.

Our environmental commitments have also led us to pursue strategic alliances, built about environmental needs. To fulfill our commitment to contribute to plastics recycling, we helped found the Council for Solid Waste Solutions, which promotes industry—and consumer awareness. We have also built and operated plastics recovery and sorting facilities that will assist us in developing polymer materials suitable for recycling.

These opportunities to eliminate or reduce the environmental impact of our own processes, to assist customers in doing so, and

195

to sell these services to others is why I speak of corporate environmentalism as a form of competitive advantage. Companies that cannot run environmentally sound operations or whose customers are beset with intractable problems of their own will find it difficult to compete in the marketplace of the future. We believe that market leadership and environmental leadership now go hand in hand.

Du Pont still has many problems—and the solutions to our problems are not all clearly worked out. The economy is still uncertain, for example, and difficult conditions always put ambitious commitments to the test. At the same time, Du Pont is encountering aggressive, world-class competition in virtually all of our major businesses. Our ability to accomplish important tasks—environmental goals, among them—which under more favorable conditions could easily command high priority, will be critically tested in a climate in which some businesses are struggling.

Also, it is not certain yet that the environmental ethic called for by the current state of public expectations and world affairs, and which we see growing at Du Pont, is firmly rooted across all levels of management. We believe that at both the very top and at the lower levels of our organization, the environmental imperative is strong, but we may have some way to go before we can say with confidence that our ethic permeates the entire company.

Finally, we do not know that all our goals are truly achievable. Some people surmised when we announced our goals that we were listing objectives that were sure bets. That is by no means the case. All our goals are "stretch" goals. They can only be achieved with real effort or with substantive change, and in some cases with technology that we have yet to develop. Only time will tell whether we succeed in accomplishing all of them. We are convinced, however, that we have started a trend within the company that could not be easily reversed.

The Future

As our work on establishing an environmental ethic and on improving environmental performance continues, we are also looking ahead to what the future might hold. Increasingly, there is talk in the international business community of the concept of "sustainable development." This notion was introduced by the World Commission on Environment and Development in a report titled,

196

Our Common Future, which was presented to the U.N General Assembly in 1987. . . . The report stressed that environmental and economic issues are interrelated and that environmental issues do not respect political boundaries. It emphasized that the problems of poverty and underdevelopment cannot be solved unless we have a new era of growth in which developing countries play a strong role and reap substantial benefits. The report also argued that in the traditional model of industrial development, wealth was created without regard for environmental consequences of production. This approach has led to increasingly severe environmental disruptions around the world. *Our Common Future* suggested an alternative approach, sustainable development—defined as meeting the basic needs of all the world's people today without compromising the ability of future generations to meet their needs.

Sustainable development has been greeted with some skepticism among industrialists because it could be interpreted as a variation on the old "limits to growth" theory. My opinion has been that sustainable development is simply common sense, and events sooner or later would have required industry to invent the concept or some close corollary if it didn't already exist. As former U.S. EPA administrator William Ruckelshaus said, sustainable development is economic activity that increases prosperity without destroying the environment on which economic activity depends.

The difficulty may be that some in business and industry continue to be guided by an outmoded philosophy. For a long time, industry took for granted two basic assumptions: One was that resources for industrial development and production would always be available somewhere on the globe and enable industrial growth to proceed without constraints. The other was that the earth could absorb the byproducts of industrial societies indefinitely without undergoing fundamental environmental changes. These assumptions no longer hold—if, in fact, they ever did.

Superficially, many environmental issues seem to revolve around ideological, aesthetic, or political views because that's the way they are presented and argued. But at the core, our most pressing issues, such as atmospheric ozone, greenhouse effect, and rainforest destruction, are usually the result of taking resources for granted or of overloading an ecosystem with some byproduct of industrial civilization. Sustainable development—perhaps "sustainable production"—is a recognition that we cannot deny physical realities.

There can be no doubt that industrial growth and development must continue. But it must continue within the bounds of ecological possibility. Industry, as society's producer, has a special role to play in creating a sustainable society. Industry must protect the environment and at the same time produce products at a fair price and provide employment. Furthermore, I maintain that the only sector in modern society that can solve many of our largest environmental problems is industry. Environmental problems that we characterize as regional or global are fundamentally problems of economy and production. Other sectors can analyze the problems of and plan to deal with the infrastructure needs—such as transportation, waste disposal and land use. But the remediation of existing problem sites, the procurement of raw materials, the minimization of waste and emissions, and product stewardship are problems that only industry can correct.

Some of us in the industrial community are working on ways to balance the multiple responsibilities of industry. In 1991, I participated in the second World Industry Conference on Environmental Management in Rotterdam. The industrialists at that meeting were from all around the world. At the meeting, we ratified a document called the Business Charter for Sustainable Development.

[Ed. Note: This charter is presented in Chapter V.]

This document defines 16 principles that industry needs to adopt to make sustainable development a working model for producers around the world. Among the principles are concepts such as process improvement, employee education, technology transfer, and prior assessment of environmental impact. It was clear to us at the conference that the participation and commitment of developing nations are necessary to make sustainable development work. If developing nations follow the traditional path to industrialization, the environmental destruction in their own countries and around the world is predictable.

The Du Pont story is a comprehensive discussion of the elements of leadership, policy and action that define an environmentally proactive corporation.

198

Like most of the case studies reported in this book, it touches only lightly on what is as yet undone, what is not being done right, and what past errors need to be corrected. While some readers might wish the text paid greater attention to those matters, as stated before, the purpose of this book is to stress the positive side of corporate environmental performance for the guidance of others wishing to follow in an environmentally progressive direction.

And, of course, Du Pont and other companies will not lack for critics calling attention to any missteps or omissions, as the next selection makes eminently clear.

■ ■ ■

Environmental activists have pressed for years for a major assault on industrial pollution. The following remarks by Brent Blackwelder, acting president of Friends of the Earth, accompanied the publication of FOE's 112-page critique of Du Pont's environmental record. His remarks concentrate on what Friends of the Earth sees as misleading corporate environmental advertising.

Friends of the Earth *(statement by Brent Blackwelder, acting President)*

With the publication of this report on the Du Pont Company—"Hold the Applause!"—Friends of the Earth is formally launching a continuing series of investigative reports that will critically review, and where necessary call into account, the environmental and/or energy policies of major corporations and industrial trade associations. The primary purpose of these reports is to examine the advertising and promotional claims, "green" marketing strategies, "environmentally friendly" technologies, "sustainable development" proposals, and other environment-related initiatives now being pursued by major corporations and trade groups. We offer our perspective not to discourage companies from legitimately bringing their environmental achievements to the public, but rather to encourage them to do so when they have made solid environmental progress.

Since last September, Du Pont has been running a national television advertisement with "applauding wildlife," which purports to tell the public about its new policy for putting double hulls on oil tankers to help prevent oil spills. The net effect of this ad, however, is to mislead the public about Du Pont's role in the environment, when in actual fact it is the single largest corporate polluter in the United States.

While Du Pont's Conoco may deserve credit for ordering double hull tankers before other oil companies did, it does not deserve the clean maritime and environmental image that this advertisement bestows upon it and all of Du Pont. In fact, in our analysis of this advertisement, we discovered that no Conoco double-hulls are yet in the water; that Conoco tankers operate primarily in the Gulf of Mexico; that Conoco's petroleum fleet is comprised of six vessels; that two Conoco supertankers used to haul oil for others will not be double hulled; and that a number of the maritime mammals and waterfowl depicted in the advertisement are not found in the areas where Conoco's tankers operate.

Du Pont, on the other hand, is the nation's No. 1 corporate polluter, releasing some 348 million pounds of toxics into the environment. That is more chemical pollution than the combined total of Allied Chemical, Ford Motor, and Union Carbide put together! Du Pont's total pollution in 1989 was 14 times more waste than Dow Chemical, 20 times that of Chrysler, and 30 times that of Mobil—companies that all rank within the top 100 U.S. polluters.

To add insult to injury, Du Pont's Edgar Woolard has taken a leadership position in industry spreading the gospel of "corporate environmentalism"—a term which may very quickly become an oxymoron if it isn't already. Unfortunately, Mr. Woolard's vision of the environmental fix is not necessarily one that will resolve the problems of the planet anytime soon.

We believe that the current round of "feel good" environmental advertising and corporate-initiated green campaigning require a counter voice of criticism and accountability. While some of the environmental changes now emerging in corporate America are genuine and welcome, a good many are superficial, some are downright diversionary, and a few are being specifically designed to preempt more stringent public policies from emerging.

Friends of the Earth sees a clear need for a public voice on the other side of Madison Avenue in matters of green advertising. Our case studies will bring some balance to the views of corporate leaders and their image-marketers. For the real measure of corporate environmentalism is not simply a few new green product lines or a single-problem fix, but rather genuine environmental protection that permeates the entire company—from remote reaches where natural resources are extracted, to how factories are designed, the amount of energy used, and the "life cycle" qualities of consumer and industrial product lines.

These are the arenas where solid environmental progress must be made, and where American businesses can make a major difference.

By launching our campaign, we hope to encourage solid environmental progress among America's corporate leaders and discourage environmental hype and chicanery. But we are putting corporate leaders on notice that we will be watching.

■ ■ ■

Interestingly, as the debate over corporate advertising programs continues, so does the debate over double-hulled tankers.

Extracts from an article appearing in the January 30, 1992 issue of Journal of Commerce *outline the elements of the situation:*

The Journal of Commerce

LONDON—The number of major oil spills from tankers fell sharply over the past decade, with the improvement continuing last year. Figures published Wednesday by the London-based International Tanker Owners Pollution Federation Ltd. show that the average number of oil spills a year is now only about one-third of the level seen during the 1970s. A total of 91 spills of more than 5,000 barrels were recorded during the 10 years to 1989, compared with 252 in the 1970 to 1979 period. In 1991, there were just seven spills of more than 5,000 barrels. In volume terms, the amount of oil spilled in the 1980s was 1.2 million metric tons, against 3.5 million tons in the previous decade—a reduction of about two-thirds. Evidence of the improvement comes at a time of heated international debate about tanker design...

* * * * * * *

The federation's study found that many oil spills in recent years were due primarily to hull failure or fires and explosions, "which suggests that no single tanker design is likely to offer a panacea."

* * * * * * *

An International Maritime Organization committee has concluded that double hulls would be most effective in preventing oil leaking into the sea after a grounding, while a tanker built with a mid-deck through the cargo tanks may be better in other circumstances.

* * * * * * *

Marine underwriters said this week that the cost of insuring a double-hull tanker probably would be higher than a single hull because of the danger of a gas buildup between the hulls, a greater risk of corrosion in the more inaccessible parts of the ship, and more expensive repair costs.

The tanker controversy underscores the difficulty of addressing a complex—and contentious—issue in a short TV "bite," and the irritation of knowledgeable observers when anyone attempts to do so. It also points out the tentative nature of many scientific conclusions, the danger of generalities, and the opportunities for the politicization of science that such uncertainty allows. When on such fluid ground, businesses—and environmental groups—that are cautious in their claims will seem most responsible in the long run.

X.
PITFALLS OF THE REAL WORLD

Most of the corporate activities described in the previous chapters covered matters in which managements could take the initiative. Chief executives can, without outside interference, change company policies, restructure the organization, set goals, design programs, measure results, work with natural allies, and communicate with the general public on their own terms, as long as they comply with applicable laws and regulations.

But, of course, the world in which companies operate does not always give corporate leaders the chance to set the agenda. Other strong and vocal groups have different perceptions, different objectives, and different priorities—often at odds with what they and others see as standard corporate behavior. This chapter highlights four types of "real world" situations that the environmentally progressive company needs to understand and respond to if it is to be a successful agent of sustainable development.

Not in My Back Yard

Any local government official facing the need to locate a site for a waste-disposal facility has run into the Not In My Back Yard (NIMBY) syndrome. The public wants its waste to disappear, but not into a hole next door, thank you. Siting new industrial facilities is no different. As the environmental hazards or unpleasantness of industrial emissions get more and more attention, the economic advantages of a nearby factory become outweighed by the perceived negatives of having it as a neighbor. Thus, consumers may enjoy the products of a plant, but not the plant itself, perceiving that as neighbors they are bearing all of the risks and only some of the benefits of its presence. One way for a company to remain well accepted by a host community, or to have a wider choice of new sites, is to clean up the emissions of its present operations. Here is an example of how one company approached the NIMBY problem.

Allied-Signal, Inc. *(from an article in* Toxic Substances Journal*)*

Ground was broken early in 1985 for a new Corporate Technology Center (CTC) on the site of the Allied-Signal, Inc., headquarters in Morris Township, N.J. Many talents were brought to bear to secure Planning Board approval, including research, construction engineering, public affairs, and law.

The CTC building is designed as a three-story structure to house over 50 wet or dry laboratories dedicated to various aspects of materials research and technology, employing about 200 people to be relocated from other older labs on the site. In presenting the petition for approval to the Planning Board, the challenge was to demonstrate that the presence of the proposed CTC laboratory involved no risks that would endanger the surrounding community.

New Jersey is highly industrialized and the home of many chemical and pharmaceutical companies. There is a serious hazardous waste-disposal problem in the state.* New Jersey contains fully 10 percent of the sites on the "Superfund" list. There exists a strong community awareness and fear of chemicals, or "chemophobia" as it has been called. This has resulted in intense advocacy in New Jersey for both community and employee "right-to-know" legislation.

Furthermore, when Allied was ready to submit its application, it would be preceded by a hearing for a new facility proposed by another respected company in Morris Township. The other application was already receiving intense public scrutiny, and its well thought out and convincing case for safety was presented by some of the leading research people in the United States from both within the applicant company and the supporting academic community. The neighbors, however, resisted with passion, and had their own scientific experts.

[Ed. Note: It is interesting that to a businessman—Allied, in this instance,—the other application was "well thought out and convincing,"

---

*See, for example, a discussion of EPA's clean-up strategy at the Pitman, N.J., Lipari landfill (which EPA considers the nation's most hazardous waste dump) in *Chemical Engineering News*, December 2, 1985.

though not so in the eyes of the neighbors. Learning from the other company's experience, Allied added an early, participative dialogue with the community to its own technical efforts to ensure maximum safety, in hopes of gaining greater citizen understanding and support.]

Finally, during the period both applications were before the Planning Board, the Bhopal incident occurred in India. The worst fears of a group opposing a chemical facility in their neighborhood had been realized at Bhopal.

Allied decided to share with the community its plan to build the CTC laboratory. To that end, two meetings were held with the neighbors to present the laboratory to be built, its location, the changes on the site that would be made to accommodate it, and the types of research activities contemplated. Specific descriptions of the environmental, safety, and health controls to be instituted within the building were described. The neighbors were given the opportunity to raise questions. Contacts were also made with other local opinion-forming groups, to inform them of plans and potential impacts, and thus eliminate rumor and misinformation.

Allied's headquarters in Morris Township has been one of the largest employers in the Township for many years, as well as the leading contributor to local charities in Morris County. The perceived impact of the corporation is generally very positive. Allied executives enjoy congenial working and social relationships with local officials. Nevertheless, in view of the high community awareness, the chemophobia, the other concurrent hearing, and the Bhopal incident, as well as Allied's experience a decade earlier with Kepone,* Allied prepared itself for detailed scrutiny.

To that end, a program was entered into to reevaluate Allied's environmental, health, and safety assurance system of protection, with particular emphasis on research programs that were to be housed in CTC.

The program involved four main efforts:

- to inspect all the existing laboratories on the site for unknown concerns or existing problems to be immediately corrected;

---

*See "Allied Chemical's $20-Million Ordeal with Kepone," *Fortune Magazine*, September 11, 1978.

205

- to construct worst-case analyses (vis-à-vis both employee and public safety) on hazardous materials to be used in CTC;
- to bring in outside experts from Arthur D. Little, Inc., to perform an independent analysis of Allied's health, safety, and environmental programs; and
- to prepare a detailed Environmental Impact Assessment for presentation to the Planning Board.

This program was undertaken to provide an independent analysis in order to develop the case for the CTC application.

[Ed. Note: At this point, the original article details the survey undertaken by Allied and outside experts to review the procedures of the existing laboratories, the improvements that could be incorporated into the new one, and the steps taken to avoid uncontrolled risk, even in the event of a worst-case accident, to the surrounding community.] As a result:

A number of modifications were made to existing programs to satisfy the condition that no potential impact on the community would occur under the worst-case assumptions. For example, a control program is in place to limit inventory to minimal amounts necessary, and semiannually to remove materials no longer needed. Particularly hazardous chemicals have been flagged and may be brought on site only after special permission/review by health professionals. Control designs for the new research building were augmented to include the fitting of all drains with traps requiring positive override before discharging to a central containment tank.

Before the hearings began, the Planning Board Technical Coordinating Committee was given a copy of the detailed Environmental Impact Document prepared by Allied with Jason M. Cortell and Associates, Inc., as well as a representative list of the materials intended for use in the CTC laboratory. The fire and police departments were contacted to enable them to evaluate and support the information on public safety that would be given the Planning Board. The project was also discussed with representatives of the local hospital to assure coordinated emergency-response planning.

Allied's petition to the Planning Board was presented by a top local attorney from one of Morris Township's prominent law firms. The presentation began with the Vice President of Research for the

Corporation and his research directors describing the activities planned for CTC. Technical aspects of construction and building use were described by architects, construction engineers, traffic experts, etc., who answered questions from the Planning Board and the public in their fields of expertise. Then, the Allied manager of environmental, health, and safety matters for the Morris Township site and independent environmental experts from Arthur D. Little, Inc., and Jason M. Cortell Associates gave testimony based on the program of prior independent assessment.

The emphasis in the testimony was on Allied's system of hazard evaluation by professionals, on materials control, and particularly on the Tier System of review of the projects, which forces problems to be identified and dealt with before materials are handled, as well as the Audit program,* which verifies that the required control systems are indeed in place.

The public was given ample opportunity to ask questions as they arose. The hearing process was detailed and lasted for several months of one- or two-hour biweekly sessions. The outcome of the process was approval from the Planning Board for the building of the CTC laboratory in Morris Township.

Certain important lessons were learned in the course of this project:

- Obtaining Planning Board approval in a developing suburban community for constructing a research laboratory handling hazardous materials is very difficult and quite expensive. Thorough preparation is required.
- The case must be presented in an open manner, and the community should feel that there is candid disclosure of the potential hazards and the control systems.
- Preparation should include (1) review of the potential hazards of the proposed facilities, (2) meeting with the community before the Planning Board process starts, and (3) demonstration of a history of carrying out responsibilities. Of course, that history must, in fact, be there.

---

*Allied's Audit Program is described in Chapter III.

- Independent testimony by a recognized and reputable expert or experts unquestionably enhances the Planning Board's comfort factor.
- Flexibility and willingness to adopt reasonable conditions that will meet technical or political needs may be essential for approval.

The Allied experience in Morris County points out a number of important strategies for dealing with the "NIMBY" problem. Even presumably desirable industrial installations (such as laboratories) can be frightening if the nature of their work is perceived to be secret and their materials hazardous. The media attention given to toxics makes the situation especially difficult for chemical companies. It is no longer possible to rely only on a community's desire for jobs and tax revenues to gain support for a new (or even a replacement) facility.

To respond to local concern, Allied began with careful preparation of its case, especially including a detailed analysis of risks. The facility they proposed was designed to handle these risks. They used both outside experts and Allied personnel in this process, which meant that in presenting the subject to the community, third parties could testify as to its safety.

Allied recognized that community approval of the project was voluntary. The company was early, open, and candid in presenting its findings and plans. Because it had been a long-time and respected member of the local community, it had a positive reputation to draw on. Time-consuming and costly as Allied's effort was, it was successful.

Increasing citizen concern for the environment makes it likely that many applications for permits to build new plants will need to be based on similar planning, documentation, and outsider support in order to be successful. A strongly positive environmental reputation at existing facilities may well become the deciding factor in gaining approval to build—a competitive asset stemming from a progressive approach to the environment.

Living with Regulations

To address its growing environmental concerns, the United States has relied heavily on legislation to regulate corporate environmental behavior (as opposed to relying on financial instruments, jawboning, or voluntarism). Its legal structure includes such landmark federal laws as:

1969: National Environmental Policy Act (NEPA)
1970: Clean Air Act, Amended in 1977 and 1990
1970: Occupational Safety and Health Act (OSHA)
1972: Clean Water Act, Amended in 1987
1972: Federal Insecticide, Fungicide and Rodenticide Act (FIFRA)
1976: Toxic Substances Control Act (TSCA)
1976: Resource Conservation and Recovery Act (RCRA), Amended in 1984 by Hazardous and Solid Waste Amendments, and in 1988 by the Medical Waste Tracking Act.
1980: Comprehensive Environmental Response Cooperation and Liability Act (CERCLA), Amended in 1986 by Superfund Amendments and Reauthorization Act—SARA.

In addition, some states and cities have enacted different or supplemental laws to deal with special local conditions (i.e., Los Angeles smog) or to introduce a more restrictive regime than could be adopted nationally. Regulations are the means by which all this legislation is converted into detailed rules that can be understood by those whose practices they govern and enforced by the agencies and, if necessary, the courts. In the United States, both laws and the regulations they spawn are the product of political give and take, in the end usually satisfying no constituent group completely, and, as a result, occasionally lacking consistency or a solid scientific foundation.

Whatever its imperfections, the resulting body of law has been responsible for major headway against the problems the proponents and legislators set out to address. However, the large portfolio of environmental regulations now in place presents a complex and often frustrating problem for even the largest companies and stimulates a desire on their part to somehow find a better way. Here is how two of them express their feelings and frustrations:

AT&T *(from the company case history)*

AT&T takes its environmental responsibilities seriously, but feels itself hindered, not helped, in its environmental efforts by the ever-increasing number and complexity of regulations. This increase transcends the federal/state level. Cities are now in the act.

While well-meaning, of what real value to global problems is a San Diego, California ordinance on ozone-depleting substances?

209

Such environmental problems are global, universal problems demanding integrated, world-wide solutions. Single-shot activities such as the San Diego ordinance do little more than confuse and complicate the issue. And imagine—under the recently signed Clean Air Act—each state implementing procedures and forms different from all others in terms of information required and solutions mandated.

National—and multinational companies like AT&T, with facilities of some type in virtually every state or city—could be strangled by many different forms—provisions—plans. There needs to be a uniformity—a standardization—of such plans. There needs to be a "rule of reason" so that industry moves forward responsibly, government obtains what it needs, the environment is protected, legal requirements are met, and everyone benefits.

Today, Europe faces profound environmental problems. But there is also in Europe a sense of a business/government partnership to address those common problems. In the United States, however, adversarial relationships, in which uniquely technical problems are handled by more and more laws and regulations, can drive up costs with no corresponding improvement in environmental pollution.

Domestic businesses face over 80,000 pages of environmental regulations promulgated by the federal and state governments just since 1981. Over 35 regulations per working day.

That's a burden to read—much less to assess the impact of all these regulations on global operations. Technical people in Environmental & Safety Engineering Division read through over 10,000 pages of Federal regulations each year.

Today, there is an opportunity for all—individuals, corporations, government bodies, and environmental groups—to form partnerships, networks, and alliances. Such partnerships and alliances can find ways to promote the voluntary commitment of principled people and institutions.

AT&T's frustration with the complicated and multi-level regulatory climate in the United States is shared by many companies. They and some other observers have concluded that regulations, especially those based on faulty science or exacting prescriptions of how to do something, rather than call for what is to be done, are sometimes inefficient, discouraging to innovators, or counterproductive.

210

Some critics view company attempts to influence regulation only as foot-dragging intended to hinder progress toward more responsible corporate behavior, as indeed it has been on occasion. On the other hand, many thoughtful managers believe it is not only their right but their duty to work with government and other interested parties to set environmental goals and standards that are:

- Cost effective, balancing risk avoided with resources expended.
- Based on sound science and technically feasible or within reach.
- Attainable by the deadlines proposed.
- Designed, where possible, to utilize market mechanisms.
- Balanced to avoid giving one competitor unfair advantage over another.

It seems right that corporations should indeed speak out, in a constructive way, on public policy issues. One test of corporate sincerity will be the degree to which companies work for balance in the overall public interest, rather than seek narrow victories for immediate corporate advantage. When a problem needs to be addressed by regulation, the company response should be to support reasonable proposals—perhaps its own— rather than simply objecting to the ideas of others. Here is an instance in which this approach has been followed with apparently useful results:

Chevron *(from the company case history)*

In the late 1980s, it became clear that the development of cleaner burning fuel formulations represented yet another step in reducing air pollution and one that could provide fairly quick progress. As a company that makes and markets gasoline, Chevron obviously has a vital interest—and some real responsibility—to help deal with this issue.

Toward the end of the past decade, ideas and proposals on new fuel formulations started floating through regulatory agencies, including the EPA and the California Air Resources Board, or CARB. A few of the proposals appeared downright draconian, suggesting recipes that were astronomical in cost. Some of the formulations were designed to cut certain emissions and would likely have succeeded in doing so. Ironically, these often increased the output of other equally undesirable emissions. Few of these early government proposals had foundations in solid, scientific ground.

211

By that point, it was awfully clear to Chevron that it had better not sit around waiting to react to some recipe that would make it almost impossible to even make gasoline, or which appeared destined to do as much harm as good. The company felt it would be far wiser if it offered to help these agencies develop the best means of cutting fuel-related pollution. And the term "best" means a technology that provides real environmental improvement cost-effectively, not only for the industry but for the public at large. "Otherwise," says Dixon Smith of Chevron U.S.A. Products Company, "We'd all be paying an extremely high price for 'improvements' of marginal or even dubious benefit."

Chevron and several other gasoline-producing companies thus began sharing technical information on fuel reformulations with CARB and EPA scientists, who were already working with their own data. "Some of the information that we passed along might well be considered proprietary technology," Smith explains. "It's the kind of thing that would give any business person some pause. To an extent, it sure did for us. But in the end, we concluded that it was critical for the CARB and EPA people to have the best information possible on which to base their regulatory standards."

Regulations based on poor science usually lead to poor results. What inevitably follows then is frustration, anger, and even more regulations, sometimes just as ineffectual and harmful.

"Our technical people worked with the CARB and EPA people primarily as scientific advisors, not as advocates for our particular approach to reformulated fuels," Smith notes. We have other folks in Chevron to handle advocacy; unfortunately, politics is a big part of the environmental picture. But on the science front, we believe we developed an exceptionally cooperative, effective, and collegial working relationship with our government counterparts."

The EPA served as the centerpiece of the effort, drawing together experts from environmental groups, the automobile and petroleum business, and other interested parties. The teamwork resulted in an EPA reformulated gasoline program that is now the industry's cornerstone. In California, CARB adopted a "Phase 2" fuels-reformulation requirement that was announced late in 1991. It was largely weighted toward technology developed through a joint automobile and oil-industry research program. The formula seems to offer some solid environmental benefits. It's expensive, costing about 16 cents per gallon more than conventional fuel. The vast majority of consumers, no matter what they tell public opinion pollsters about wanting to help the environment, are unlikely to pay that great a per-gallon premium if a cheaper alternative is available. But if every gasoline marketer must sell such reformulated fuel, there simply won't be an alternative. We'll all be playing on a level field.

[Ed. Note: Chevron makes the excellent point that regulations should apply equally to all competitors, not exempt those with shallow pockets or of small size. Such political bias discriminates economically against those who do clean up and reduces the benefits to the environment.]

Historically, industry has often opposed new regulations by arguing how much it costs the business. It's a legitimate concern but also a bit self-serving. More important—and it's something business, environmentalists, and regulators should consider—are the people who might really be harmed by the higher costs. Nevertheless, Chevron remains optimistic about the next generation of reformulated fuel standards, if they're needed. Because of the process we've just gone through, we've developed a running and open dialogue with the regulators, a climate of good cooperation, and a growing sense of trust. The right technology can indeed yield cleaner-burning fuel. It will cost a little more to improve the environment, but should not be so much that it puts an unreasonable burden on the industry, or the often overlooked consumer. We can now tackle new regulations with a balanced approach.

The cooperative effort Chevron cites is notable for several reasons:

- *It engaged regulators, environmental groups, and the auto and petroleum industries in a joint effort;*
- *It sought a scientifically sound solution based on the public's interest both in cleaner air and reasonable fuel costs; and*
- *Chevron separated its scientific input from its advocacy function, raising the level of trust.*

In a world with limited resources to solve many problems, constructive participation in the regulatory process by knowledgeable corporations can have a beneficial effect. But companies that view themselves as environmental leaders will be closely watched to see if they follow such a course in their government relations. While other groups will undoubtedly have views that differ from company positions, and debate is both necessary and healthy, an industry retreat to a policy of knee-jerk opposition to change will greatly damage the credibility of the movement to corporate environmentalism that the companies quoted in this book believe is under way.

Finally, it should be noted that not all environmental problems are global; some are regional or local and need to be addressed on that basis. And, desirable as voluntary action is, reliance on it alone may not always be sufficient or even in a responsible company's self-interest. Voluntary action can impose costs on the volunteer not borne by less responsible competitors; well-drafted regulations can even the burden and ensure that the irresponsible player is not rewarded.

Liability

The uniquely American system of assigning liability and assessing damages presents a real-world challenge to the participant companies, and EPA's Superfund program provides a dramatic example.

Here is how a leading insurance company executive presents his view of how this program is working—or not working—to clean up toxic waste sites, an effort with which few companies, environmentalists, or the EPA are happy.

American International Group *(extracted from an article by Maurice Greenberg, Chairman of AIG, in issue #4, 1991 of* World Link*)*

Mitigating the effects of past pollution is one of the most significant environmental issues facing industrialized nations. When the U.S. Congress rushed to create Superfund in 1980, few could have anticipated the problems that would result over the ensuing decade. At the heart of these problems lies Superfund's liability system.

It is important to recognize that this liability system is first and foremost a fund-raising mechanism. As mandated by the Superfund law, the U.S. Environmental Protection Agency conducts site-by-site searches to find those responsible for the waste and then forces them to pay for the cleanup. To ensure that the EPA would be able to raise adequate cleanup funds, Congress created a liability scheme under Superfund of unprecedented reach and severity.

The scope of Superfund's inclusive liability approach is worth noting. Superfund imposes liability without the necessity of finding fault or even knowledge. It imposes it retroactively, with no statute of limitations, and whether or not the disposed waste actually caused harm. Finally, Superfund liability is joint and several, meaning that any single party can be required to pay the total cost of cleanup at a site, regardless of its own percentage of waste at the site, and then face the task of trying to collect from other parties. This liability can apply to almost anyone who has had a link to a Superfund site. This includes anyone who ever generated, transported, disposed of, or arranged for disposal of waste at the site; and it includes past and current site owners and operators.

Instead of advancing cleanup, the EPA has focused on fundraising. The result is that Superfund has become a litigious nightmare for those it has targeted. Business of all sizes, local governments, nonprofit organizations, individuals, and, in turn, the liability insurers for all these parties have spent billions of dollars on protracted litigation debating who should pay for cleanup. Thus, Superfund's environmental goals have been undermined by the firestorm of litigation arising from use of the liability system to raise money to pay for cleanup of old hazardous waste sites. To help document how this process has worked and to illustrate its dire consequences, American International Group, Fireman's Fund Insurance Companies, and Crum and Foster Insurance Companies commissioned a series of site studies around the United States. The preliminary results are shocking. We have found hundreds of companies and insurers mired in costly litigation and protracted negotiations, with little or no actual cleanup under way. One company executive referred to the liability system as "extortion." Others noted that Superfund's absolute liability forces parties to settle for a specific (and in their view inequitable) amount of liability, rather than risk even more costly and time-consuming negotiations or litigation. At one site in New York state, the legal and consulting fees paid to apportion liability have almost equalled the total estimated site-cleanup costs. The negotiations and litigation continue at this site, with actual cleanup still years away.

Our site studies reveal how fund-raising and the accompanying debate over who should pay have delayed cleanup and wasted resources. As the studies are completed, we are sharing the findings with the EPA, Congress, and other interested parties. We have undertaken this site-by-site research as part of an effort to prompt a comprehensive review of Superfund's liability system and consideration of alternative funding mechanisms.

We believe the current system must be changed fundamentally. To this end, we have proposed a simple trade: replacing Superfund's liability system to raise cleanup funds at old sites with a broad-based fund, which we call the National Environmental Trust Fund. The fund would be paid for across all sectors of our economy without regard to liability.

As an incentive for responsible waste management, our proposal would retain Superfund's liability scheme for current and future waste generation. But at old sites, the fund's resources would be used solely to pay for cleanup on a ''no-fault'' basis—rapidly, efficiently, and without the transaction costs of Superfund.

We are exploring various funding mechanisms for the trust fund, including a small premium surcharge collected on all commercial insurance and an equivalent amount for ''self-insureds.'' Whatever funding approach is adopted, it should meet the test of being sufficiently broad-based so that cleanup costs are shared across all economic sectors, eliminating the inequities of the current system. Old hazardous-waste sites are the residue of economic progress; and just as we have all benefited from it, we must share the costs of environmental cleanup.

It is worth noting that in addition to describing a problem of great magnitude, Mr. Greenberg goes the next step and suggests a way of solving it. While few are happy with Superfund, not all will agree with Mr. Greenberg's proposals. Any better approach than the present one, however, is likely to come about only through cooperation among industry, environmentalists, communities, and the federal government.

■ ■ ■

The liability problem is indeed ''real world'' to some participant companies.

Royal Dutch/Shell Group *(from the company's case history)*

One new and worrying development concerns the legal position of companies in relation to environmental risks, by which past environmental performance to then-acceptable standards is judged by today's knowledge and standards. The original lack of awareness of long-term effects (e.g., from waste disposal) may no longer be accepted as a defensible argument. Similarly, the concept of product liability shifts the onus onto the producer to show no fault. If the liability can arise several links down the chain from the original producer or supplier, there are serious implications for the manufacturer. Such all-embracing responsibility for a product or waste has become a significant consideration in investment decisions.

The fact is that Shell companies may have to withdraw from certain activities if faced with unpredictable and uninsurable potential risks (e.g., unlimited liability) for the consequences of a failure or accident including those attributable to human error and those where negligence is not a factor. Already Shell has reached just such a position, deciding in 1990 to stop shipments in Shell-owned vessels of crude and fuel oil into all U.S. ports except the Louisiana Offshore Oil Port (LOOP).

[Ed. Note: Shell explains that the LOOP exclusion is because of the port's location 30 miles offshore and the very careful control of operations exercised by the port authorities.]

This, because ship-owners face largely uninsurable liabilities and damage claims in the event of an accident with consequent pollution in U.S. territorial waters. In most of the rest of the world, there are international conventions that enable ship owners to limit their liability except in cases of negligence. These conventions also make funds available for clean-up and compensation.

■ ■ ■

For some companies and their executives, the liability matter involves more than money damages or staying in business. In a recent seminar sponsored by Booz, Allen & Hamilton, a leading environmental lawyer confirmed these concerns. Here is a summary of his remarks:

217

James A. Rogers, *Partner, Skadden, Arps, Slate, Meagher & Flom*

In the 1990s, the possibility of criminal liability for environmental violations may well be a greater threat to corporate governance than a possible hostile corporate takeover. Increasingly, the federal and state governments are pursuing individuals and corporations under the criminal provisions of the environmental laws, and now even a persistent "non-knowing" violation can spawn a grand jury investigation. This dramatic increase in prosecutions (roughly 33 percent per year) is due to several factors:

- State and federal governments believe that there is widespread public and Congressional support for criminal actions.
- At the local level, environmental prosecutors gain greater popularity for prosecutions.
- There are many more federal investigators and experienced criminal attorneys and much more practical guidance as a result of more real world experiences with these laws.
- The courts have accepted the government's theories of criminal conduct, including minimal knowledge of facts and law to establish a "knowing crime" on the part of individuals.
- Corporate entities are particularly vulnerable because the law charges them with the collective knowledge of all the employees.
- There is an information overload. Even the larger and more sophisticated companies cannot keep up with the many complicated changes in environmental regulations. At many corporations, the sophisticated day-to-day environmental rules have simply "passed the corporation by."

In our experience, the risk of criminal action against individuals and corporations is often the result of reports to government agencies by disgruntled employees. Also, corporations often pay too little attention to statements in insurance or environmental audits that later are interpreted by prosecutors as showing knowledge of problems.

Under the new Sentencing Guidelines, it is no longer enough to have an effective program to ensure environmental compliance. And those individuals with direct responsibility for corporate environmental compliance may want tailored employment contracts and may seek greater compensation—more commensurate with their individual exposure.

Many companies are outraged by lawsuits that threaten them with massive damages and criminal liability for actions not known to be harmful at the time they were taken, or perhaps not even taken by them. Their wrath is aimed at aspects of the American tort system that they believe to be unfair and counter-productive. Clearly, the costs of litigation, remediation, and paying damages relating to the practices of former decades place today's U.S.-made products at a disadvantage in international competition, and the threat of similar future attack based on hindsight discourages experimentation with innovative new ways of dealing with waste.

On the other hand, fear of liability is a powerful stimulus for increased attention to all the possible consequences of any new innovation before it is released. But because it is impractical—perhaps impossible— to analyze all the ripples a new product may cause (remember that for many years CFCs were considered a miracle of efficiency and safety, and DDT a life-saver), unexpected negative impacts followed by after-the-fact sanctions for damage are likely to remain a part of the American corporate experience.

In a perfect world, environmental tort law, as well as environmental standards, would be harmonized globally. It is not within the scope of this book to predict when that will happen. Until it does, even those companies that maintain high environmental standards worldwide may be tempted, as Shell was, to flee from the clutches of the American judicial system to safer harbors elsewhere.

And, for the great majority of companies that have no intention or wish to relocate, Dr. Peter Sandman has some good advice. He points out that most people sue "not to get rich, but to get even. Good communication, stressing listening and openness, will reduce their incentives, and thus can greatly reduce the liability lawsuits to be dealt with."

■ ■ ■

Casualties of Protecting the Environment

Increased environmental protection does not always build a company, for doing what is right may eliminate products, jobs, or even whole businesses.

> If we cannot afford to protect the environment, we should get out of the business.
>
> ■ *David Kearns, President and CEO (until 1990) Xerox Corporation*

Monsanto *(from the company case history)*

Not all of the changes are painless. While corporate environmentalism presented new opportunities, it also placed an additional burden on smaller plants. This, combined with other business factors, resulted in the shutdown or consolidation of several operations.

S.C. Johnson Wax *(from the company case history)*

While the company had in place a key technical advance of using hydrocarbon propellants for fluorocarbon propellants, the ban was for all Johnson products, even where no substitution by hydrocarbons was possible. Entire Johnson product lines were lost, including, specifically, popular antiperspirants and hair sprays in the Personal Care line. The decision was not only unpopular in some of the aerosol industry circles, but also unpopular with some of Johnson management, who were skeptical of the company's ability to recoup the potential loss of business.

Unfortunate as plant and product shutdowns may be, it is worth noting that environmental improvement also creates jobs in goods and services needed for remediation and protects other jobs by enhancing the long-term competitiveness of proactive companies. Like plants or products that fail to meet functional, cost, or quality expectations, those that fail environmentally must expect to be casualties of the changing business scene.

■ ■ ■

Cumulatively, these rocks and shoals of the real world pose extensive navigational problems for corporate leaders, dwarfed only by the threat to their businesses implicit in a decision to do nothing to improve their environmental performance.

XI.
SCENARIOS
FOR
PLANNING

A number of participants mentioned the need for incorporating the environment into their strategic plans. In recent years, corporate planning has evolved from a numbers exercise, concentrating on projecting trends along a most likely path, to a more conceptual approach dealing with various future possibilities, enabling planners to prepare for a variety of uncertain eventualities. Royal Dutch/Shell has been a leader in this new technique. After consulting with outside experts, including environmentalists, they have developed two possible future scenarios (published in January 1991) that pay considerable attention to the environmental concerns of their world-wide group of companies, most of which are heavily engaged in the energy business. With changes in detail, a similar set of scenarios could be developed to address any company's future, including its environmental concerns.

The following material is abstracted from the Shell publication "Global Scenarios for the Energy Industry: Challenge and Response," which the company uses to test existing strategic options and to stimulate new ones. Shell describes the process as "helping managers to live the future in advance." The global scenarios from which the following material is extracted are updated every two or three years; regional or local scenarios that complement are prepared in the interim.

Royal Dutch/Shell Group *(from Shell's publication "Global Scenarios for the Energy Industry")*

Long-term forecasting is not a very successful enterprise. Some of the most important events of the last two years caught most observers off guard. Notwithstanding this difficulty, the future is too important to be ignored. The Shell approach to strategic planning is, instead of forecasts, to use scenarios, a set of "stories" about alternative possible futures. These stories promote a discussion of possibilities other than the "most likely" one and encourage the consideration of "what if" questions. They also help us recognize more of what is going on around us, including the early, weak signals of change, and illuminate the uncertainties and issues that are critical for the future. Scenarios lead to better decisions if they improve our understanding of the world.

The World of 1990

The only solid basis we have for discussing the future is information about the past and the present. In 1990, the present is a time of promise but also of considerable risk. In these scenarios, we concentrate on three areas of potentially far-reaching change:

- geopolitics;
- international economics; and
- the natural environment.

Geopolitical Changes

The most spectacular evidence of geopolitical change has been the cascading "domino" collapses of communist regimes in Eastern Europe and the Soviet Union. These upheavals have been caused by deep economic and environmental problems and nationalist and ethnic tensions.

The United States of America has also declined in economic importance and power, relative to Western Europe and Japan. Partly because of faster growth in other parts of the world, and partly because of slow productivity growth, low savings, and large budget deficits at home, the United States no longer has as dominant an international economic position.

In Western Europe, fears of "Euro-sclerosis" have given way to "Euro-optimism." The momentum of the European Communities (EC) 1992 programme has raised the possibility of closer monetary integration, leading ultimately to economic and political union.

The very rapid economic growth of East Asia also has geopolitical consequences. Japan and the four Newly Industrializing Countries [Hong Kong, Singapore, South Korea and Taiwan] have enjoyed extended periods of growth and are now widely seen as models of successful development, but have produced dislocations in other countries that have provoked friction and protectionist responses.

The International Economy

The lengthy expansion of the world economy since 1982 suggests that in some respects there are strategies for economic growth that work and have been learnt. Market-oriented policies have been effective, notably in East Asia, and have won recent converts in Latin America, Africa, Eastern Europe, and elsewhere. The dramatic increase in international economic interconnection has important advantages, but has also resulted in greater interdependence and scope for disagreement. The clearest examples of disagreement are in the Uruguay Round negotiations of the General Agreement on Tariffs and Trade (GATT).

One important symptom of these frictions is the rise in unilateral restrictions and bilateral deals. Another symptom of economic difficulties is that average per capita incomes in much of Latin America, Sub-Saharan Africa, and Eastern Europe fell over the 1980s. *(See Fig. 7.)*

Environmental Concerns

The third important area of change is man's impact on the natural environment. Although concern about environmental degradation is not new, it has recently been heightened. This has been due to a combination of:

- increasingly severe degradation in many areas;
- improved scientific understanding and measurement capability; and
- changed personal values—especially in wealthy countries, as people move up the hierarchy of needs and focus on "quality of life."

These changes in perspective have been reflected in new economic models, which point out that sustained economic output depends not only on investment in man-made assets, but also on the maintenance of natural assets, such as clean air and soil. *(See Fig. 8.)*

These scenarios emphasize the approach taken to reduce global warming and raise fundamental questions about the combustion

Figure 7. Growth in Gross Domestic Product Per Capita

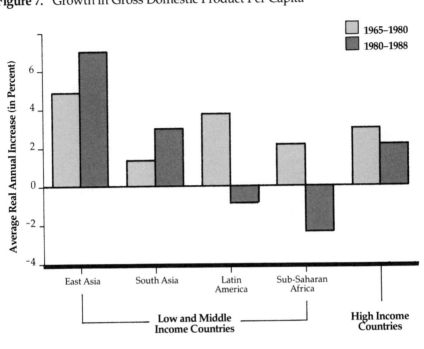

Source: A. Kahane, *Global Scenarios for the Energy Industry: Challenge and Response,* Shell
International Petroleum Company Ltd., England, 1991, p. 3

of fossil fuels. The unprecedented international cooperation required to tackle these sorts of global problems could have important political implications.

The position of developing countries is crucial in global environmental discussions. Developing countries are often the most directly
affected by environmental degradation, and they will make an increasing contribution to global problems as their populations and
economies grow. On the other hand, they have fewer resources
available to move towards sustainable development.

Framing Scenarios

These three areas of change—geopolitics, economics, and environment—are interrelated. New international mechanisms and
alliances for dealing with international political problems have to be
found. The consensus in favor of multilateral solutions, previously

Figure 8. The Two Loops of Sustainable Economic Growth

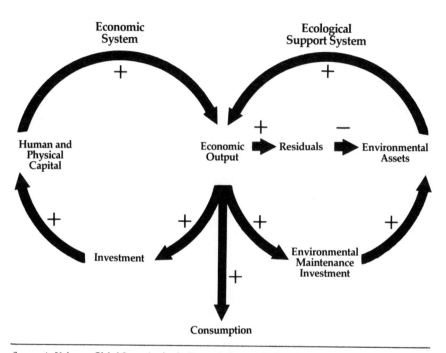

Source: A. Kahane, *Global Scenarios for the Energy Industry: Challenge and Response,* Shell International Petroleum Company Ltd., England, 1991, p. 4

held together by a dominant United States, is in doubt. Environmental concerns can be divisive, with significant disagreements over the seriousness and urgency of the problems (especially global warming), but may also be an important force for cooperation through the perception of a common threat.

Developments in all three of these areas may therefore lead to fundamental changes in international relations. The role of the nation-state itself is under scrutiny; increasing migration of capital, people, information, and pollution makes national borders less relevant.

These are all important signs of structural change in a global system under stress. However, the direction of change is not at all clear. These scenarios suggest two possible directions—two alternative interpretations of the present signs of change. *(See Fig. 9.)*

Figure 9. Two Alternative Interpretations of the Present Signs of Change

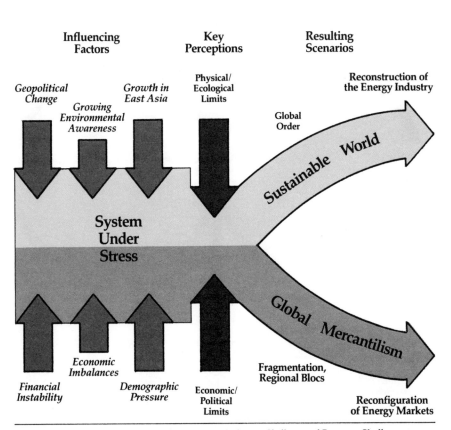

Source: A. Kahane, *Global Scenarios for the Energy Industry: Challenge and Response,* Shell International Petroleum Company Ltd., England, 1991, p. 4

In the first scenario, Global Mercantilism, the primary challenge of the 1990s turns out to be the weakness and instability of current international economic and political systems. The structural response is fragmentation and regionalization. In the second scenario, Sustainable World, the primary challenge turns out instead to be how to deal with common problems, especially ecological problems, such as global warming. Here the response is cohesion (and also coercion) and a broadening of international systems.

226

Global Mercantilism

In this scenario, the new post-Cold War international order proves to be weak. Regional conflicts are destabilizing. The current GATT negotiations fail. Financial instability is accentuated by deregulation and rising interest rates. Faced with a downturn, politicians focus on national economic difficulties, and there is little international leadership. Continued frustration over trade and investment imbalances leads to increased protectionism. Overall, response to the downturn is ineffective and confrontational, and it turns into a recession as severe as in the early 1980s.

The result is increasing emphasis on regional pacts—functional, if variously defined, blocs—particularly the EC and North America. Japan and the NICs find their access to these markets substantially constrained and therefore place more emphasis on Asia-Pacific markets, building up a web of bilateral alliances centered on Japan.

The failure of global institutions, and a lessened appreciation of common interests, mean less aid and assistance to poor countries. Countries that are not in a bloc have severe difficulties in this scenario, and the gap between rich and poor countries widens further.

Within the regional blocs, the primary policy objective is to become economically efficient and competitive. Governments adopt hands-off, market-oriented policies and accept the resulting dislocations and volatility; there is little sympathy for industry special pleading.

Economic policy has a dual character: inter-bloc economic exchanges are politically managed, but intra-bloc exchanges are market oriented, with very competitive domestic markets coexisting with government support for national champions in international markets.

Environmental concerns are not very high on the political agenda. Although local and regional problems are tackled, there are too many international disagreements for a consensus to be reached on difficult global issues. *(See Fig. 10.)*

Implications for Energy

Internationally, crude oil is a key traded commodity, and oil markets are therefore strongly influenced by the fundamental changes in the rules of international trade. Emphasis is placed both

227

Figure 10. The Logic of Global Mercantilism

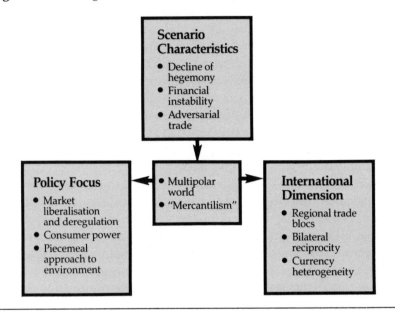

Source: A. Kahane, *Global Scenarios for the Energy Industry: Challenge and Response,* Shell
International Petroleum Company Ltd., England, 1991, p. 5

on regional self-sufficiency—which means that production from countries outside of OPEC (Organization of Petroleum Exporting Countries) is kept up—and on reciprocal alliances between producers and marketers (''you can have access to my downstream market only if you allow me access to your reserves'').

One result is that proportionally less oil falls under OPEC control. Together with volatile economic growth, this makes OPEC management of oil prices very difficult and cyclical over-capacity and under-capacity leads to a price rollercoaster. Within the intra-bloc mega-markets, oil-price swings force consumers to emphasize flexibility, fuel-switching, and the development of spot markets. Electric and gas utilities are radically affected by the promotion of common carriage and independent electricity generation.

Sustainable World

In this scenario, the international economic frictions that have been in the headlines can be resolved, and attention focuses instead

228

on the resolution of common problems, including environmental ones. There is widespread consensus on recipes for economic stability and growth and cooperation among the largest economies. Danger of a failure in international trade interdependence is seen to be too great for "divorce" to be a feasible option. Regional conflicts are dealt with effectively by large power alliances. In general, there is a recognition of common interests and the continued development of institutional structures to deal with them.

At the same time, international concern grows over all kinds of environmental degradation. There are continued, noticed environmental problems, which are perceived as breached limits. Global warming is believed to be a serious threat. In rich countries, the environment rises to the top of the political agenda and stays there, so that the necessary agreements are reached and action is taken.

Concern about environmental problems is not limited to rich countries. Many of the problems are most acute in poor countries, which are heavily dependent on natural resources, especially forestry and agriculture. However, the central political question is how poor countries can be brought on board. The rich countries lead, providing carrots of aid and technology transfer to encourage sustainable projects, recognizing that economic growth is a prerequisite to achieving environmental objectives. At the same time, there are "sticks" of sanctions and trade barriers against environmental offenders. Coercion is an important aspect of this scenario, with the rich deciding that new global arrangements (on trade, security, environment, etc.) are necessary and, in effect, imposing these priorities and arrangements on the poor.

Two additional political elements are important. There is a three-pronged dynamic interaction between "leader" and "laggard" countries, whereby the former pull up the latter:

- politicians compete to be seen as the most "green";
- technology, developed by the leaders, is less expensive for the laggards; and
- the leaders need to encourage the laggards if their own efforts on global problems (for example, reduced carbon dioxide emissions) are to be effective. Both economic instruments, including taxation, and re-regulation play a role. Environmental

229

investments inspire invention and innovation, leading to profitable new economic activities. *(See Fig. 11.)*

Figure 11. The Logic of Sustainable World

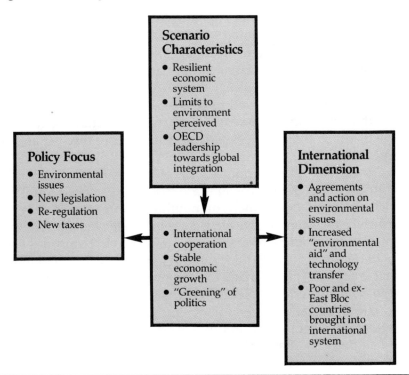

Source: A. Kahane, *Global Scenarios for the Energy Industry: Challenge and Response,* Shell International Petroleum Company Ltd., England, 1991, p. 7

Implications for Energy

The primary effect of Sustainable World on the energy industry is greatly increased pressure to reduce the industry's impact on the natural environment. Five aspects are important. These are:

- Tightened regulation of emissions from energy facilities.
- Higher standards for the quality of energy products.
- Switching to cleaner fuels.

- Improvements in the efficiency of energy-using devices.
- The re-design of whole energy-using systems, such as transportation and housing.

The technology already exists to move forward in all of these areas. In many cases, however, economic and other incentives are insufficient for substantial take-up. Even when they are adopted, it takes a long time before the effect is significant because the systems are so large.

Both market instruments and command-and-control regulations are important in implementing these measures. One essential ingredient is greatly increased final energy prices to end-users.

Although final prices are raised significantly (for example, through a large carbon tax), energy consumption per dollar of Gross Domestic Product (GDP) falls because of improved energy efficiencies, and so the burden of energy costs relative to GDP is not much higher than historic levels. In this sense, the high energy prices are economically manageable.

These measures have radical implications for the energy industry. Growth in total world primary energy supply occurs much more slowly. There is a substantial shift in the mix of fuels, especially (over this period) from coal to natural gas. However, even such a scenario—which postulates very severe policy intervention—does not result in reductions in global emissions of carbon dioxide sufficient to meet the Toronto target of a 20-percent reduction by 2005. Therefore, if the current scientific consensus is correct, some global warming will occur, even in Sustainable World, although much less than in Global Mercantilism. *(See Fig. 12.)*

Conclusion

These scenarios present two radically different images of the future. In Global Mercantilism, the main global challenge is dealing with the decline in the hegemonic position of the two superpowers and instability in international markets. The response is fragmented, with neo-mercantilist economic policies and the establishment of markets.

In Sustainable World, the central challenge is dealing with common problems, especially global warming: the response is cohesive,

Figure 12. Global Emissions of Carbon Dioxide from Burning Fossil Fuels

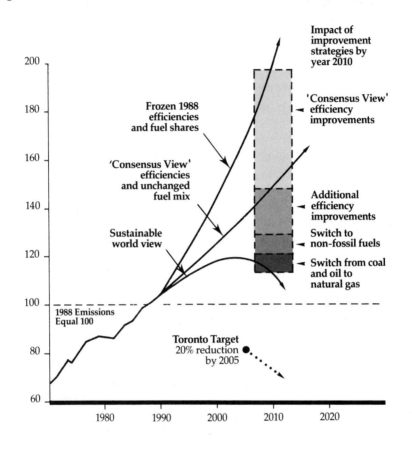

Source: A. Kahane, *Global Scenarios for the Energy Industry: Challenge and Response,* Shell
International Petroleum Company Ltd., England, 1991, p. 8

with enhanced international cooperation (as well as coercion) and
new global institutions and mechanisms. *(See Fig. 13.)*

The two scenarios are alternative interpretations of the present. As such, their purpose is to sensitize us to recognize signals
of possible changes in the world—which will probably include elements of both scenarios—and to enable us to respond quickly and
appropriately. They are less reassuring than conventional forecasts,
but more challenging—and therefore more useful.

Figure 13. Summary of the Scenarios

	Global Mercantilism	**Sustainable World**
Challenge	Hegemonic decline and economic instability	Degradation of the environment (especially through global warming)
Response	Multipolar world and mercantilism	International cooperation and management
Implications For Energy	New rules for business and reconfiguration of markets	New values for fuels and reconstruction of the energy industry

Source: A. Kahane, *Global Scenarios for the Energy Industry: Challenge and Response,* Shell International Petroleum Company Ltd., England, 1991, p. 9

Shell's use of planning scenarios rightly recognizes that a company must anticipate the world as it may be, not as it "ought" to be. Yet, if the presumptions on which this book is based—

- *World population will double by about the year 2050;*
- *Social and political stability will depend on increasing global per capita wealth; and*
- *The implied increase in global economic activity, using presently installed industrial practices, would overwhelm the world's ecological systems*

prove correct—then leaders in business, governments, and the environmental movement need to put aside their short-term and often conflicting goals and join in a global effort to move toward the "Sustainable World" scenario, for it promises to be far happier than the one described by "Global Mercantilism."

233

XII.

A LOOK INTO THE FUTURE

No participating company has concluded that environmental pressures will go away or that the "good old days" of little concern will come back. That's not surprising, both because all the participants were selected on the basis of their increasing environmental efforts and because the old days, whether good or not, are indeed dead and gone. Even at a time of economic difficulty, public calls for environmental improvement remain strong.

While most companies see the future as an extension of present trends, what they choose to stress is quite varied.

■ ■ ■

> A voluntary program frees participating organizations from the restraints normally caused by government regulation and bureaucracy and, most importantly, it is the most cost-efficient way to stimulate change.
>
> ■ *Margaret Kerr, Vice President*
> *Northern Telecom—1991*

Monsanto *(from the company case history)*

The more companies embrace environmental stewardship, the more they will undertake voluntary initiatives. The more voluntary initiatives are pursued, the more performance-based standards will effectively replace command-and-control regulations. Performance standards that employ positive, free-market incentives do the job of environmental clean-up more effectively, advancing protection more rapidly.

235

The public's environmental antennae are still up high and are not likely to lower anytime soon, and, since our employee base is fed by society, environmentalism inside will increase to match the pressure from the outside. The most responsible companies will be those sought by the most talented recruits, which, in turn, will help us achieve our objectives even faster.

While some product lines and operations may be discontinued if they can't meet tough targets, those that remain will have a competitive advantage in the marketplace. They'll be produced with less waste and related expense.

Environmental goals and commitments are no longer seen as only a cost of doing business. The environment *is* our business; it is as integral to the success of Monsanto as are new products, quality, service, a favorable return to our shareholders, and dedicated and talented employees.

■ ■ ■

Monsanto's call for voluntary initiatives in lieu of prescriptive command-and-control regulations is in line with a recent EPA program, which can be summarized by quoting from two EPA press releases:

United States Environmental Protection Agency *(from press releases)*

February 7, 1991

EPA Administrator William K. Reilly today asked over 600 U.S. companies to reduce voluntarily pollution caused by 17 high priority toxic chemicals. The goal is to reduce, by one-third, the total releases and transfers of the 17 target chemicals by 1992; and to reduce them by one half by 1995.

"As I travel around the country," Reilly stated, "I am meeting industrial leaders who are ready to step up to the plate as good corporate citizens to help reduce troublesome pollutants. The support for this effort from chief executives is encouraging—in particular, in the chemical, petroleum and pulp and paper industries."

"The voluntary pollution prevention initiative launched today will reinforce, rather than replace, the regulatory program to protect human health and the environment, including the standards and the incentive provisions to be
developed under the new Clean Air act," Reilly said.
"There is a two-fold design to this voluntary initiative, to
help reduce toxic pollution ahead of schedule by encouraging companies to act now rather than wait for statutory
deadlines and by stimulating interest in reducing wastes
at the source as a cost-effective way to comply with both
existing and future requirements."

[Ed. Note: This effort became known as the 33/50 program.]

July 19, 1991

EPA Administrator William K. Reilly today announced the
first results of the 33/50 Program that seeks voluntary reductions of toxic emissions by industry. To date, according to
Reilly, more than 200 companies have committed to reducing their emissions at industrial facilities an average of 50
percent by 1995, which would yield an overall reduction
of over 200 million pounds of toxic releases.

"I am tremendously excited by industry's willingness to
make ambitious voluntary commitments to environmental protection," EPA Administrator William K. Reilly said.
"This program is a promising experiment to see if voluntary goals can work, alongside our conventional regulatory
approach, for achieving quick environmental results."

Many of the first-round companies that have not yet signed
up for the program have indicated that they will in the coming months. In addition, EPA is currently contacting thousands of other companies (about 6,000 in total) to seek their
participation in the 33/50 Program.

*[Ed. Note: All companies participating in this book that were among EPA's
initial group of 600 candidates have signed onto the 33/50 program.]*

Royal Dutch/Shell Group *(from the company case history)*

> Our future must be one in which Shell companies excel in environmental performance; one in which we actively support governments in developing sensible policies to deal with environmental problems; and one in which we are open about our policies and practices and performance.
>
> ■ *L.C. van Wachem, Senior Group*
> *Managing Director*
> *Royal Dutch/Shell Group of*
> *Companies*
>
> —*from a letter sent by Mr. van Wachem to the Chief Executives of all Shell operating companies; 1990.*

The environmental challenge ahead is formidable. Global solutions have to be found that are adaptable to a multiplicity of countries in different developmental stages. Somehow, in striving for real sustainable development through the proper stewardship of man's physical environment, society has to harness, not destroy, the energy of enterprise. In a world of changing social values, one of the main tasks is to balance the environmental challenge with economic development.

With stakeholders rightly demanding proper environmental stewardship, industry must participate constructively in the development of standards and in the whole international environmental debate. It must proffer experience and understanding to enable a balanced view to be taken. Closer industry cooperation with governments is inevitable. Yet, legislation alone cannot achieve the optimal result; it is up to industry to find new, less environmentally harmful, ways of meeting society's needs, but, to do so, it must be given adequate running room.

No one can pretend that unfortunate incidents and unacceptable lapses in environmental standards are about to be relegated to the past; a risk-free society remains a dream. Of course, work will continue to devise means to avoid repetition; and evolution in knowledge and in "state of the art" technology will help. There will be times when multinational enterprises are pioneers in seeking the best standards of proper environmental care. Because of their wealth of industrial experience in widely differing environments, their managerial, technical, and scientific expertise, they are well placed to take the lead in global environmental stewardship. Indeed, Shell companies' depth of knowledge is one of their greatest strengths.

■ ■ ■

Northern Telecom *(from a speech by Vice President Margaret Kerr)*

It's clear that we've entered an era in which global corporations have the opportunity to play a significant role in environmental problem-solving as owners, partners in joint ventures, and as suppliers of technology in many developing countries. We must continue to explore new ways to transfer environmental technology, through organizations such as ICOLP, through global funding mechanisms such as those supported by the Montreal Protocol, and through new delivery systems such as the cascading of technology within developing countries.

If we are to make a difference as global companies, we must be prepared to work with other stakeholders to share information and facilitate the prompt adoption of safe, environmentally acceptable operating practices and methods on a global basis—and here I'm talking about not just strengthening our relationships with governments, as ICOLP has done in Mexico, but with environmental groups, the scientific community, and the media.

We must also work harder at enlisting support from our suppliers, our customers, and even our competitors. We must draw on their technical expertise, their experience in finding new alternatives and processes, their enthusiasm and commitment to change. And they, of course, must be encouraged to draw on our strengths. In some cases, this will require putting aside adversarial relationships in favor of greater cooperation and consultation. We can no longer support competing demands on the environment, but must "co-evolve" within its limits.

From my perspective in the telecommunications industry, I believe that the rapid changes in the global economic landscape have been a major stimulus in this ongoing evolution. We've clearly shifted to an information-based economy that is in the throes of globalization.

Industry's greatest strength today is its flexibility in determining where and how it will pursue new growth opportunities. It is exactly this kind of flexibility and adaptability that ensures we're well-positioned in the search for global solutions to what are very clearly global environmental problems. The challenge is simple enough to define: companies that do not adjust their business strategies to embrace the concepts of sustainable development will find themselves faced with greater constraints and penalties on their operations—plus the hostility of an increasingly aware public. In contrast, companies leading the environmental wave will find themselves possessed of technologies and competitive advantages that will result in business opportunities and new growth.

■ ■ ■

Most participating companies view the future as presenting increasing environmental challenges—perhaps clouds with a silver lining, but clouds nonetheless. Southern California Edison believes that, for it, an environmentally demanding future means bigger markets and better business, given appropriate community and government support. Here, echoing the enthusiastic words of its chairman, is how it sees its future.

Southern California Edison *(from the company's case history as reported by its chairman)*

Many times there are great business opportunities in meeting environmental needs.

■ *John Bryson,*
Chairman and CEO
Southern California Edison

All businesses—large and small—will have to change their ways of doing things, even though it will involve a little inconvenience and change in lifestyles. But if current trends continue, in the year 2000, California commuters will waste up to 900,000 hours each working day fighting traffic—three times more than in 1988.

Obviously, some things are going to have to change. Business can greatly help to make this happen by proactively understanding and meeting environmental concerns. The key to environmental improvement at the least possible economic cost will be for government and regulatory agencies to allow market-based, least-cost solutions to problems. Government should set broad policy goals and allow private industries to determine the most cost-effective way to meet those goals. The alternative approach—what we have come to refer to as ''command and control'' regulation—leads almost inevitably to more costly and less effective solutions to problems.

We are encouraged by the willingness of the U.S. Environmental Protection Agency nationally and the California South Coast Air Quality Management District [AQMD] locally to consider widespread use of incentives, emissions credits, and the establishment of a market for emissions allowances. Locally, the AQMD has also shown a real willingness in recent years to use more goal-oriented approaches to solving our air-quality problems rather than command-and-control.

Creative initiatives by business can provide real improvements at relatively low cost. Unocal had one good idea when it spent $6 million to buy 8,400 high-polluting old clunker cars. That removed more pollution than $150 million dollars worth of refinery emission-control equipment.

At Edison, we are very excited about the potential of transportation electrification. This includes electric vehicles—EVs—and electrified mass transit. The California Air Resource Board has mandated that 2 percent of all new vehicles sold in the state in 1998 be non-polluting—10 percent in 2003. Only electric vehicles meet that test. Even counting the emissions from power plants associated with recharging the batteries of electric vehicles, they are 97 percent cleaner than internal combustion vehicles. We're working with vehicle developers like General Motors, Ford and Chrysler to make EVs more economical and practical. At first, we expect most users will be business fleets rather than individuals. But we're confident that the benefits of EVs will ultimately win the hearts of the general public.

Edison is also helping plan and power the electrified light-rail systems being built for the greater L.A. area. One line—the Blue Line, between L.A. and Long Beach—is already operating. Two more—the Green Line, between Norwalk and Los Angeles International Airport and the Red Line, between L.A. and North Hollywood—are under construction. Additional rail mass transit lines are under consideration.

Because Southern Californians commute long distances to work and face ever-increasing traffic congestion, the time is right for more commuter trains. There is some thought about powering them with diesel engines to achieve faster start-up of the projects. We believe these lines should be electrified at the outset. Diesel locomotives used today for freight and Amtrak operations in Southern California already contribute emissions equal to all of Edison's L.A. Basin power plants.

Two-thirds of smog in the Los Angeles Basin comes from automobiles. The other one-third comes from fixed sources—from Mom-and-Pop drycleaners to manufacturers to backyard barbecues. It is possible to reduce emissions from many of these sources with new advanced electric technologies. These electrically based technologies, or electrotechnologies, today can provide environmentally superior solutions to an array of industrial problems. They make more efficient use of primary energy resources, using less source-fuel energy to get the job done than the older technologies they replace.

Southern California Edison's "future" goes beyond Mr. Bryson's optimism over new markets. In 1991, the company issued their "No Regrets" CO_2 Management program, which it describes as follows:

On May 20, 1991 Southern California Edison Chairman John Bryson announced the adoption of an energy resource strategy that is designed to reduce carbon dioxide (CO_2) emissions by 10 percent over the next decade and will mitigate potential effects of global warming. SCE also announced the goal of an additional 10 percent reduction by the year 2010. This announcement was made jointly with officials of the Los Angeles Department of Water and Power (LADWP), who have adopted the same reduction goals using a similar resource strategy.

The development of our energy plan coincided with the release of a report by the National Academy of Sciences (*Policy Implications of Greenhouse Warming*, 1991) that concludes, "Despite the great uncertainties, greenhouse warming is a potential threat sufficient to justify action now." The NAS report states that greenhouse gas emissions reductions in the range of 10 to 40 percent are achievable at little or no cost.

Chairman Bryson stated, "The actions we are taking make sense environmentally, scientifically, and economically. Taking prudent steps to reduce CO_2 emissions today will ensure we'll have no regrets later."

* * * * * * *

We characterize this as a "no regrets" energy plan, meaning that Edison has developed a resource plan that emphasizes energy efficiency resulting in an environmentally sensitive and economically responsible resource acquisition program. This plan incorporates (1) energy efficiency, (2) renewable energy resources, (3) efficiency improvements in existing power plants, and (4) switching to lower carbon-based fuels.

* * * * * * *

In total, this plan is designed to reduce Edison's CO_2 emissions from the current 31.8 million tons/year to about 28.3 million tons/year by the year 2000, and in 2010 down to 25.9 million tons/year. These emissions reductions are expected to occur despite the fact that Edison will serve 12 million people in the year 2000, up from our current 10 million. By 2010, Edison will serve 14 million people.

In addition to these environmental benefits, we believe that the real success of our "No Regrets" CO_2 Management Program can be measured by our internal commitment to address the global warming issue and our leadership in the voluntary corporate management of CO_2 emissions.

■ ■ ■

One of the most vigorous proponents of a new environmental role for his company and the chemical industry is Frank Popoff, chairman and CEO of Dow. Here is how he describes, in his own words, what lies ahead.

243

The Dow Chemical Company *(by Frank Popoff, chairman and CEO)*

The future of the chemical industry and The Dow Chemical Company depends on the strong commitment to protection of the environment as this complex global concern takes center stage in the 1990s. However, in this era of keen environmental consciousness, when perception is the most important reality, it's no longer enough to have a strong commitment to environmental quality or to do good work. To succeed in the next decade and beyond, we must be publicly accountable and publicly visible.

In the 1970s, just when we were beginning to understand and make some tangible contributions to environmental quality, our industry and our company adopted the attitude that what went on within our fences was nobody's business but ours. In the name of protecting our proprietary interests, we shrouded ourselves in a veil of secrecy. The public saw this as a sure sign that we had something to hide. People didn't really care how much we knew—they just wanted to know how much we cared, and they wanted to see evidence of action on our part.

In the 1980s, our arrogance became tempered by increasing public concern and seasoned by an open exchange of data with regulatory agencies. By the 1990s, we were encouraging and empowering all our employees to be practicing environmentalists through waste reduction incentives and technology innovation. Today, I think that we have made genuine progress in the eyes of the public. But there's always more to do.

We must emphasize continuous improvement in our environmental performance while communicating with our many audiences. Our objective is to be and be seen as part of the solution to the world's environmental problems by working in cooperation with everybody concerned—and that means everyone. There's a great deal that we still don't know, and claims and counterclaims abound, but we intend to keep working toward meaningful dialogue with all who will come to the table. And that table now stretches around the world. Our industries are global. Our problems are global. Our critics are global. So our priorities must be global.

So where do we go from here? We must campaign on three fronts. We need collective action, first, *as individuals* and as individual

244

enterprises, second, *as units,*—industry associations in particular, and third, *as partnerships*—the broader the better. For Dow, this means being one of the leaders in ushering in a new era of cooperation on environmental issues. And cooperation is emerging as the system of the future, the process leading to change.

At Dow, we are forging effective partnerships and working relationships with all parties who sincerely want both a better living standard and a better environment. One unique partnership, for example, involves the private sector and conservation groups with federal and state interests to conserve wetland habitat areas in the United States, Canada, and Mexico.

To win the hearts and minds of people in all countries, we know we must be "up front" and "out in front" on the great environmental issues ahead. And above all else, we must continue to demonstrate not just compliance, but leadership beyond compliance.

■ ■ ■

What are the common threads in the future that participating companies see?

- *A belief that industry participation and enterprise is essential to achieving global sustainable development.*
- *Learning from each other and continuous improvement toward the ideal of eliminating pollution.*
- *An increase in partnerships with environmentalists and others, including governments, to communicate and to solve environmental problems.*
- *An understanding that multi-national corporations must facilitate the diffusion of good technology to less-developed regions.*
- *A desire to see voluntary action supplant regulations, while recognizing the need for public accountability.*
- *A belief that a strong environmental effort is a long-term competitive necessity and, in some cases, the avenue to new business opportunities.*

XIII.
AFTERTHOUGHTS

The preceding chapters include many specific insights or conclusions a reader might draw from the material presented. It does not seem necessary to summarize all of those editorial comments here. However, ruminating on what the company stories are telling us prompted some thoughts worth sharing.

Most Major Changes are Very Recent

While several company reports stressed many years of attention to environmental matters, the high level of commitment seen today is clearly of recent vintage. As noted earlier, a large number of respondents pointed to events of the 1980s—the accident at Bhopal, the Exxon Valdez oil spill, the release of SARA Title III Data—and the pressures arising from them as major stimuli for change. Quite a few followed on with new company policies, organizational restructuring, and more aggressive pollution-prevention programs in the late 1980s or early 1990s. The operating results of these changes in corporate approach—in the form of reduced emissions and lessened environmental impact—are still not generally visible in many cases.

Perceptions of Corporate Environmental Progress Vary

Most managements of participating companies are presently trying to instill a new corporate culture in their enterprises—one that includes an environmental ethic as part of the group of intangible values that have traditionally included *health* and *safety* and, more recently, *quality*. Several indicate that the need for a new environmental attitude is more easily accepted by senior management and younger workers than it is by experienced middle-level employees who may remain a reservoir of old ways of thinking or, perhaps, skeptical about whether management "really means it." These people, after all, are veterans of past confrontations with environmental critics and well-indoctrinated in any past company policies of resistance or reluctant compliance.

The newness of a company's more positive environmental stance, and its as-yet-incomplete acceptance by all employees, can lead to a divergence between what senior executives see as their environmental progress and what outside observers conclude the companies are, in fact, doing. For example, a chief executive who has made public commitments to a new environmental approach, reorganized his company to implement it, approved programs and capital expenditures for better environmental technologies or remediation, and made environmental speeches for a couple of years inside and outside the company is likely to believe sincerely that his (or her) firm is on a new path of which it can be proud. In his view, it is doing the right thing, and should be so perceived, even if the job is only partially complete.

On the other hand, outside critics are naturally wary of words, and so far that may be all they have to go on. Company programs are often too new to have had much demonstrable effect. Capital projects may take two or three years from conception and funding to operation. Official emissions data are not available for several months following the calendar year they cover. Financial, technical, and human resource limitations prevent companies from attacking every problem first. Unexpected new threats may be discovered as older ones are brought under control. And so there may as yet be few or even no tangible improvements to show for changes recently set in motion. Distinguishing between hypocrisy and the beginnings of real change requires great wisdom.

For all these reasons, the actions that are convincingly real to the chief executive may be dismissed as corporate "hype" by citizens' groups. If a member of such a group also has a friend among the company's unconverted employees, his or her suspicions may be "confirmed" by disparaging comments from what seems to be "the horse's mouth." One executive had it right when he said, "Don't trust us, track us," but that takes time and some means of independently verifying results.

Communicating Credibly is Difficult

Meanwhile, a number of companies report frustration that their efforts to communicate their new environmental policies do not seem to be terribly convincing to the public at large. What to communicate, when, to what audiences, and by what media clearly present companies with challenges vastly different from those customarily met in selling products. In this area, companies have had more to say about the problem than about successful solutions.

Much work obviously lies in front of companies, their communications consultants, and the advertising agencies that represent them if their stories are to be credible. "Listening" is mentioned occasionally, but the value of saying "I'm sorry" not at all. Whether such an attitude is the result of legal advice or corporate pride is unclear, but it is in any event a barrier to credible communication with critics.

Some companies cling to the belief that a command of the scientific facts can "prove" their rectitude and are frustrated when it does not. In taking this position, they overlook human nature. Most citizens do not want to—or cannot—make scientific judgments. Much more convincing to them is corporate recognition of their fears, a sincere effort to deal with the causes, and, thus, the establishment of emotional common ground. Yet, sound science is necessary as a basis for policy formulation if the public interest is truly to be served. It may not be the only thing, but it is important to both companies and their critics.

Until communications intermediaries really understand what the environmental community, citizens, and committed company leaders are saying, their messages may continue to sound superficial and unconvincing, or worse yet, false and hollow. For the environmentally aware company, "greening" Madison Avenue may become a high priority. Peter Sandman's thoughtful words of advice in the chapter "Beyond Corporate Walls," may be very difficult for companies to follow, but they are worth heeding nonetheless.

Cooperative Efforts May Be Easier Locally than Nationally

A counterpoint to the problems just mentioned is the apparent success several companies have had in establishing relationships with citizen groups in communities where plants are located. This is clearly a step worth emulating widely, and one from which much can be learned.

Getting positive results in a local situation may be relatively easy, however, compared to national or international cooperative effort. Nearby citizens usually have a positive stake in a local plant. It provides jobs, directly or indirectly, to many of their families and neighbors. Its managers may be friends of long standing, local civic leaders, or contributors to local causes. And the existence of the plant is a fact of life. It is there.

The aim of the citizen group is to retain the plants' benefits while reducing its real or apparent threat or unpleasantness—a goal quite similar to that of the plant manager. So common ground is not only literally underfoot, but within close reach in a figurative sense. But all bets may be off if the local community is already frightened and has closed ranks against the company. The trick is preventive medicine. Begin dialogue before a crisis hits.

Establishing cooperative efforts with outsiders on a national or global level may prove more difficult. Unlike management and citizens in plant communities, it is harder for companies and environmental critics to recognize their mutual interdependence on a national or international basis. Off-the-job personal friendships are less likely to exist. Critics do not depend on the company for their economic well-being. Ideological, political, and cultural differences may be impediments. In extreme cases, each side may get psychic satisfaction out of casting the other as a villain and suffer from a sense of ideological impurity when considering compromise.

Yet, the good that can result for society through more open, constructive, and conciliatory dialogue between companies and environmental and other citizen groups is immense. It is important that both corporations and their critics see the concept of sustainable development as their common ground and that in their interactions they pay at least as much attention to shared values and objectives as they do to differing viewpoints. If a desire for cooperation between environmentalists and industry could take deep root in both camps, replacing fault-finding, punishment, and defensive attitudes with a focus on results, even the resource-consuming Superfund process might be improved. These stories encourage us to believe that a number of companies, environmentalists, and citizen groups are taking steps toward this type of cooperative venture.

Economic Benefits are Becoming More Widely Recognized

Several companies recognized the economic advantages of a forward-looking environmental policy, stressing that pollution is waste and waste represents an unnecessary cost. Some went further, describing their efforts as a preemptive strike against future end-of-the-pipe equipment investments, unpredictable liabilities, or new and burdensome regulation. Others mentioned the positive effect on employee recruitment and attitude, host community acceptance, and green consumers and investors that an environmentally responsible reputation can provide. A few identified new business opportunities based on what they were learning. Most thus saw their new or increased attention to the environment as a competitive plus, perhaps even a competitive necessity.

Effect of Environmental Initiatives on Trade is Not Emphasized

Interestingly, only one company even hinted that its added costs might be a handicap in international trade. This came as a surprise given the attention now being paid to that aspect of the environmental movement by government and the media.

Perhaps the companies represented in this book are less vulnerable than other industries—copper comes to mind—might be. Producers and users of CFCs can expect, because of the Montreal Protocol, that all their competitors will have to eliminate these chemicals too. Doing so promptly may represent an advantageous head start. The chemical industry is seeking globally harmonized environmental practices through its Responsible Care program. Packaged goods producers tend to manufacture their products in the countries in which they market, and, like local competitors, can tailor local specifications to local needs. Power generators, serving discrete areas, usually enjoy predictable (though regulated) pricing, to some extent free from competition with less responsibly produced alternatives.

Finally, many companies report that their new environmental approaches may actually confer a competitive advantage, with total

251

benefits out-weighing costs over the long run. For the participating companies up-front environmental costs may not be heavy competitive millstones.

Harvard Business School Professor Michael Porter, writing in the April 1991 issue of *Scientific American,* comes to a similar conclusion empirically when he states:

> "The strongest proof that environmental protection does not hamper competitiveness is the economic performance of nations with the strictest laws. Both Germany and Japan have tough regulations. In America, many of the sectors subject to the greatest environmental costs have actually improved their trade performance, among them chemicals, plastics, and paints. Japan has become a world leader in developing pollution control equipment and cleaner, more efficient processes."

If the above suppositions are correct, they may also point to at least some of the ways that other industries might find to reduce any competitive disadvantage stemming from environmental improvement. Possibilities include harmonizing global environmental expectations for a whole industry, as in the case of Responsible Care, or incorporation of environmental criteria based on scientific knowledge into the GATT or separately by means of Montreal Protocol-type agreements. Consider, for example, what a commitment by developed-country automakers to license, or manufacture and sell only low-emission vehicles, worldwide, could eventually do for air quality in the developing nations' cities.

Some Regulatory Reflections

It is no surprise that several companies (like a number of other groups) are dissatisfied with the current state of environmental regulations, considering many of them cost-inefficient and inhibiting to innovation. While some companies hope to replace them with voluntary measures, this tack seems politically unrealistic and would probably not achieve environmental goals, though voluntary effort to improve conditions in unregulated fields can be valuable.

The plea for regulations that call for specific end results without prescribing methods seems much better justified. But an effort to overhaul the regulatory system, initiated by industry alone, is not likely to succeed since many environmental watchdogs will view it as an effort to "get off the hook." Taken up in conjunction with environmental groups, however, starting with joint agreement on objectives and building on the success of voluntary initiatives such as EPA's 33/50 program, regulatory overhaul might succeed.

Financial Instruments Were Not Widely Endorsed

Respondents paid only slight attention to the merits of government-sponsored financial instruments (fees, taxes, offsets and subsidies) in influencing environmental behavior. Apart from companies involved in power generation, which have accepted such techniques, only limited attention was given to such tools as offsets (Unocal and 3M) and "economic instruments" (The ICC Charter and Monsanto). Weyerhaeuser, for example, did not comment on below-cost sales of government timber, though such subsidies damage both the environment and large private timber owners such as itself. And only Shell, a European-based company, brought up the touchy subject of environmental taxes.

This reticence by American firms is understandable but perhaps short-sighted. American industry has been conditioned to believe that any new tax is an added tax. But the use of economic measures to conserve energy in the power-generation industry, tradeable emissions permits, and the new CFC taxes all promise greater efficiency in obtaining environmental results than would added layers of regulation. Policy research on how these concepts are actually faring might give industry more heart to look positively at a new revenue-neutral tax structure that penalized "bads" (such as emissions) in exchange for lower levies on "goods" (such as profits, savings, and employment).

The Roles of Science, Economics and Risk Analysis

Although the subject was not ignored, few participating companies stressed scientific and economic realities and the importance of comparing benefits with the costs of obtaining them. Admittedly, this concept verges on anathema to those who view the capitalist system—or its agents, the corporations—as inherently anti-social,

253

or to those who contend that involuntary risks must be eliminated without regard for cost. Yet, it seems indisputably true that society has many problems to face (not all of them environmental) and finite resources with which to do so.

As in any human endeavor, this calls for an assessment of both needs and means. Here, the conventional corporate approach to decision-making has great merit, provided environmental and other social concerns are given proper weight—an issue progressive companies must address. Once they have developed a way to weigh alternatives, preferably in consultation with outsiders, they deserve support in tackling the most pressing problems first and tolerance for leaving until later those of lower priority.

Pressure to do everything at once can only lead to confusion and a waste of society's resources, ending in less environmental improvement than could be achieved by a more systematic and analytical approach. EPA's recent effort to prioritize environmental issues and to compare the views of scientists with those of the general public is a helpful step. To be fully effective, however, it must go hand in hand with an effort to understand and deal with public fears and outrage.

Property Rights

This subject was left untouched by the respondents. Free markets are predicated on property ownership and the right of owners, as buyers and sellers (subject to some limits imposed by governments in society's interest), to exchange goods and services freely. Prices reflect supply and demand, and they rise to discourage overuse of scarce resources and to stimulate the search for cheaper substitutes.

Unfortunately, many environmental services, such as the use of land, water, and air as dumping grounds for waste, or biodiversity's genetic warehouse, are "unowned" and, therefore, unpriced. Since they seem then to be "free," they are overused, with no disciplinary mechanism, such as rising prices, in place to protect them.

Similarly, natural assets that must endure indefinitely— especially land—are often exploited by current "owners" without regard for the needs of the unborn successors to their fee title, or of those who will depend in the future on the services the land

254

provides. Policy researchers need to seek options for establishing ownership and value of the resources of the global commons, and for evaluating the benefits accruing to future generations, using lower discount rates than those normally applied by people looking only at their own lifetimes.

These difficult international and intergenerational questions of ownership and equity, and the political debates they raise, pose obstacles that must be overcome on the way to sustainable development. To the extent they can be factored into industry's cost and price calculations, they will be addressed far more efficiently than if they must be brought under control by empirical regulation arrived at by political give and take.

A Broader Perspective Will be Needed

Few companies mentioned poverty or population growth among their concerns. Their view of environmental problems tends to be limited to the immediate impact of their own products and processes, and most worry mainly about conditions in the home country. This is understandable, but in the longer term a broader vision is needed to carry the day.

> I've not heard many corporate CEOs speak out on the need to restructure the global energy economy, or to limit the number of children per couple to two, for example. They are prepared to think about how they might reduce pollution at their factories. But not anything more fundamental than that, in many cases.
>
> ■ *Lester Brown, Director,*
> *Worldwatch Institute*
>
> (from "Watching the World Environment," Claes Sjoberg, Tomorrow Magazine, vol. 1, no. 1, 1991

Global problems will require global, not national, responses. Industry has much to contribute to overcoming poverty in developing countries, and much to gain by doing so. Multinational companies should be prime agents of technology cooperation and diffusion, as well as beneficiaries of growing markets in a developing world.

Restraint of population growth through family planning can be aided by new industry-developed technologies. Yet, few (if any) United States pharmaceutical firms are doing any research on new contraceptive technologies—an example of how a globally preeminent U.S. industry can be chilled into inaction by fear of tort liability and political opposition from family planning opponents.

These matters, too, provide opportunities for policy research to help unlock industry's potential for addressing a vital environmental problem. We would expect the widening environmental perceptions of business leaders to eventually embrace the holistic views now typical of environmental thinkers.

Surprisingly little attention was paid to industrial environmental problems abroad by the several participating companies that do a great deal of their business outside the United States. A number of reasons may explain this domestic focus. Environmental groups are perhaps more aggressive and well organized in the United States and Canada than elsewhere, and responding to them captures a company's full attention. The U.S. legislative, regulatory, and judicial climate is more adversarial and poses greater immediate threats. U.S. public attitudes may be more demanding. U.S.-based companies have less ability to influence foreign legislation, and so spend less time reacting to it.

Managers of such companies, no matter how international their business, tend to hail from the headquarters country, and so think principally in terms of its political environment. In this regard, Shell differs, especially in its approach to planning, and seems to set a standard for how all multi-nationals will eventually need to look at their environmental future. As American companies broaden their environmental horizons beyond national concerns and the rhetoric of "similar standards worldwide," their ability to diffuse the best of their practices will be similarly enhanced. Only then will industry be positioned to contribute its full share to global sustainable development.

Education and Leadership Will Continue to be Critical

Educational initiatives like those of Allied-Signal and Tufts University can play an important long-term role in environmental progress, and further industry support of such programs seems well justified. To these efforts might be added mid-career environmental management courses along the lines of those offered in general business management by Harvard, M.I.T., and others.

Continued movement toward sustainable development depends heavily on the ongoing engagement of the leading companies and their CEOs. Besides supporting what is already apparently under way, CEO leadership is necessary to incorporate environmental factors fully into corporate strategic plans, to forge cooperative links with national and international environmental groups, and to work with like-minded citizens and public officials to develop a framework of effective environmental policies on both a national and a multilateral basis. They can expect continued public and environmentalist pressure to hasten their efforts.

Equally important is the leadership of committed CEOs in persuading less aware peers to join in the march, to energize trade associations, and to persuade reluctant governments that attention to environmental protection will be economically and politically beneficial, not damaging. The environmentally progressive CEO will have no time to rest on his—or her—oars.

At the End of the Rainbow

Business leadership has often been assailed as being self-interested or greedy, much to the distress of many socially responsible businessmen. Yet, often a dedication to the principal *social* mission of business—to use resources efficiently to produce valued goods and services—measured by success in achieving long-term growth and profit—reinforces that stereotype.

Doing right by the environment, bringing the world's economic activity into harmony with its ecological system, is a vital challenge that few but business leaders can really meet. It is a chance for them to leave the black chapeau at the hat check counter and pick up a white one instead. It is a chance to initiate the good instead of react defensively to the bad. It is a chance to leave the world a better place for all our grandchildren. Our participating companies report they are taking up the task. We wish them well in its accomplishment—and we will be tracking how they do with interest.

■ ■ ■

APPENDICES

Appendix 1
Participating Contributors

The AES Corporation
Roger Sant, Chairman and Chief Executive Officer
Allied-Signal, Inc.
Jonathan Plaut, Director, Environmental Compliance
American International Group
Maurice Greenberg, Chairman and Chief Executive Officer
AT&T
David Chittick, Vice President, Environment and Safety Engineering
Tom Davis, Manager E&S Engineering Affairs
Bank of America
Richard Morrison, Senior Vice President
Briggs Nursery, Inc.
Bruce Briggs, Chairman
James Robbins, Research/Education Manager
Chevron Corporation
Kenneth Derr, Chairman and Chief Executive Officer
Dennis Bonney, Vice Chairman
William Crain, Vice President & Director
Rod Hartung, Vice President
Bill Mulligan, Manager, Health, Environment & Loss Prevention
Dixon Smith, General Manager for Strategic Planning and Business Evaluation
Jay Stuller, Senior Editor, Public Affairs Department
The Dow Chemical Company
Frank Popoff, Chairman and Chief Executive Officer
David Buzzelli, Vice President, Environment, Health and Safety

Pat Brink, *Environmental Issues Communication Manager*
Du Pont
Edgar S. Woolard, Jr., *Chairman and Chief Executive Officer*
Bruce Karrh, *Vice President, Safety, Health and Environmental Affairs*
Justin Carisio, *Executive Writer*
Friends of the Earth
Brent Blackwelder, *Acting President*
International Chamber of Commerce
Nigel Blackburn, *Director*
S.C. Johnson Wax, Inc.
Samuel C. Johnson, *Chairman*
Jane Hutterly, *Director of Environmental Actions—Worldwide*
3M
Robert Bringer, *Staff Vice President, Environmental Engineering and Pollution Control*
Thomas Zosel, *Manager, Pollution Prevention Programs*
Monsanto
Nicholas Reding, *Executive Vice President*
Mike Pierle, *Vice President*
Diane Bartolanzo, *Manager, Public Relations*
Donald L. Meade, *Community Affairs Superintendent*
National Wildlife Federation
Jay D. Hair, *President*
New England Electric System
John Rowe, *President and Chief Executive Officer*
Jeffrey Tranen, *Vice President*
Northern Telecom
Margaret Kerr, *Vice President*
Pacific Gas and Electric Company
Grant Horne, *Vice President, Corporate Communications*
Diane Fong
The Procter & Gamble Company
Edward L. Artzt, *Chairman and Chief Executive Officer*
Royal Dutch/Shell Group
Richard Tookey, *Director of Shell International Petroleum Company*
Peter Bright, *Head of Environmental Issues, Group Public Affairs, Shell International Petroleum Company*
Adam Kahane, *Head of Socio-Political, Economic and Technological Studies in Group Planning*

Skadden, Arps, Slate, Meagher & Flom
James A. Rogers, Esq., Partner
Southern California Edison
John Bryson, Chairman and Chief Executive Officer
Charles McCarthy, Senior Vice President
William Ostrander, Manager of Environmental Services
TransAlta Utilities
Ken McCready, President and Chief Executive Officer
Tufts University
Anthony Cortese, Dean of Environmental Programs
United Technologies
Robert F. Daniell, Chairman and Chief Executive Officer
Unocal
Barry Lane, Manager, Public Relations
Weyerhaeuser
George Weyerhaeuser, Chairman
Richard K. Long, Vice President, Corporate Communications
Donna Brown, Director of Communications
Xerox Corporation
James Mackenzie, Director, Environmental Health and Safety
Art Zuckerman, Manager, Public Relations Programs
Abhay Bhushan, Manager, Environmental Leadership Programs
Zytec Corporation
Ron Schmidt, President and Chief Executive Officer
John Dudek, Value Analysis Manager

Appendix 2

Corporate Profiles

The AES Corporation*

Annual Revenue:	$190 million
Employees:	440
Headquarters:	1001 North 19th Street
	Arlington, VA 22209
Business:	Operates 4 electric power plants co-generating energy for sale to utilities.

Environmental Recognition

Corporate
- 1988 *Power Magazine* Environmental Protection Award for "success in using waste material as an energy source"
- 1989 Council on Economic Priorities America's Corporate Conscience Award for Environmental Responsibility

Individual
- Roger W. Sant, Chairman of the Board and Chief Executive of AES is Vice-Chairman of the Board of the World Resources Institute, a member of the Boards of the Environmental and Energy Study Institute, and the World Wildlife Fund, and a member of the National Council of the Environmental Defense Fund

Allied-Signal, Inc.

Annual Revenue:	$12,300 million
Employees:	105,800
Headquarters:	P.O. Box 4000
	Morristown, NJ 07962
Business:	Diversified multinational manufacturer of aerospace and automotive products and chemical and engineered materials.

---

*WRI Supporter, FY 91 and/or 92.

Environmental Recognition

Corporate
- 1980 Touche-Ross Award for Environmental Excellence
- 1988 Allied-Signal Program of Environmental Excellence featured in UNEP *Industry and Environment* Journal
- 1991 The President's Environment and Conservation Challenge Award for Education and Communications

AT&T*

Annual Revenue:	$37,300 million
Employees:	323,700
Headquarters:	550 Madison Avenue New York, NY 10022
Business:	Information movement and management; provides telecommunications and computer products, systems and services.

Environmental Recognition

Corporate
- 1990 Council on Economic Priorities Corporate Conscience Award for CFC reduction program
- 1991 New Jersey Governor's Award for Outstanding Achievement in Pollution Prevention for low solids fluxer work
- 1991 U.S. EPA Administrator's Award (Region II) for corporate recycling program
- 1991 National Environmental Development Association Honor Roll Award for CFC reduction program
- 1991 National Association for Environmental Management Environmental Excellence Award for CFC reduction program
- 1991 President's Environment and Conservation Challenge Awards citation for CFC reduction program

American International Group

Annual Revenue: $10,200 million
Employees: 34,000
Headquarters: 70 Pine Street
      New York, NY 10270
Business: Insurance

Environmental Recognition

Individual
- Maurice R. Greenberg, Chairman and CEO, is a member of the Business Council on Sustainable Development

Bank of America

Total Assets: $96,000 million
Employees: 68,000
Headquarters: 555 California Street
      San Francisco, CA 94104
Business: Commercial banking

Environmental Recognition

Corporate
- 1991 Citation—President's Environmental Challenge Award

Briggs Nursery, Inc.

Annual Revenue: Not available (privately owned company)
Employees: 150
Headquarters: 4407 Henderson Boulevard
      Olympia, WA 98501
Business: Wholesale nursery

Environmental Recognition

Corporate
- Briggs Nursery's environmental efforts have been cited in a number of trade publications, including, *Balls and Burlaps* and *Greenhouse Grower*

Chevron Corporation*

Annual Revenue:	$42,000 million
Employees:	54,000
Headquarters:	225 Bush Street
	San Francisco, CA 94104
Business:	Exploration and development of crude oil and natural gas reserves, operation of refineries, and marketing petroleum products; manufacture of petrochemicals; mining of coal.

Environmental Recognition

Corporate
- 1987 The Izaak Walton League's Clean Water Award (Pascagoula Refinery)
- 1988 National Institute for Urban Wildlife's Distinguished Conservation Award
- 1989 Renew America's Environmental Achievement Award
- 1990 The National Environmental Awards Council's Environmental Achievement Award

Individual
- Kenneth T. Derr, Chairman and CEO, is a member of the Business Council for Sustainable Development and the President's Commission on Environmental Quality

The Dow Chemical Company*

Annual Revenue:	$16,600 million
Employees:	62,100
Headquarters:	2030 Willard H. Dow Center
	Midland, MI 48674
Business:	Diversified manufacturer of chemicals, metals, plastics, agricultural products, pharmaceuticals and consumer products.

Environmental Recognition

Corporate
- 1989 World Environment Center Gold Medal for international corporate environmental achievement
- 1989 Electric Power Research Institute Innovative Technology Award for development of advanced coal gasification technology
- 1989 EPA Excellence Award for outstanding implementation of a hazardous waste program (Russellville, AK facility)
- 1990 Renew America Environmental Achievement Award for Dow's Waste Reduction Always Pays (WRAP) program
- 1990 Wildlife Habitat Enhancement Council certification for meeting high standards of wildlife protection (Joliet, IL and Granville, OH facilities)
- 1990 National Environmental Development Association Earth Day Honor Roll in recognition of WRAP program
- 1990 Michigan Audubon Society's Corporate Award for Dow's environmental commitment
- U.S. Occupational Safety and Health Administration Star Award for outstanding performance in the areas of employee health and safety (facilities in Louisiana, Texas and Arkansas)

Individual
- Frank Popoff, President and Chief Executive is a member of the Business Council for Sustainable Development and the President's Commission on Environmental Quality

Du Pont*

Annual Revenue:	$30,000 million
Employees:	140,000
Headquarters:	1007 Market Street
	Wilmington, DE 19898
Business:	Diversified chemicals, specialty products and energy company.

Environmental Recognition

Corporate
- 1987 World Environment Center Gold Medal for International Corporate Environmental Achievement
- 1990 Rene Dubos Environmental Award
- 1990 EPA Stratospheric Ozone Protection Award
- 1991 The Vision for America Award presented by Keep America Beautiful, Inc.

Individual
- Edgar S. Woolard, Jr., Chairman and CEO is a member of the Business Council for Sustainable Development

S.C. Johnson Wax, Inc.*

Annual Revenue:	Not available (privately owned company)
Employees:	14,000
Headquarters:	1525 Howe Street Racine, WI 53403
Business:	Manufacturer of chemical specialty products for home care, insect control and personal care.

Environmental Recognition

Corporate
- 1990 National Environmental Awards Council Certificate of Achievement
- 1990 State of Wisconsin Governor's Award for Energy Innovation
- 1990 U.S. Department of Energy Award for Energy Innovation
- 1991 World Packaging Organization International Worldstar Award
- 1991 American Forestry Association Global Releaf Award
- 1991 Environment Canada Environmental Achievement Award
- 1991 Wal-Mart Environmental Achiever Award
- 1991 U.S. EPA Region V Administrator's Award Program Certificate of Recognition for Excellence in Recycling

- 1991 Ontario Lieutenant Governor's Conservation Award
- 1991 President's Environment and Conservation Challenge Award

Individual
- Samuel C. Johnson, Chairman, is regent of the Smithsonian Institution and a member of its Executive Committee; a member of The Nature Conservancy International Advisory Committee and the Conservancy's National Board of Governors, and a member of the Business Council for Sustainable Development

3M

Annual Revenue:	$13,000 million
Employees:	89,600
Headquarters:	3M Center
	St. Paul, MN 55144
Business:	Diversified manufacturer of a wide variety of products, including pressure-sensitive adhesive tapes, specialty chemicals, magnetic recording products and health care products.

Environmental Recognition

Corporate
- 1984 World Environment Center Award for 3P Program
- 1985 Minnesota Governor's Award for outstanding environmental achievement
- 1988 Council on Economic Priorities Corporate Conscience Award
- 1989 National Wildlife Federation Corporate Conservation Council Environmental Achievement Award
- 1991 Citation Recipient—The President's Environment and Conservation Challenge Award
- 1991 EPA Stratospheric Ozone Protection Award

Individual
- Allen F. Jacobson, retired Chief Executive Officer is a member of the President's Commission on Environmental Quality and the Business Council for Sustainable Development

- Robert P. Bringer, Staff Vice President, Environmental Engineering and Pollution Control, is Chairman of the National Wildlife Federation's Corporate Conservation Council

Monsanto Company*

Annual Revenue:	$8,900 million
Employees:	41,000
Headquarters:	800 North Lindbergh Boulevard
	St. Louis, MO 63167
Business:	Manufacturer of chemicals, pharmaceuticals, agricultural products, man-made fibers, and plastics.

Environmental Recognition

Corporate
- 1985–88 Texas Water Commission Exemplary Plant awarded to Monsanto's Chocolate Bayou plant
- 1989–90 Reclamation Excellence Award for reclamation of land at company's phosphorus mine in Idaho
- 1990 Environment Foundation Commendation for performance at Ruabon, Wales plant
- 1990 National Resources Conservation Society Conservationist of the Year Award for wildlife programs at Columbia, Tennessee site
- 1990 Iowa Lung Association award for emission reductions at Muscatine, Iowa plant
- 1991 Renew America Environmental Achievement Award for wildlife enhancement programs at Columbia, Tennessee site

New England Electric System

Annual Revenue:	$1,900 million
Employees:	6,000
Headquarters:	25 Research Drive
	Westborough, MA 01583

Business: Public electric utility holding company. Subsidiaries include three retail operating companies, two wholesale generating companies, and three transmission service companies.

Environmental Recognition

Individual
- John W. Rowe, President and CEO is a director of the Environmental and Energy Study Institute, and the Alliance to Save Energy; he is also a member of the Clean Air Act Advisory Committee

Northern Telecom Limited
Annual Revenue: $6,800 million
Employees: 60,000
Headquarters: 3 Robert Speck Parkway
                 Mississauga, Ontario L4Z 3C8 Canada
Business: Manufacturer and supplier of telecommunications equipment.

Environmental Recognition

Corporate
- 1991 U.S. EPA Stratospheric Ozone Protection Award

Individual
- Paul G. Stern, Chairman and CEO, is a member of the Business Council for Sustainable Development

Pacific Gas & Electric Company
Annual Revenue: $9,500 million
Employees: 26,200
Headquarters: 77 Beale Street
                 San Francisco, CA 94106
Business: Public utility supplying electric and natural gas service.

Environmental Recognition

Corporate
  - 1990 Renew America Environmental Achievement Award
  - 1990 State of California Environmental Affairs Agency Air Pollution Reduction Award
  - 1991 Renew America Environmental Achievement Award and Environmental Success Index
  - 1991 National Institute for Urban Wildlife Outstanding Conservation Award
  - 1991 California Council, American Institute of Architects' Presidential Citation (energy conservation standards through planning and design)
  - 1991 President's Environmental Challenge Award—Environmental Quality Management
  - 1991 National Wildlife Federation's Corporate Conservation Council Environmental Achievement Award

The Procter & Gamble Company
Annual Revenue: $24,100 million
Employees: 89,000
Headquarters: One Procter & Gamble Plaza
                 Cincinnati, OH 45202
Business: Manufactures household and personal care products.

Environmental Recognition

Corporate
  - 1990 Family Circle Green Chip Award
  - 1990 Keep America Beautiful Visions for America Award
  - 1991 Council on Economic Priorities Honor Roll of companies recognized for social/environmental responsibility
  - 1992 World Environment Center Gold Medal for International Corporate Environmental Achievement

Individual
  - Edwin L. Artzt, Chairman and CEO, is a member of the President's Commission on Environmental Quality

271

Royal Dutch/Shell Group of Companies*

Annual Revenue:	$106,000 million
Employees:	137,000
Headquarters:	30 Carel van Bylandtlaan
	2596 HR The Hague, The Netherlands
Business:	Exploration, production and processing of oil and natural gas; marketing of petroleum-derived products.

Environmental Recognition

Corporate
- 1989 Alaska Outer Continental Shelf Region of the Minerals Management Service Conservation Award for Respecting the Environment
- 1990 U.S. Department of the Interior Minerals Management Service Gulf of Mexico Outer Continental Shelf Region Conservation Award for Respecting the Environment
- 1990 U.S. Department of the Interior Minerals Management Service Conservation Award for Respecting the Environment
- 1991 U.S. Department of the Interior Bureau of Land Management Partners in the Public Spirit Award for protection of public lands

Individual
- Lo van Wachem, President of Royal Dutch Petroleum Company and Senior Group Managing Director is a member of the Business Council for Sustainable Development
- Sir Peter Holmes, Chairman of the Shell Transport and Trading Company is a member of the Advisory Council of Worldwide Fund for Nature U.K.
- John Collins, Chairman and Chief Executive of Shell U.K. is Chairman of the U.K. Government's Advisory Committee on Business and the Environment

Southern California Edison Company

Sales:	$6,500 million
Employees:	17,000
Headquarters:	2244 Walnut Grove Avenue
	Rosemead, CA 91770
Business:	Public electric utility

Environmental Recognition

Corporate
- 1981 John and Alice Tyler Ecology Award for commitment to alternative and renewable energy
- 1989 National Institute for Urban Wildlife Outstanding Conservation Award
- 1990 U.S. Department of Energy ''Energy Innovation'' Award
- 1991 South Coast Air Quality Management District Clean Air Award
- 1991 Citation Recipient—The President's Environment and Conservation Challenge Award

Individual
- John Bryson, Chief Executive Officer of Southern California Edison is a member of the Boards of Directors of the World Resources Institute and California Environmental Trust, and a member of the National Commission on the Environment.

TransAlta Utilities

Total Revenue:	$1,068 million
Employees:	2,600
Headquarters:	110 12th Avenue, S.W.
	Calgary, Alberta T2P 2M1 Canada
Business:	Public electric utility

Environmental Recognition

Corporate
- 1990 Alberta Chamber of Resources Reclamation Award

273

Individual
- Ken F. McCready, President and Chief Executive Officer is a member of the Business Council for Sustainable Development and Chairman of the Alberta Roundtable on Environment and Economy

United Technologies, Inc.

Annual Revenue:	$21,700 million
Employees:	192,600
Headquarters:	United Technologies Building Hartford, CT 06101
Business:	Diversified manufacturer of aerospace and defense, building and automotive products, systems and services.

Unocal Corporation

Annual Revenue:	$10,000 million
Employees:	17,500
Headquarters:	1201 West Fifth Street Los Angeles, CA 90017
Business:	Exploration and production of crude oil and natural gas; manufactures petroleum products, chemicals and fertilizers.

Environmental Recognition

Corporate
- 1991 Citation from the Los Angeles County Board of Supervisors (for SCRAP program)
- 1991 Izaak Walton League Honor Roll Award (for SCRAP program)
- 1991 Society of Consumer Affairs Professionals in Business Outstanding Program Award (for SCRAP program)

Weyerhaeuser Company

Annual Revenue:	$9,000 million
Employees:	40,600
Headquarters:	33663 32nd Avenue South Federal Way, WA 98003

Business: Grows and harvests timber and manufactures forest products.

Environmental Recognition

Corporate
- 1983–91 Appeared on *Fortune* Magazine list of "Most Admired Companies" (included criteria for responsibility to community and environment)
- 1991 Rocky Mountain Elk Foundation Corporate Citizen of the Year Award

Individual
- Charles W. Bingham, Executive Vice President is Vice President of the Board of the Mountains to Sound Greenway Trust
- John P. McMahon, Vice President for Timberland External and Regulatory Affairs serves on the Board of the Washington Chapter of the Nature Conservancy

Xerox Corporation

Annual Revenue: $17,900 million
Employees: 110,000
Headquarters: P.O. Box 1600
Stamford, CT 06904
Business: Manufactures document processing products and systems.

Environmental Recognition

Corporate
- 1988 National Energy Resources Organization Energy Conservation Award
- 1989 U.K. Secretary of State for the Environment Business and Industry Commitment to the Environment Award
- 1989 Malcolm Baldrige National Quality Award (and between 1986–90 national quality awards from the governments of Mexico, the Netherlands, Canada, France and the U.K.)

275

- 1991 The Institute of Packaging, U.K., Silver Star Starpack 91 Award

Zytec Corporation

Annual Revenue: $50 million
Employees: 750
Headquarters: 1425 East Bridge Street
Redwood Falls, MN 56283
Business: Designs and manufactures electronic power supplies for equipment manufacturers of computers and electronic office, medical and testing equipment.

Environmental Recognition

Corporate
- 1991 Minnesota Quality Award
- 1991 Malcolm Baldrige National Quality Award

Appendix 3

Bank of America has developed a sophisticated control system which breaks down its environmental improvement program into individual tasks, assigns responsibility for their accomplishment, and reports progress towards scheduled completion dates. The entire report covers four areas or "Themes":

- *Theme #1: Environmental Practices*
- *Theme #2: Consumption & Recycling*
- *Theme #3: Water*
- *Theme #4: Forests*

Their 1991 Midyear Report for Theme #1 is reproduced below to illustrate the technique.

Bank of America *(as submitted by Richard Morrison, senior vice president)*

Environmental Principles
Goals and Action Steps
1991
Mid Year Report

Theme #1—Environmental Practices
Develop policies and procedures that encourage responsible environmental activities of borrowers and suppliers and discourage borrowers and suppliers that treat the environment irresponsibly; ensure BAC's own environmental activities are exemplary; encourage employees and customers to adopt sound environmental practices.

Goals

1) Implement credit policy that add an environmental element to loan decisions.

Action Steps

a) Distribute environmental credit policy (Dorfman). 1st Qtr. POLICY DISTRIBUTED.

277

GUIDELINES FOR ADMINISTRATION OF CREDIT POLICY ARE BEING DRAFTED AND SHOULD BE DISTRIBUTED 3RD QTR.

b) Establish lines of communication for consultation on environmental matters with each division credit administration (Morrison). 1st Qtr.
CONTACTS ESTABLISHED WITH EACH GROUP SENIOR CREDIT OFFICER. ACCOUNT OFFICERS HAVE BEGUN CONSULTING ON ENVIRONMENTALLY SENSITIVE ISSUES, ESPECIALLY PROJECT FINANCING AND TIMBER RELATED CREDITS IN THE PACIFIC NORTHWEST.

2) Identify environmentally oriented industries that present lending opportunities, especially those where Bank of America can play a catalyst role in building the industry.

Action Steps

a) Investigate creation of Environmental unit as part of Industries Specialties Group (Sacasa). 2nd Qtr.
U.S. DIVISION IS IN PROCESS OF ASSESSING ALTERNATIVES. SOME TYPE OF ENVIRONMENTAL INDUSTRY FOCUS LIKELY TO BE ESTABLISHED BY YEAR END.

b) Identify at least one industry segment representing a lending opportunity and develop marketing plans (Morrison). 4th Qtr.
EFFORTS TO DATE HAVE BEEN CONCENTRATED ON RECYCLING INDUSTRIES, ESPECIALLY MARKETS FOR MATERIALS COLLECTED THROUGH RECYCLING.

3) Work with State of California and Commercial Banking Division to develop a loan guarantee program to enable small businesses to clean up/prevent toxic wastes and install air pollution control equipment.

Action Steps

a) Develop recommended guarantee program and gain credit policy approval (Morrison). 2nd Qtr.
CONTACTS ESTABLISHED WITH SOUTH COAST AIR QUALITY MANAGEMENT DISTRICT AND CALIFORNIA

DEPARTMENT OF COMMERCE SMALL BUSINESS AD-
MINISTRATION. BOTH AGENCIES WILL PILOT DIRECT
LOAN PROGRAMS AND ARE BEGINNING TO DEVELOP
GUARANTEE PROGRAMS.

b) Support necessary state/federal legislation/regulation to enable
creation of program (Brown). 4th Qtr. N/A

4) Make periodic reports to Credit Policy on prevailing environmental issues related to specific industry groups.

Action Steps

a) Present briefing papers on the following subjects to Credit
Policy Committee (Henry):
   (i)   Lead   1st Qtr.
   (ii) Asbestos   2nd Qtr.
   (iii) Underground storage tanks   3rd Qtr.
   (iv) To be determined   4th Qtr.
   LEAD PAPER PRESENTED. ENVIRONMENTAL SERVICES
   EXPLORING WAYS IN WHICH A BANK POLICY PERTAIN-
   ING TO HOUSING FINANCING MIGHT BE IMPLE-
   MENTED, IF IT IS DECIDED TO ADOPT A POLICY.

   ASBESTOS PAPER REVIEWED BY VICE CHAIRMAN,
   CREDIT POLICY COMMITTEE. INFORMAL WORKING
   GROUP IN COMMERCIAL BANKING TO DEVELOP PROP-
   ERTY VALUATION GUIDELINES.

5) Establish purchasing policy to add environmental element to vendor and product selection.

Action Steps

a) Develop a policy statement applicable to all BAC suppliers
which will attempt to ensure environmental responsibility
(Lynch). 1st Qtr.
ACCOMPLISHED. LITERATURE PROVIDED TO ALL SUP-
PLIERS NOW STATES ENVIRONMENTAL RESPONSIBIL-
ITY WILL BE A FACTOR IN SELECTION.

b) Establish a certification program to ensure compliance with
the above policy (Lynch). 1st Qtr.

PILOT CERTIFICATION PROGRAM INITIATED WITH GREEN CROSS. FIRST CERTIFICATION EFFORTS ARE WITH ROCKY MOUNTAIN BANKNOTE, A MAJOR SUPPLIER. FULL PRODUCT CYCLE CERTIFICATION WILL ALSO INVOLVE CERTIFYING FOUR MAJOR PAPER MILL SUPPLIERS.

c) Evaluate with Corporate Real Estate and Human Resources purchases have an environmental element (Schikore/Cammidge). 4th Qtr.
EVALUATION PROCESS IN CRE WILL BE CENTERED AROUND NEW PURCHASING AND INVENTORY SYSTEMS THAT ARE UNDER DEVELOPMENT.

INTERIM COMPANY STORE CATALOG PUBLISHED WITH SOME NEW ENVIRONMENTAL ITEMS. NEW CATALOG TO BE PUBLISHED BY 4TH QUARTER WITH SPECIAL ENVIRONMENTAL SECTION.

OCCUPATIONAL HEALTH AND SAFETY REVIEW OF PURCHASES IS BEING CONDUCTED ON AN ONGOING BASIS BY CORPORATE SAFETY.

AWARDS FOR LENGTH OF SERVICE HAVE BEEN REVIEWED AND DETERMINED ENVIRONMENTALLY SOUND.

6) Ensure BAC disposes of waste through safe and responsible methods.

Action Steps

a) Identify all products being disposed of from our major distribution facilities (Lynch). 1st Qtr.
EXISTING PRODUCTS HAVE BEEN IDENTIFIED. IDENTIFICATION IS ONGOING SINCE NEW PRODUCTS ARE CONTINUALLY INTRODUCED.

b) Identify alternative disposal methods (Lynch). 1st Qtr.
SEE THEME #2 ITEM 2(B) FOR PRODUCTS BEING RECYCLED.

c) Ensure all California buildings of 100,000 sf or greater dispose of waste properly (Schikore). 4th Qtr.

SYSTEM BEING ESTABLISHED TO TRACK VENDOR AND CONTRACTOR COMPLIANCE WITH DISPOSAL LAWS.
  d) Present funding documentation to Managing Committee for new underground fuel storage tanks and clean up for S.F. Data Center (Schikore). 3rd Qtr.
  PRESENTATION TARGETED FOR SEPTEMBER.
  e) Purchase automotive Freon recovery/recycle system (Zugnoni). 1st Qtr.
  ACCOMPLISHED. THREE RECYCLE SYSTEMS PURCHASED.
  f) Contact Du Pont for alternatives to Freon (Zugnoni). 1st Qtr.
  PRODUCT NOT READY FOR DISTRIBUTION (ONLY FOR NEW VEHICLES AT THIS TIME.)

7) Ensure that environmental issues, including maximum use of public transportation by employees, are separately delineated in the business justification for all premises projects.

Action Steps

  a) Obtain consensus from CRE Executive Council to include an environmental section in all business justifications (Schikore). 2nd Qtr.
  SIXTY FIVE ITEM ENVIRONMENTAL CHECKLIST DEVELOPED AND IMPLEMENTED. MUST BE COMPLETED FOR ALL PROPOSALS GOING TO MANAGING COMMITTEE. SUMMARY VERSION TO BE INTEGRAL PART OF COMMITTEE PRESENTATIONS.

8) Research current environmental issues in the workplace and take the initiative to make improvements where needed.

Action Steps

  a) Prepare all U.S. staff and bank occupied premises for No Smoking policy implementation (Schikore/Cammidge). 1st Qtr.
  ACCOMPLISHED

9) Ascertain feasibility and, to the extent possible and practical, implement Environmental Principles in BAC's non-US units; adapt goals as required by local circumstances.

Action Steps

a) Target Canada, Mexico, United Kingdom and Japan as initial countries; identify local point person (Sacasa/Bartolucci). 2nd Qtr.
CANADA HAS ESTABLISHED DESK TOP RECYCLING PROGRAM IN TORONTO. WILL MOVE TO OTHER BRANCHES LATER THIS YEAR. PURCHASE OF RECYCLED PAPER HAS COMMENCED.

MEXICO COUNTRY MANAGEMENT COMMITTED AND READY TO COMMENCE IMPLEMENTING A PROGRAM.

UNITED KINGDOM CORPORATE REAL ESTATE HAD ESTABLISHED 30 ITEM ACTION PLAN COVERING ELECTRICITY, GAS AND WATER CONSERVATION WITH EXPECTED COMPLETION BY YEAR END. GREEN IDEAS IN ACTION PROGRAM INITIATED WITH 44 IDEAS RECEIVED. REVIEW OF COMPUTER REPORTS INITIATED WITH VIEW TO REDUCING PAPER CONSUMPTION. NEARLY ALL AUTOMOBILES CONVERTED TO UNLEADED FUEL. RECYCLING PROGRAM PUT IN PLACE.

TAIWAN HAS BEEN SUBSTITUTED FOR JAPAN AND HAS COMMENCED IMPLEMENTING A PROGRAM WHICH IS PLANNED TO INCLUDE EMPLOYEE EDUCATION, CONSERVATION AND RECYCLING INITIATIVE WITH OTHER TAIWAN COMPANIES, AND FINANCING OF TAIWAN'S POLLUTION CLEAN UP.

b) Join forces with American Chamber of Commerce to include environmental responsibility as a major agenda item (Sacasa/Bartolucci).
ISSUED RAISED WITH INTERNATIONAL BODY. IMPLEMENTATION PLANNED FOR EUROPE AS A TEST.

c) Include Environmental Team agenda as integral part of individual business unit strategies (Sacasa/Bartolucci). 2nd Qtr.
WBG WILL CONCENTRATE ON THE FOUR TARGET COUNTRIES LISTED IN (A) ABOVE INITIALLY. OTHER COUNTRIES WILL BE ADDED AS APPROPRIATE. EUROPE WILL BE INITIAL FOCUS.

d) Consider development of training programs for correspondent banks in and outside the US (Sacasa/Bartolucci). 4th Qtr. FEASIBILITY STUDY INITIATED TO TEACH FOREIGN BANKS, ESPECIALLY EASTERN EUROPE AND LATIN AMERICA, HOW TO SET UP AN ENVIRONMENTAL PROGRAM.

10) Educate and motivate employees toward environmentally responsible behavior at work and off work.

Action Steps

a) Expand and enhance employee transportation policy and program (Cammidge). 4th Qtr., On going
   (i) Educate employees about alternative forms of transportation to work through printed medium, rallies, staff meetings, and video. Conduct management briefings on transportation issues (Cammidge).
   SENIOR MANAGEMENT IS REVIEWING A POSITION PAPER ON ALTERNATIVE TRANSPORTATION INCENTIVES. TELECOMMUTING PILOTS BEGUN IN LOS ANGELES AND CONCORD.
   (ii) Encourage employees to participate in Rideshare Week using printed medium and incentives (Cammidge).
   RIDESHARE WEEK IS IN OCTOBER. DRAFTS OF COMMUNICATIONS HAVE BEGUN.

b) Conduct an environmental Ideas in Action campaign to solicit "green" ideas from employees. Create an environmental evaluation team to determine which ideas should be accepted (Cammidge).
   ACCOMPLISHED. 399 IDEAS RECEIVED, 23 ADOPTED FOR A TOTAL PAYOUT OF $4318. OF THOSE NOT ADOPTED, 190 WERE DUPLICATES AND 177 WERE EVALUATED BUT DECLINED.

c) Develop education for employees on environmental issues (Cammidge/Rhody). Ongoing
   NEWSFRONT INSERT PUBLISHED WITH CHECKLIST OF ENVIRONMENTALLY BENEFICIAL ACTIONS INDIVIDUALS CAN DO. ARTICLES IN *ON YOUR BEHALF* AND *NEWSFRONT* COVERED VARIOUS ENVIRONMENTAL

ISSUES. INFORMATION PIECE HAS BEEN PREPARED FOR NEW EMPLOYEE WELCOME PACKAGE TO FAMILIARIZE THEM WITH THE BANK'S ENVIRONMEN-TAL PROGRAMS. ENVIRONMENTAL HOTLINE ESTAB-LISHED TO ANSWER EMPLOYEE QUESTIONS. "CHECK-LIST FOR ENVIRONMENTALLY SOUND OFFICE" PREPARED AND SCHEDULED FOR DISTRIBUTION 3RD QUARTER.

d) Publicize environmental volunteer opportunities to employees (Cammidge). Ongoing.
ARTICLE PUBLISHED IN APRIL *ON YOUR BEHALF*. "EARTH ACTION" DATABASE CREATED TO KEEP LIST OF INTERESTED EMPLOYEES AND INFORM THEM OF ENVIRONMENTALLY ORIENTED EVENTS. 80 NORTH-ERN CALIFORNIA EMPLOYEES IN DATABASE SO FAR.

e) Incorporate environmental activities in the BankAmerica Club activities (Cammidge). 1st Qtr.
ENVIRONMENTAL PRINCIPLES HAD THEIR OWN TABLE AT VENDOR FAIR DURING BANK-WIDE BANK-AMERICA CLUB OFFICERS CONVENTION IN SAN LUIS OBISPO. ALSO GOT A SPEAKING SLOT TO ENCOUR-AGE INCORPORATING ENVIRONMENTALLY BENEFI-CIAL EVENTS AND PROJECTS IN CLUB ACTIVITIES.

MAILED INFORMATION TO CLUBS ON THE ENVIRON-MENTAL GRANTS PROGRAM TO ENCOURAGE CLUB INVOLVEMENT IN ENVIRONMENTAL PROJECTS.

f) Involve retirees in the environmental programs of the Bank (Cammidge). Ongoing.
ENVIRONMENTAL PROGRAMS WAS GIVEN SPEAKING SLOT AT PRESIDENT'S MEETING. LETTER TO RETIREE CHAPTER PRESIDENTS IN MARCH ASKING FOR INFOR-MATION ON ENVIRONMENTAL ACTIVITIES THEY ARE DOING GOT VERY LIMITED RESPONSES. RESEARCH WILL BE CONDUCTED TO SEE WHAT MIGHT INTEREST RETIREES.

g) Develop an environmental ideas notepad for distribution among Bank employees (Cammidge). 3rd Qtr.

PROJECT CANCELLED. BENEFIT DOES NOT JUSTIFY
THE EXPENSE.

11) Run cause-related promotion to encourage customer support
for the environment.

Action Steps

a) Identify a key concern for the initial promotion (Hall). 2nd
Qtr.
DIRECT MAIL PROGRAM PLANNED FOR AUGUST
WHICH WILL TEST CONSUMER REACTION TO ENVI-
RONMENTAL INCENTIVE. COMMITMENT MADE TO
WORK WITH CONSERVATION INTERNATIONAL ON A
CAUSE RELATED MARKETING PROGRAM.

12) Provide leadership in the private sector to encourage other corporations to develop environmental awareness campaigns
among their employees and customers and to follow sound environmental practices in their own activities.

Action Steps

a) Encourage corporations in areas where BAC has a large market share to establish/coordinate their environmental programs with ours (Morrison). 4th Qtr.
SEE PAGE 10 ITEM 3(D) "RECYCLED PAPER INITIATIVE"

Note: A number of activities related to the environment are being
undertaken by the credit structure of the bank. These include
expansion of environmental risk assessment to non-Cali-
fornia subsidiaries and selected overseas locations. The activities also include education of account officers in Commercial Markets and World Banking Groups to recognize
environmental risk. Therefore, these activities are not included as part of implementing the Environmental Principles. However, in that conditions are placed on credits which
cause prospective borrowers to adopt more responsible environmental practices, the bank has promoted an environmental benefit. Those instances will be tracked by the Environmental Services Unit.

About WRI

World Resources Institute is a research and policy organization help-ing governments, the private sector, environmental and develop-ment organizations, and others address a fundamental question: How can societies meet human needs and nurture economic growth while preserving the natural resources and environmental integrity on which life and economic vitality ultimately depend?

WRI's books and reports present accurate information about global resources and environmental conditions, analyses of emerg-ing issues, and creative yet workable policy responses. To deepen public understanding, the institute also undertakes briefings, semi-nars, and conferences and offers material for use in print and broad-cast media.

In developing countries, WRI provides field services and tech-nical support for governments and nongovernmental organizations working to ensure the sustainable use of natural resources.